MYSTERY
of the MARIE

Quest of a daughter to surface the real story to
the shipwrecked *Marie* and seven men lost at sea
expanding the frontiers of infrared
June 7, 1960.

By
Teresa Newton-Terres
with
James Pence

TNT Press
A Division of Project-TNT, LLC

Dear Hillary,

You asked me in 2010 for an article; but, the story deserved; no, needed more. This is the first half ... second half I intend to launch/@ the 60th in 2020.

TNT 😊 Rom 8:28

MYSTERY OF THE *MARIE*

Quest of a daughter to surface the real story to the shipwrecked *Marie* and seven men lost at sea expanding the frontiers of infrared June 7, 1960.

Copyright © 2017 by Teresa Newton-Terres

www.Project-TNT.com

ISBN-13: 978-0-9791447-2-1
ISBN-10: 0-9791447-2-8

Jacket design: Bernard Erlinger-Ford
Jacket image of author: Ryan McInerney
Image of Diego S. Terres, Sr. at helm, author's archives.

In memory of seven men:
Dr. Niel Freeborn Beardsley
Loren Dale Howell
Paul Timothy Lovette
Harold Herbert Mackie, Jr.
Hugh James McCaffrey
James Russell

Diego Santos Terres, Jr

In honor of women like my mother,
Marian Streeter Terres,
who during challenging times
put her Trust In God.

(Roman 8:28)

Marie Commemoration Artwork by Teresa Newton-Terres

Contents

"One of the strangest boating accidents
of the 1960's
was the disappearance
of the *MARIE*."

Eugene Wheeler & Robert Kallman
Shipwrecks, Smugglers and Maritime Mysteries [1]

Preface

In June 1960, Santa Barbara stood still for several days after the *Marie*, a refurbished World War II landing craft, and the seven men aboard her failed to return from testing top secret equipment off Santa Cruz Island. The mystery of the boat's disappearance continues to this day, not least because it happened at the height of the Cold War.

Several of the men on the *Marie* were strong, capable outdoorsmen, skilled in the art of tracking—and survival. They were friends who began learning outdoor skills as young boys in scouting adventures, then honed those skills in the armed forces, and later assisted in one of America's most secret initiatives.

Solving the mystery of the *Marie* was the only item on my bucket list. It is a question I knew I had to answer because my father, Diego Santos Terres, Jr, was one of those men. He was the youngest engineer on the team, and helped design, build, and test a watertight casing that would take a top-secret device on its first underwater mission. He was Jimmy to his family and Jim to friends and colleagues.

To me he was Daddy.

My father was lost at sea when the *Marie* went down. I was only two years old when he disappeared. For most of my life, the question of what happened that day has surfaced and swirled like foam upon a wave. As far back as I can remember, there was talk of a Russian submarine and a possible kidnapping. Was the *Marie* tragedy a shipwreck? Or was something more sinister at work? What, exactly, happened that day? That question has also been floating on the minds and hearts of seven families who lost their husbands and fathers.

In my desire to learn more, I embarked on a journey of discovery into seven men and the purposes for which they lived and died. One of those men was a scientist who participated in a top-secret project that hastened the end of World War II.

His presence on the *Marie* signaled that it was no casual mission.

When men lose their lives in service to their country, they deserve special recognition. The *Marie* shipwreck event is a story of seven men: Dr. Niel F. Beardsley, L. Dale Howell, Paul T. Lovette, Harold "Hal" H. Mackie, Jr., Hugh James "Jim" McCaffrey, James "Jim" C. Russell, and my father, Diego "Jim" Terres, Jr. These seven were ordinary men doing their job, and in the process made the ultimate sacrifice during a critical time in history, a time when nuclear war was an ever-present danger.

This story has been submerged beneath an ocean of secrecy for over fifty years. It is time for the *Marie* tragedy and its secret project to re-surface, to provide the surviving family, friends, community, and nation the opportunity to remember an event that shook Santa Barbara. It is time to honor the scientist, engineers, scuba-divers, and crew of the *Marie*—men who worked together, and died together.

The full story may never be known. Yet my search for truth revealed a Heavenly Father's goodness in operation. My journey began with what, I believed, was a simple question. What happened? Yet, I failed to realize the Goliath I stood before –giant issues that threatened to overwhelm me many times. Nevertheless, by taking on this Goliath, I found peace where I had frustrations, I gained courage serving things that matter most, and I became grateful where I once had a chip on my shoulder. Through an abundance of relationships, collective memories, and a crumbling wall of secrecy, at least part of the story surfaced.

And my appreciation of America's motto, "In God We Trust" grew.

Part-I HARBORS

FIG. 1: Diego Santos Terres, Sr. searching for his son.
His younger son, Albert, stands behind.

CHAPTER 1:

A Window To The Past

The handwritten note from my aunt Norma read, "Found this in the basement and thought you might want."

Whatever was in the package I found on my front porch, it was old. The odor of mildew stung my nostrils as I opened the package and drew out a heavy book. The words *Scrap Book* were imprinted on the dark leather cover.

I assumed it held family memories. Aunt Norma was keen on slipping various family treasures my way.

I'd found the package on the doorstep of my home at Fort Shafter in Hawaii. I had zipped home early from a Project Management Institute (PMI) luncheon, but I didn't have time to explore the scrapbook. I had a special goal for the afternoon.

Replacing my heels for flip-flops and skirt for shorts, I headed out the half-mile walk to the legendary Palm Circle, where the movie *Pearl Harbor* was being filmed. Earlier in the month, I had tried to get on as an extra, but the casting crew only wanted women who were nurses with white caps and uniforms.

I wanted to be one of the bodies floating in the harbor.

I was a licensed scuba diver and willing to cut my hair short and bob around dead in Pearl Harbor's waters, but I couldn't convince anyone to take a chance on me. So, today I was determined to do the next best thing: be a fan in the crowd watching the filming. A rainbow brightened the sky as I headed toward the filming location.

"Simple wonders of the Rainbow State," I said to myself, smiling.

Thus, the scrapbook that would change my life sat unopened for a few more hours.

When I finally opened it, the first thing I saw was a small black and white photo of my grandfather. He wore a heavy coat and binoculars hung around his neck. He held a soda bottle in one hand and grasped the helm of a sailboat with the other. Standing behind my grandfather was Uncle Albert, my father's younger brother. Grandfather peered in one direction; Albert looked the other way.

The headline above the photo read, "Search on for *Marie* Victims."

I flipped to the next page and then the next as I read other headlines: "Six Santa Barbarans Lost at Sea; Body of 7th Found," "Testing Secret Gear," "SECRET MISSION," "Six Feared Victims of Shark Pack."

I glanced over more pictures and maps. One had a photo of my father. His dark eyes looked directly at me as if he were trying to tell me something.

Grandmother never spoke about my father or the shipwreck.

As I turned the pages, it slowly dawned on me that this scrapbook was her attempt to understand the tragedy that took her son.

The heavy tropical air felt thick and I found it difficult to breathe.

The scrapbook was part of grandmother's personal effects, willed to her surviving son, my Uncle Albert. My father was her firstborn, but because he was no longer living, Grandmother's assets were distributed equally between my uncle, my three brothers, and me. Most notable of those assets was what our family called "the Goleta property," a block of stores with two apartments on the second floor.

After Grandmother's death, the Goleta property was sold and the proceeds distributed among her heirs. My share later helped pay my college expenses.

"It will all be yours one day," Grandmother told me many times as I played with her collectables and personal things, dressing up in her clothes, jewelry, high-heels.

She gave many of those possessions to me while she was alive: Spanish combs, white lace mantilla, crocheted bedspreads, a steamer trunk, a spindle rocking chair and dresser that had traveled from Spain, and her treasured lace maker.

I cared for these things because, even when I was young, I felt a sense of responsibility toward family treasures. Now, perhaps Grandmother's greatest treasure had been entrusted to me.

At first, I saw the scrapbook as a connection to my identity that my father couldn't provide. I didn't realize it was also a pathway that led to the secrets of the shipwreck that changed the course of my life. I have grappled with where to begin telling this story. Some might argue it began when my father and his friends began scuba diving in the waters off Santa Barbara. Others might say the story began when dad and mother took leave from Navy duties to marry and honeymoon at the family's cabin in California's Sierra Nevada Mountains. Still others will argue this story began with Pearl Harbor and our nation's transformation to peace time after World War II, or even that the story began with a California Cultural History Project. For me, the story began the day my eyes scanned the images and artifacts preserved in my grandma's—mi abuela's—scrapbook. That moment was like the first light of a new dawn.

CHAPTER 2:

Memorial

When people ask me what my mother died of, I say, a broken heart. It would be natural to assume that I was talking about the death of my father. That assumption would be wrong.

The man who broke my mother's heart did so many years after my father's death.

Mother checked into an assisted living facility after calling me and saying, "Get that man out of my life. I should have listened to you and never married him."

Sadly, she learned that even if you are married for only a year, you can't just tell your spouse to leave your home if he doesn't want to. My brothers and I initiated divorce proceedings on my mother's behalf, trying to remove this man from her life. Twice she had to appear before a judge. At her first appearance, she needed two of my brothers to escort her by the arm. But despite all this man had done to her, she wouldn't say a word against him.

"If you can't say anything good, don't say anything at all," said afterward.

Thus, the court ruled that he could stay in Mom's condo.

When word reached me in Hawaii, I prayed about how to handle this situation. I wanted to help her understand she didn't need to lie or embellish her testimony. She only needed to tell the truth.

A second court date was set.

At her second court appearance, Mother needed a walker, a nurse, and two of my brothers to escort her. The results were better this time. The man was given thirty days to vacate the premises. However, it was a hollow victory. By the time mother's condo was vacated and returned to order, her health had so declined that she never returned.

When I received the call about her death on July 6, 2002, I can't say I wasn't prepared. I had hoped she could hold on for three more days, when I planned to fly for the seventh time in six months to San Francisco to stay with her. Instead, my husband Ken and I were now on an airliner, traveling to her funeral.

The head flight attendant gave us drinks after we boarded and settled into our first-class seats. I noticed her nametag, *Teresa Fernandez*. I wasn't in a talking mood and didn't mention that my name was also Teresa, and my Grandmother Terres' maiden name was Fernandez. However, in time our paths would cross again.

I took a deep breath as I sank back into my seat. Ten months had passed since the September 11 attacks, and I felt like I was living in a war zone. Every military command center in Hawaii was on high alert. This meant that as we came and went from our home on Fort Shafter or Ken's work at Camp Smith, soldiers, barricaded behind sand-bag bunkers and fortified housing, aimed machine guns at us. Ken knew what it felt like to have people aiming weapons at him, but the experience was new for me. Because we were also subject to search, getting out of Fort Shafter and to the airport tried everyone's patience.

Airport security was also high and searches of our vehicles, luggage, and carry-on bags were routine. Traveling by air had once been pleasant; now it was characterized by suspicion.

****

As our flight got underway, I thought of the last time my mother, three brothers, and I had been together. It was the weekend of the Old Town Goleta Cultural History Project.

I had made calls to my family alerting them to a historical collection effort that was underway. That's why Grandmother's scrapbook about the shipwreck had been sent to me.

Sometime earlier my dad's cousin, Beatrice, called me. "My uncle Diego built Goleta up and you need to get involved. I think Laura Funkhouser, director of the project, lives in your grandparents' old apartment in the center of Old Town." Old Town Goleta is nestled in the valley between the ocean and Pacific Coast Mountains on the north side of Santa Barbara, California.

Bea was a retired Santa Barbara school teacher and self-appointed standard bearer for the building guidelines that preserved Santa Barbara's splendor. The beauty of red-tiled roofs, white stucco walls, low profiles, and turquoise trimming—standards established after the town was demolished in the June 1925 earthquake—contributed to the city being recognized today as America's Riviera.

I called and introduced myself to Laura Funkhouser. As Beatrice thought, Laura was living in the apartment on Hollister where my father grew up. Laura told me, "We're locating Goleta's Old Town folks and recording their stories before they are lost."

She explained that time was of the essence if her team was to be able to capture the tales from a humble working-class community that lived in Old Town. In 1959 Goleta was said to be the fastest growing city on the Pacific west coast, but then growth stalled and passed over Old Town.

Developers were now trying to label Old Town as "blighted." They wanted to demolish it and erect a large strip mall, not considering the town's uniquely historic heartbeat that traced directly back to the Chumash Indians.

I didn't need any more persuasion. I wanted to help with the project.

After reviewing Grandmother's scrapbook, I contacted my Aunt Norma and asked her to send any other family items of interest she had. Soon I was opening more family history: four carousels of slides and two metal boxes containing twenty-four 8mm film canisters. A few labels caught my eye: Family trips to Spain 1950, 1954, 1968; Goleta buildings; Beach Days; Family Gatherings; and Teresa Dancing.

My free time quickly became consumed with compiling a composite of the films and images that would serve the Cultural History Project. My composite included a twenty-minute film, with scenes of Old Town buildings my grandfather built; Goleta's first Magnolia Parade, filmed from my grandparent's balcony in the 40s; WWI & WWII memorial dedications at the school my father attended; the first Chamber of Commerce actions; and gatherings at the beach.

Dr. David Russell, a Professor of Oral History at UCSB, volunteered to conduct interviews, so I spearheaded a Saturday family gathering that included time for recording memories about my grandparents and life in Old Town Goleta.

"Please compile a list of the participants, a brief bio, and a sentence telling what they are interested in hearing from the others," Dr. Russell requested.

I did that, but no one in my family mentioned the shipwreck.

When the day came for the family interview, we gathered at the Community Center. I displayed the scrapbook about the shipwreck along with other memorabilia.

No one flipped through any of the scrapbook's pages.

The interviews progressed along an expected path until one question came from out of the blue. Interviewing a panel of five people from the older generation, the professor asked, "Why do you think Goleta stood still as if placed in a time capsule since the 60's?"

The panel members looked at each other and had no input to offer.

Dr. Russell moved on to another question.

My mind lingered on the question.

Could the shipwreck of the Marie *have stalled the progress of the town? Was I the only person who wondered about that?*

I knew that the tragedy took my father, the oldest child of the Diego Terres, Sr. family. But in preparing for the Cultural History Project I learned that the shipwreck also claimed the only son of Goleta's first mail carrier. I also knew that the Raytheon-based project team operated from an office that was located across from the Santa Barbara airport, less than one mile down the road from Grandmother and Grandfather's apartment and the Cultural History Project interviews.

Surely the professor knew about Goleta, my father, and the shipwreck.

****

The flight attendant's voice broke into my thoughts. "Please return to your seats and prepare for landing."

After touching down in San Francisco, Ken and I made a quick stop at my mother's condo. Order had been restored to the two-bedroom, one-bath unit. I picked up a box of clean bedding and one of Mother's photo albums, and then we headed out of the city and up into the Sierra Nevada Mountains to our family's cabin.

Mother was four when she helped my grandfather build the cabin. She loved to tell about the time he cut pumice boulders for the cabin's fireplace. "Folks driving by slowed to watch me carrying those huge boulders."

In 1932, my grandfather was given one year to clear the land and build a structure before he could get a permit for the cabin in the National Forest. Originally it was tiny, but over the years it had been expanded to 400 square feet, nestled on a third of an acre in a historical community of cabins. What space the cabin didn't have, its wrap-around deck did.

As Ken drove, I reflected on recent events. Working with the history project had made me more inclined to ask Mother about her memories, and she was delighted to share them. The next time she visited me in Hawaii, we looked at Grandmother's scrapbook together.

I asked her about a newspaper photo that showed three women waiting in the Coast Guard's office the first night when they searched for survivors. "What are you doing here?"

"Knitting," said mother. "Do you remember the salmon-colored sweater with the cable pattern edging the cuffs and buttons? You wore it to threads in your dance classes."

I remembered it well. I had found the sweater in a bag in the garage. It was soft. It was also perfect as a warm-up sweater for dancing. Back then, the movie *Flashdance* with its tattered clothing style was the rage, and I enjoyed Mom's sweater until it was threadbare. I knew she had knitted it, but I didn't know it helped calm her mind while people searched for my dad.

"That was the only thing I ever knitted," said Mom. "Busy hands are happy hands." It wasn't the first time I had heard her use that expression.

"Later, you came across a sweater that reminded you of it and bought it for me," I reminded her. "That one is still on my shelf."

I told her about one of my oldest memories. "I was pulled by an arm and it was dark outside and inside," I said. "We went into a home down the block, where the girl with curly red hair lived. People were whispering. I knew something was up, and to this day the memory has stuck."

"Most likely it was the early hours when our neighbors helped me escape the paparazzi," she said. "It took all I had to take care of you four kids. So, when the search dragged on…" her voice tapered off. "Finally, our neighbor drove me and you kids the ten-hour drive up to the cabin."

Ken and I were drawing close to the base of the mountain, so we stopped for gas and switched seats. He knew I loved the winding two-lane road leading up to the cabin, so he let me drive the last leg of our journey.

****

We planned to hold Mother's memorial in a mountain meadow. My oldest and youngest brothers, Jim and Don, lived in California and had arrived earlier. They were in charge of locating a suitable meadow for the memorial. It took longer for my other older brother, Rick, to fly in with his wife and daughter from the Middle East, where he worked in the oil industry. Additionally, my daughter Dete flew in from Washington, D.C. Uncle Albert and his new wife Lynda soon arrived, along with other family and friends.

We held Mother's memorial outdoors, in a place our family now calls "Marian's Mountain and Meadow." It was an intimate ceremony attended by special family and friends. Beautiful morning light rose above the mountain in the distance, and the warm colors danced across the grassy meadow encircled by tall pine trees. As we gathered, someone read Psalm 23 and the Lord's prayer.

We scattered mother's ashes on the far side in the heart of the meadow wildflowers.

She loved the cabin, and had spent her summers there as a child. I couldn't think of a more suitable place to honor her life and spread her ashes. She worked there while Dad was deployed with the Navy on the USS Yorktown. And she had brought us kids here to play each summer and winter. We had all crossed this meadow on horseback riding and backpacking adventures into the Emigrant Basin of the higher Sierra Mountains.

When the ceremony was complete, we quietly piled into the four-wheel-drive vehicles in which we had arrived. Back at the cabin, I noticed some of Mother's ashes lingering on my brother Jim's pants.

"Mom always was on my butt!" Jim said as he brushed away the ashes.

****

That afternoon one of my cousins said, "Aunt Marian would want us to take care of the cabin business."

I groaned inwardly. This was a moment I'd dreaded.

The family cabin was under the jurisdiction of estate laws and Mother's trust. As the co-executor of the trust, along with Ken, Mother gave me the freedom and authority to do whatever I believed wise.

There was one small problem.

At that time, no one knew that Mother had named Ken and me as co-trustees. I didn't want to be disrespectful to my brothers by springing this detail on them before other family. So, I avoided the issue.

"Mother's estate business, including the cabin, will not be conducted today," I said. "We will just have to contend with the details as best we can later."

For me, at least, the cabin had always been an emotionally-charged place. I always felt that I couldn't clean enough, or paint enough, or get my brothers to help enough to please my mother. I preferred the power and passion of the Pacific Ocean to the babbling brooks and lakes near the cabin. But on this day, I didn't want my frustrations with Mother or the quaint brown and green trimmed cabin to overshadow her memory.

****

After a dinner of Mother's cabin chili beans, my brothers built a bonfire and we circled around the campfire and burned the wooden box that had held her ashes.

"I was prepared for mother's death," said my brother Don.

It is what Don didn't say that reminded me of a recent interview I saw on TV.

"When you lose a parent when you are young," a well-known star of Charlie's Angels said, speaking of her own father's loss, "anyone you love from then on you see die a thousand deaths as a shield for your heart."

Although our mother's death had been expected, what remained unspoken was that none of us were prepared for the loss of our father.

CHAPTER 3:

Change of Command

"What can they say but no?"

I had encouraged Ken to pursue the command of the National Guard Professional Education Center (PEC) back in his home town of Little Rock, Arkansas. Command of the PEC was the most prestigious assignment in the National Guard Bureau. Founded in 1974, the PEC was the National Guard's premier training and conference center. Every year, upwards of 30,000 people came from all over the country to learn there. Ken had applied for the command twice before and been denied.

Prior to this, the Army had moved my husband, Colonel Kenneth H. Newton, between Washington DC, Pennsylvania, Kansas, Arkansas, in California where I had met and married him after he rotated in from a tour near the Berlin Wall, and our current assignment: Hawaii.

While we lived on Ft. Shafter, Honolulu, Ken worked at Camp Smith, located in the hills above Pearl Harbor. He was the senior National Guard Bureau liaison to the Commander in Chief of the Pacific as an account manager and the NGB State Partnership coordinator between courtiers like Mongolia and Alaska, Guam and Philippines.

I worked as a project management professional, serving a litany of projects and teams in a variety of industries. The work week kept us both busy, but the weekends were busier.

Ken and I played like never before in Hawaii, scuba diving, snorkeling, surfing. We chased balls around various golf courses. We bounced between a few churches where people show up in the island's traditional "Aloha" gear of flowered comfortable clothes and flip flops. I even befriended a group of retired teachers who accepted me into their dance classes of traditional Spanish and Flamenco classes, followed by coffee hour at a local bakery. We traveled regularly to the mainland for work and to visit friends and family. We were building a life worth living as empty nesters, and were planning to retire in Hawaii.

But, although he'd been denied twice before, the third time was a charm for Ken. He was offered the PEC command—a job offer he couldn't refuse.

Even though I had encouraged him to pursue the command, I had mixed emotions. I preferred the idea of retiring in Hawaii, but I knew that our destiny lay in the PEC command. That understanding didn't make it any easier as I anticipated moving to Arkansas.

In Hawaii, my personal and professional life had headed in a positive direction for almost five years. On the island, weekends were laid back and carefree. Life on the mainland would be much different. On the other hand, we would be close to our children and other relatives, something we hadn't enjoyed for some time.

Ken had two children from a previous marriage. I had a daughter, also from a previous marriage. The grandchildren would be *ours*. In Arkansas, we'd be near Ken's family, and mine would only be a quick flight away. After living in Hawaii for so long, that would be a blessing. However, proximity to family came with increased responsibilities. It was going to be a different situation for us all.

For our farewell party, I decided to host a fiesta/luau. My fiesta/luaus weren't Spanish, Mexican, or Hawaiian. Rather, they were a melting-pot of American families, friends, and fun. In the military, and especially overseas, gatherings and celebrations fill the void created by separation from family members. Most of our neighbors had an entertainment specialty such as Valentine's parties, Christmas cookie exchanges, wine tastings, and so on.

My specialty was the *Hawaiian Fiesta/Luau*.

Ever since we'd arrived on the island, we had hosted a yearly fiesta/luau around the May 5th Cinco de Mayo festivities. I rarely could be with my family in Santa Barbara for my hometown's summertime Old Spanish Days festival. Instead, I brought my hometown food, music, dancing and children's laughter into my life. And it made my heart sing.

On the day of the big event, we set up tables and covered each with a bright red and black tablecloth. This would be our fifth fiesta, and our neighbors' children were looking forward to the annual event. Some of the children helped make tissue-paper flowers, stuff piñatas, fluff the girly skirts, and fill confetti eggs. Other children prepared an act for the floor show. With over 100 people expected to attend, Ken and I had a routine that was more like organized chaos.

The evening began with three candy-filled piñatas for both kids and adults. Next came a pot-luck dinner, which featured my grandmother Terres' *paella* as the main course. After that came the floor show.

On this final Fiesta, the show began with a parade of little beauties swirling their skirts. The teen girls had helped them dress-up in frilly old dancing costumes and added a finishing touch of red lipstick. After they swirled their skirts to a lively music piece, I led them in a ribbon-like formation behind me. Then I seated them around the outline of the makeshift stage. Next, a mock bullfight commenced as sounds of *España Cani* announced the matador's entrance. Swishing a black and red cape, a neighbor with a flair for a bullfighter's role came onstage. The bull, played by a group of boys huddled under a blanket with one of their fathers in front wearing a bull's head, plodded into the arena. The addition of the father was strategic. Over the years I had learned that, left to themselves, boys will try to steal the show and kill the bullfighter.

The floor show continued as a family of children sang. Next a group of youths presented a precision break-dance to a Latin beat. My Spanish-dancing friends and I followed up by dancing *Seviallans* (a dance my grandparents probably danced), and then we got everyone up dancing in a Conga line.

For the grand finale we distributed dozens of confetti eggs and everyone crushed them over each other's heads as an endowment of new life and prosperity.

In the midst of the fun, I stopped. *What would the folks in Arkansas think of my fiestas?*

Shortly after our farewell fiesta, we left our Hawaii home. We sent one car and our household belongings off on a two-month boat journey to our new home in Arkansas. In the meantime, we lived out of suitcases.

After we closed the door on our island bungalow, we checked into a hotel where we could wake to the sunrise over Diamondhead and Waikiki's crystal blue waters. Not long after, Ken's Hawaiian finale melody floated through the air waves as Kona winds began swirling up a tropical storm we boarded an airliner and headed to Arkansas.

****

I recovered from our whirlwind move in a hotel room on one side of Little Rock, Arkansas while Ken went off to the National Guard Professional Education Center (PEC) to prepare for the traditional Change of Command ceremonies.

The first time I set foot on PEC was for what I understood used to be called a "ladies luncheon" but had now been renamed the *Family Program Luncheon*.

I felt uncomfortable, but tried to at least look the part. My make-up was fresh. My hair, that I had grown long to fit in with the Hawaiians, was now in a neat bun. I knew how to sit at a head table, with my legs and feet pointing in the right direction. And I was wearing a new, white outfit.

I pointed to the decoration on the head table—a bird in a cage—and said to the person sitting beside me, "I feel like that bird."

More than fifty men and women were at the event. My stomach churned when they asked me to say a few words. I should have assumed they would ask me to speak, but I wasn't expecting it. Public speaking has always unnerved me. I wanted to inspire and impress; I felt like a blabbering bimbo.

"I don't know you, but thank you for what you have done and will do. I am honored to be here, and I hope I get to know each of you personally," I said, and then sat down.

But that wasn't the worst part of the luncheon.

They named me the Family Program Leader.

That evening, I gave Ken a rundown. "They named me the Family Program Leader," I said. "I thought I was the Commander's spouse. Keep a pretty face. Host a gathering or two. Cheer on the Commander. Eat chocolate bon bons. Family Program Leader is a role that has serious responsibilities."

I had strong reservations about the responsibilities the title implied, and I feared people's unrealistic expectations. I was a professional with years of experience running my own business. When the PEC command was awarded to Ken, my business went into limbo. I enjoyed working with men in a project-oriented world. I found comfort in the well-outlined structure of a good plan. Even my fiestas were organized on my terms and my timing.

I was raised with three brothers and a busy, widowed mother. I had learned a few hostess tips and tricks over the years, because I was observant. And I liked acting in school, so I found some comfort in playing "the role" of the good wife. But I was not at all looking forward to leading the Family Program, whatever that entailed.

****

The next day a traditional Change of Command ceremony took place. It was April 2003 as Colonel Kenneth Harold Newton became PEC's 11th Commandant.

I was seated in the front row and during the ceremony I would stand to receive a presentation of flowers from Ken, a symbol of his respect and gratitude for the service I would offer in this command assignment. Our children and grandchildren sat in the row behind me.

In a half circle of seats were military, civilian, staff, families and special guests.

Three leather high-backed office chairs sat before us in an open space. These seats would soon be filled by the guests of honor: the outgoing commander, the incoming commander (Ken), and their boss, who had flown in from Washington D.C.: Ken's friend, Colonel Nuttall .

Military traditions always touch my heart and soul. In such ceremonies, the participants share in a historical milestone that marks a link in a legacy's chain. After the parade of the honored guests comes a prayer, then the U.S. flag is marched in, followed by the national anthem and pledge of allegiance. During the ceremony, Ken would be handed a flag, symbolic of the responsibilities that were changing hands.

My emotions soared as I was reminded of where I fit in the context of America and its military, why I make the necessary sacrifices, and in whom I put my trust—not man, but God.

****

After the ceremony, we went back to our hotel, packed up our things, and moved into our Arkansas home. I smiled when I opened the front door of our large townhome. Although it looked small and humble from the outside, the front door opened into an expanse of glass, a rock fireplace, and wood beams above and around an inner atrium. In the distance, I could see the ninth green of a golf course beyond the living room. It wasn't Hawaii, but it had a unique beauty all its own. The home was not new to us. We bought it over ten years earlier when we lived here under a different assignment. We kept the townhome in hope that Ken might someday get the PEC command.

We entered our townhome, with nothing but suitcases, my laptop and a rental car. Our furniture wouldn't arrive for another month. It had been years since we last had to "camp out" in a house, but we had done it in the past. We blew up an air mattress and placed it against one wall in the master bedroom.

The doorbell rang.

"Hey Newtons." Our friends Steve and Lana Russell stood grinning at the front door when Ken opened it. Steve reached out and placed a set of car keys in Ken's hand. "It's yours until your car comes from Hawaii."

Soon the doorbell rang again. Larry and Sherri Sims stood holding a box. "Thought you may need these until yours come in." They placed the box on the kitchen counter.

Inside, I saw pots, pans, dishes, silverware and a coffee pot with a filter and bag of coffee. "See you," they said as they retreated.

Next, Philip Lipsmeyer, the man who had hired Ken for a starter job at PEC thirty years earlier, stopped by. Ironically, after the Change of Command ceremony he was under Ken's command.

"You remember Philip Lipsmeyer," Ken said to me as he followed Philip out the door. The two returned shortly with two folding chairs and a table.

"The campsite's shaping up," Ken said.

I tried to look as though I shared his enthusiasm, but I didn't. As if a month without furniture weren't enough, I began having nightly sweats as menopause set in.

As we lay in bed that night, trying to go to sleep, a distant siren blared a tornado warning.

It was going to be a long month.

CHAPTER 4:

Raytheon

The months passed and we settled into our new life which, I must admit, had its perks. Ken arrived home one Friday evening with an invitation I couldn't refuse. I had grown used to his regular travel, usually for face-to-face meetings with his bosses in Washington D.C. Sometimes, however, he traveled to different places around the country. This time, he was planning to attend a workshop offered by the Harvard Business School in Boston, MA.

"Why don't you join me," Ken encouraged. "You could enjoy exploring the Freedom Trail by day, and we can dine together each night on seafood."

I sorely missed the crystal blue comforts of Hawaii, and I was emotionally exhausted because my new life had little routine. Our household goods had arrived months earlier and the boxes were long put away. I had begun upgrading areas of the townhome and bought new furniture and accessories. On top of that, I was still trying to wrap up my mother's life in California. Clearing out and selling her condo was no easy task, and neither was dealing with her husband as she died two weeks shy of the finalized divorce. Moreover, I had reestablished some professional connections on the mainland and in Arkansas and was trying to make a difference in the PEC's Family Program.

In short, I needed a break.

"That sounds wonderful," I said, but I knew that I couldn't hide from my burdens indefinitely. The next chance I had, I got on the Internet to discover for myself what I might find in Boston.

One of the articles in Grandmother's scrapbook had a photo of Raytheon officials from MA, standing stiffly as they looked at the hatch-covers recovered from the *Marie*.

I Googled *Raytheon and MA* and a selection of links filled the screen. I clicked through to the Raytheon website, which listed offices in Waltham, a western suburb of Boston.

I poked around the site for historical information about Raytheon. They listed some corporate milestones: "The first commercial microwave oven, miniature tubes for hearing aids, the Fathometer depth sounder, the mass production of magnetron tubes, early shipboard radar, the first successful missile guidance system, a space communications system, mobile radio telephones, the first combat-proven air defense missile system and Terminal Doppler Weather Radar."

Did my father die helping develop one of these?

I searched for a safety record but didn't find anything.

I also wanted to discover who the man at the top was. When I found a bio for Mr. William Swanson, the Chairman of the Board and CEO, I discovered that he and my father had three things in common: they graduated from the same school (California Polytechnic University, San Luis Obispo), same program (Engineering) and they both started their careers with Raytheon Santa Barbara, located on Hollister in Goleta.

A tingle ran up and down my spine.

The men on the *Marie* were involved in a Raytheon-related project.

There must be someone at the headquarters who could meet with me and tell me what happened.

The news articles in Grandmother's scrapbook were confusing. I needed someone to help me unravel this mystery. Mr. Swanson might not have time to meet with me, but perhaps he knew someone who would.

How could I arrange a meeting with someone so important and so busy?

At that time, the National Guard Professional Education Center's Family Program was organizing a charity golf tournament and one of my responsibilities was helping find corporate sponsorships. I wasn't comfortable with the task, but since Raytheon had a building at the Little Rock airport, I thought maybe I could accomplish two things at once: obtain Raytheon's sponsorship for the Charity Golf Tournament and get information about the *Marie* tragedy.

On the website, I found a contact number for Raytheon HQ.

I didn't have much time to set up a meeting with Raytheon in Boston. I worried about what to say and how to tell someone about a charity event I knew little about or a shipwreck I knew even less about.

I had worked with company executives and military leaders and knew that they all relied on administrative assistants who were usually very approachable. The following Monday, I called the contact number and asked for the name and office number of Mr. Swanson's secretary. They gave me the contact information for a lady named Ms. Moore.

I called Ms. Moore's number.

"Ms. Moore," a pleasant voice answered.

"I just found out that I will be in Boston this week. How would you recommend that I attempt to get a meeting with Mr. Swanson?" I asked.

"Well, you can send a letter or e-mail to him through me, and I can see what I can do to help you," she said. "Mr. Swanson has a pretty busy schedule," she added.

I took a long deep breath as I hung up the phone. There was no time for a letter, so I decided to draft an e-mail.

All that day I wrestled with what to say. I wanted to make a good impression but I also wanted Raytheon to act. *Why didn't I simply state that I was interested in meeting with Mr. Swanson to discuss the potential for Raytheon's sponsorship in a National Guard Charity Golf Tournament? Then I could casually add that I also had a personal interest in meeting with him.*

I tried to consider Mr. Swanson's perspective. I remembered a section from my project management training on how to get people to comply with needs. I got out a blank worksheet and scribbled in responses to see what might germinate. I believed I had to pique Raytheon's interest. Perhaps they would be interested in knowing more about who was approaching them (friend or foe). They might also be interested in positive media and innovation as their website suggested.

Driven by desire and the clock's countdown before my blastoff to Boston on Wednesday, I scribbled out a message on a notepad, pounded it out on my keyboard and sent it off. It seemed like a simple connection to get my foot in the door. As it turned out, it was more like a crazy idea I believed would hook the "big fish."

When Ken returned from PEC, I showed him what I had written and sent. I felt like a kid holding out a valentine for her parent.

The Commandant shook his head and took a deep breath. "You tend to try too hard," Ken said as he continued into the master bedroom to remove his uniform.

"So, you think I oversold my ideas?"

"This makes you look like an unrealistic dreamer." Ken was direct. He was used to dealing with soldiers. "Focus on one thing and build rapport. Shipwreck or fundraising."

My heart sank. I thought I had been so clever.

Did Ken hear me say that I already sent it out? It wouldn't be the first time that I had to swallow my pride, backpedal while holding my head high and acting as if I had everything together. I choked back tears and wished I had run it by him the night before. I knew that Ken was consumed with his work, and burdening him with mine wasn't wise. However, the fundraising activity that weighed on me *was* his business.

My thumb shot up to press on one tooth that protruded slightly, my "Terres tooth" as Grandmother called it. She had taught me to do this, just as her mother had taught her, and I had taught my daughter. "The slight pressure will help to move the tooth into alignment," she used to say. Alignment notwithstanding, I also found focus and comfort by putting pressure on that tooth.

Now what? I wanted to go hide somewhere.

CHAPTER 5:

Intrigued

We packed our things and the next day, as spring flowers were beginning to blossom, we flew to Boston.

After we settled in at our hotel, I began fidgeting. I knew I had sent the e-mail to Mr. Swanson, and I had written that I would follow-up with a phone call. It's one thing to send a garbled e-mail; it's another thing not to follow through. Before the end of the work day I called, hoping that the intent of my e-mail would shine through its fog.

"This is Ms. Moore."

"I sent an e-mail to Mr. Swanson yesterday in hopes of setting up an appointment this Thursday or Friday while I was in town," I said. "Yes. I remember," she said. "Keith should be in touch. He also serves Mr. Swanson's needs." She mentioned that Raytheon's board of directors was in town that week, filling up Mr. Swanson's schedule.

"Should I come and camp outside Mr. Swanson's office in case he has ten minutes to meet face to face?" I asked.

I could hear her smile. "Mr. Swanson is really busy, but Keith should be in contact."

I hung up. The rest of the day I stayed close to the phone.

By mid-morning the following day, with no response, I gave up and went into Boston. With a guide map in hand, I followed the legendary

Freedom Trail. I tried to recall what I'd learned in school as I walked by Old State House, the site of the Boston Massacre, Faneuil Hall, the Old North Church, Paul Revere's Home, the USS Constitution, Bunker Hill Monument, and Old North Bridge site of the, "shot heard round the world."

I did a lot of sightseeing, but heard nothing from Raytheon.

I returned home disappointed. I decided to save face by not pursuing Raytheon's golf tournament sponsorship. There were plenty of other sponsors, not to mention areas where I could apply my skills to the charity golf tournament and make a difference.

My investigation into the *Marie* shipwreck might have ended there, but I received, as it were, a second chance. A few months later, Ken returned home from a long day at PEC and asked, "Want another trip to Boston? This year's National Guard Family Program conference is being held in Boston mid-September," he said. "We'll be with two other couples, but the soldiers will have to continue onto the National Guard Association of the United States (NGAUS) conference that is scheduled in Las Vegas at the same time."

My thoughts began churning. Maybe this time, I could connect with Raytheon's President or his representative. I didn't have to include fundraising mumbo jumbo.

Ken regularly attended the National Guard Association of the United States (NGAUS) conferences and I had gone with him several times. While he participated in all the workshops and proceedings, I spent as much time as possible in the exhibition hall exploring a vast array of industry leaders' gadgets and gizmos. The Raytheon booth was always a highlight. One year they were giving away *Raytheon TWS Gun Powder* jalapeno seasoning. I loved it.

I always told them my father had been a Raytheon engineer in the Santa Barbara office. At first, I didn't add that dad died serving a project team because I didn't know anything about what his team tested.

One time, a Raytheon representative responded, "Santa Barbara? The lenses for the Thermal-Eye come out of that area." He handed me an information sheet with pictures and details on the RAYTHEON THERMAL-EYE 250D and X100xp.

"Gives users the ability to see in complete darkness whether on a routine patrol, locating a lost child or tracking a fugitive."

The fact sheet showed a police officer holding the camera.

Waterproof to 9ft. My eyes caressed the listing.

The representative held out one of the hand-held infrared cameras.

"I get to touch one?" I said, truly delighted,

"Can someone turn off all the lights, so I can try this baby out?" I said.

We all smiled. It wasn't the first time they had heard that.

Was this the device that the guys on the Marie were testing?

****

I sat at my computer, preparing once again to connect with Raytheon headquarters in Boston. It seemed clear again that I needed to start at the top, with Mr. Swanson. Against Ken's advice, I located and streamlined my original e-mail. I still wanted to include my original dream.

Ms. Moore's voice on the phone was respectful and kind when I called to follow-up.

"I forwarded your e-mail to the VP of Corporate Affairs. This seemed suitable to your need. Is that okay?"

"Oh, yes. Thank you." I said.

After researching the responsibilities and background of the VP of Corporate Affairs, I called her.

"This is Teresa Newton-Terres. My e-mail to Mr. William Swanson was forwarded to you."

After an appropriate timeframe with no response, I left another phone message.

When I still had a couple days before heading east, and hadn't heard from Raytheon, I called Ms. Moore once again.

"No one has contacted you?" She sounded truly concerned.

By the morning of our departure to Boston, I had yet to receive a response.

****

It was early Sunday, September 12, 2004 when I and Ken arrived at the Little Rock Airport for our flight to Boston. Ken tried to get us seats together, but a mix-up separated us. My assigned seat was just in front of his.

As I approached my seat, I noticed a newspaper that was folded and placed in the middle of the seat. I picked it up and stuffed it into the pocket in front of me.

As we took off, a headline caught my attention, "Mystery of Scientist's '53 Death Grips Son." I took the paper and began to read the article. A subhead sounded ominous: "Did the father jump, or did the government push him?"

The article told about Eric Olson, and of his search for the truth behind his father's death. Consumed by his search, Eric lost his family, friends, and even his own health. Eric found a 1950s CIA manual, declassified in 1997 by President Clinton. The CIA manual allegedly contained guidelines for carrying out assassinations such as, "The decision and instructions should be confined to an absolute minimum of persons," and "For secret assassinations the contrived accident is the most effective technique. When successfully executed, it causes little excitement and is only casually investigated." Apparently, Eric Olson built a circumstantial case claiming that his father was the victim of "national security homicide." In 1975, after an investigation into overall abuses in the CIA revealed certain details on the Olson case, White House aides Dick Cheney and Donald Rumsfeld helped set up a meeting with President Ford, who apologized to the Olson family. The article went on to tell how the search for truth had consumed Eric Olson's adult life.

When I finished the article, I was concerned about how it found its way to my seat. Nonchalantly, I dropped my napkin in the aisle, and bending over to pick it up, I twisted and looked around to see if anyone was watching me. No one caught my eye.

I could tell Ken thought I was being weird, but that wouldn't be an unusual thought for him.

I sat back, closed my eyes, and considered what I'd just read. *Was the article placed there by a concerned hand, to inform me? To caution me? Was it a threat, telling me to go no further or risk losing what I held dear? Was it a divinely-guided coincidence?*

It seemed clear that if a divine hand placed the article in my path, the message was intended to encourage me to use wisdom. Wisdom not to allow my wellbeing, earning power, or family to be anchored down by a process of discovery, its details, or a desired destination.

On the other hand, maybe someone was trying to give me a clue that national security issues were at stake, thus raising the possibility that the *Marie* was what the article called a 'contrived accident?'

I took out a note pad and wrote: *Consider the CIA: What were they doing in the 1960s? What of the 1950 CIA how-to-do-an-assassination guide book? What of the 1975 CIA report of in-house abuse?*

My mind and heart seemed to find refuge and peace as a thought seeped in, "Fear not. I am with you. I am your God,"

Fear not — but be wise.

****

My second trip to Boston was a bust, at least as far as contacting someone at Raytheon was concerned. Again, I received no response to my requests for a meeting.

However, the trip was not a total loss. My failure to connect with Raytheon a second time left me with a challenge. I was more curious than ever, and I was now forced to go to the newspaper articles as my source for information.

What happened to Raytheon's project team on the *Marie*? I felt as if something was egging me onward. "I dare you to find out what happened." And I couldn't resist the urge to investigate.

Still, I remembered the article about Frank Olson and the CIA assassination information that had been left on my airline seat. An inner voice of wisdom seemed to whisper to me, "Stay alert and don't lose yourself."

I spread the contents of Grandmother's scrapbook on my drafting table, and read each article word for word. I also typed them into my computer, entering every date, every headline, and scanning every image. This enabled me to sort, search, and highlight details.

After I processed every news article. I organized the events in a timeline, listing the facts that were clear and those that were foggy. Interestingly, the newspapers included people's home addresses. I believed it to be a sign of the level of trust and accountability in the communities. Finally, I began to list all the people involved and associated notes in a file I labeled "Stakeholders."

One name I would become very familiar with was Dr. Niel Freeborn Beardsley.

****

I'd never heard of Dr. Beardsley before I opened Grandmother's scrapbook. I had been told that the shipwreck's mystery was intensified because a scientist was on board, but I never knew any specifics. Like my father, Dr. Beardsley was lost at sea and his body never recovered.

Did I hear that there were people who would want to kidnap him? My father along with him?

I found myself drawn to his photograph. He had white hair and a receding hairline that uniquely defined the shape of his head. His enigmatic smile, like Da Vinci's *Mona Lisa*, gave the impression that he had a secret. His glasses and narrow tie seemed fitting for a man of science, but age had softened his features and given him a gentle appearance.

Why was Dr. Beardsley at sea that June day?

He didn't scuba dive like my father. He didn't have knowledge of the area as my father and the other men. He wasn't an engineer; he was a scientist.

His obituary contained an impressive listing of his educational achievements, work, and association memberships. He was a Mason. He was a member of IRIS, whatever that was. He was also a member of The American Rocket Association.

Did that mean he was a rocket scientist?

I compiled Dr. Beardsley's background information into one file, but nothing seemed to link him to anything significant. I found no mention of any publications he had written, and only one project that he had worked on.

The Manhattan Project.

CHAPTER 6:

Propelled into a Mystery

Three years had passed since my mother's memorial service. I hadn't returned to the Santa Barbara and Goleta area since then. Now, I drove alone towards Santa Barbara, and I was nervous.

"I'm too busy," I'd told myself. It was one thing to return to my hometown with my mother; it was another to return on my own. I had just dropped Ken off at the San Jose airport after spending three days at the cabin. I was anxious because I would be spending the next week with my Uncle Albert and Aunt Lynda in their Goleta home.

I had never stayed with them before.

When I arrived, instead of going to their house I joined Al and Lynda at AJ Spurs, an upscale BBQ restaurant. They were with twenty of their friends who had gathered for dinner. AJ Spurs was noisy, full of weekend diners, enjoying the western cattle ranch and wrangling atmosphere. "Hey, this is my niece," Uncle Albert called over the crowd noise.

I was amazed at how much he looked like Grandfather Terres. He had a thin, receding hairline, round features, twinkling blue eyes, and a big smile.

I smiled politely and waved. "Hi everyone."

I was relieved that they had left an empty chair next to a familiar face, Josephine "Jo" Millet. I sat down next to Jo and began catching up. I had worked with her and her late husband on staff at the University of California at Santa Barbara (UCSB). Feeling self-conscious in the presence of twenty strangers, I focused my attention between Jo on my left and Uncle Al and Lynda on my right. At some point in the dinner I heard the words, "Raytheon retired picnic." I looked at the white-haired man sitting across from me and tried to catch what he was saying. I wanted to learn more, but I knew it wasn't the time or the place to raise questions about Raytheon or a 1960 shipwreck.

Joining the group for dinner was a delightful way to begin my time with Uncle Albert and Aunt Lynda. At the close of the evening, Lynda jumped into my car and said, "I'll show you to your room." During the forty-minute drive to her home, we chatted about the evening's events.

A wave of thoughts had been building in my mind, so I took a deep breath and asked. "I've begun poking around on the shipwreck and I'm hoping to ask Uncle Albert what he remembers. Do you think he will mind talking about it?" I asked.

"I think it would be good for Al," she said.

Was I using the shipwreck as a vehicle to discover more about my father? Was I ashamed that I knew so little about him? I was only two when he died. We weren't forbidden to discuss my father, but we never did. I didn't even know his birthday. I talked with my mother about him only twice: once at the fall of the Berlin Wall and once during her last visit with me in Hawaii.

My brother Jim and I discussed my father when we sorted through papers from the lawsuit that followed the shipwreck. And I talked about Dad with my younger brother, Don, when I gave him Dad's handwritten journal. The journal told how Grandpa Terres sold a block of buildings in Goleta to fund a trip to Spain in 1950 with his wife and two sons – Uncle Albert and Dad. Apparently, Dad recorded the story in his journal while serving on the USS Yorktown during the Korean War. I don't remember discussing dad with my brother Rick except in the course of sharing the printed journal when we gathered mid '90's in Spain.

Even though we didn't talk about my father, others remembered him fondly.

One year, I was in a lineup of horses just before the start of Santa Barbara's Fiesta Parade when a handsome gentleman, decked out in a traditional *caballo* outfit, rode up to me on his stallion. I was dressed in a white wedding gown with my Spanish comb and *mantilla*, and clinging to my rider.

"I hear you are Jimmy Terres' daughter," the gentleman said.

I looked at him and smiled, nodding but saying nothing.

Why did I want to shade my eyes behind my lace fan and mantilla?

"I knew your father. I respected him as a man and as my friend," he said, keeping a short rain on his magnificent palomino.

Blinding sunlight reflected off his silver saddle. "I appreciate the comment. Thank you," I replied.

The man gave me his name, but I didn't hear it. My head was awhirl with his first words: *I knew your father.*

I fought back tears. I didn't know my father. I felt guilty and ashamed as I became aware of how little I knew about him.

Now, as Aunt Lynda and I drove to her home, I realized that although I was interested in the shipwreck, I hoped Albert would tell me about my father. He was my father's only sibling. He had lived my father's loss and the search for him. I wanted to know more.

I needed to know more.

CHAPTER 7:

The Lost at Sea Memorial

I never asked Uncle Albert to tell me about my father, but the next morning we started a journey together one step, one conversation, and one discovery at a time. I stumbled from the bedroom and into the kitchen. The aroma of fresh coffee and warm muffins met me.

"I hope you like oatmeal bran and blueberry muffins," Lynda said.

"I sure do."

"First, I need your help. Follow me," she said and handed me a bowl. I followed her out the back door to a vine that ran the length of the house.

"Blackberries," I said, delighted.

Stepping from one stone to another on the path, Lynda rummaged through leaves to pick and hand me little black beauties. After the bowl was full, I followed her out the side gate to the front of the house. Almost immediately the fragrance of roses stopped me short. Lynda took a pair of scissors from her pocket, and stepped into a garden of some thirty bushes, all sizes, shapes, and colors. She caressed a few in admiration, and then cut some others. Returning to the kitchen, Lynda took a bowl of roses from the middle of the kitchen table and refreshed it with the ones we had just collected.

"Get yourself a cup of coffee and sit down," she said.

After breakfast, Uncle Albert said, "Get ready for a ride. There is something that I need to go find."

"I have nothing on my schedule," I said.

We went outside and he directed me to his red, Gold-wing Honda motorcycle. The skies were clear blue and the air from the California coastline crisp; perfect day for a ride.

"I have to make a stop at a local bakery to catch a couple guys first, and then we'll head downtown," Albert said. "There's something I want to show you."

He was a carpenter and heavy machinery contractor by trade, but his passion was playing trumpet. I wasn't surprised that the motorcycle sound system filled the air with music, including the Fat Cats, a group he had recorded with.

Within minutes we were at our destination. Albert motioned for me to follow him over to an umbrella-covered table where four men were sitting. "I can find these guys here every morning," he said. "We're going on a cruise together, and I have some questions."

We grabbed some chairs and sat with them on the wide brick patio. For the next hour, I listened and laughed as these men tried to outdo each other's humor.

A man called Ernie began by telling me that my uncle was part of the "Friday" group that held court on the patio. He pointed a finger at Albert. "But we'll tolerate you on an unsanctioned Monday." Ernie pointed to another patio table. "That's where the retired Raytheon engineers sit every Tuesday morning."

I didn't hear what he said next. I had already begun making plans to be at the Raytheon engineers' table the next morning.

After Albert had the information he came for, he said, "We have to be going. See you guys Friday."

Next, he took us from Goleta to Santa Barbara's harbor area. He drove past the Dolphin Family fountain at the end of State Street and onto the long, wooden wharf. We bumped along to the wharf's end. He was looking for something, but apparently couldn't find it. We turned and rode back down the wharf, and further down Cabrillo Boulevard toward where boats were docked in the Santa Barbara harbor.

Albert parked the bike and placed his helmet on the handles. "Let's walk to the end of the breakwater."

I hadn't walked along the breakwater in years. The water was calm on the marina side, but during high tide, waves crashed up on the rocks and onto the breakwater walkway from the ocean side. I remembered how much fun it was to dodge the saltwater spray.

As we walked, Uncle Albert explained what he had been looking for. "About two months ago, we came across a newspaper article that told about a monument to the shipwreck that your dad was lost on."

I couldn't believe my ears. Had someone created a memorial to the shipwreck and not invited me, one of the victims' daughters?

"You were invited," I asked?

"I had no idea the monument even existed until I read the article in the paper."

We walked from the parking lots along the marina on our left. The Santa Barbara Maritime Museum, a shop, and some restaurants were on our right. In 1960, it was the headquarters of the Coast Guard and Naval Reserve. It was also where my mother sat for hours, waiting for news of my father, and knitting the salmon sweater that I later wore out.

I inhaled deeply as we passed the marina shops toward the breakwater walkway in the distance.

I love the smell of a working harbor.

The sun was almost at its high point and the sea was calm. On our left an array of flags flapped in the wind. We walked past fishing boats and luxury vessels moored at floating docks. On the protected side of the breakwater, just before the sandbar at its end, lay a concrete slab circled by large boulders. Two benches, shaped like whale tails, sat centered on the slab. A stone boulder with a dolphin's head breaking through the top rested on the slab's edge. I sat on one bench. Uncle Al sat on the other. A bronze emblem embedded in the center displayed four dolphin images circling what looked like a star. Another bronze was embedded below the dolphin head on the rock. I read the inscription:

IN MEMORY OF OUR LOVED ONES
WHOSE LIVES AND DESTINIES HAVE BEEN
CLAIMED BY THE SEA.

An image of fish, seaweed, octopi, and the rear view of a youth's head, shoulders and outstretched arms encircled the inscription.

I looked around. Nothing explained the story of this monument. *Whom did this honor? Who designed it?* After we returned home, Albert brought me a box of scrapbooks. "You might want to look through these," he said.

I opened an album of photos of my father. I couldn't remember seeing these before. In one photo, he was a baby in my grandmother's arms. In another, he was a scout in a uniform with a tie, tilted to one side. Another picture was of him as a teen at the beach, and another photo showed him working with his dad on a roadster.

"They built and raced this with the gang on Sundays down the airstrip at the airport," Uncle Al said of that picture.

There were other images of him as a sailor, learning to scuba dive, as a young husband and father, in Fiesta gear. Through the photographs and Uncle Albert's colorful stories, I began to learn more about my father.

And it whet my appetite to learn even more.

CHAPTER 8:

Raytheon Retired Engineers

The following morning, I did what any woman on a mission would do. I put on a becoming outfit, added some rouge and slicked up my lips. Then I returned to the patio Al and I visited the previous day. I found Ernie, but no one else. I re-introduced myself and told him I wanted to connect with the retired Raytheon engineers. Ernie waved to a man at another table. "Gill, this gal wants to talk with you."

I went over to the Raytheon retirees' corner of the patio, and we had a few minutes together before his colleagues began arriving. Gill was a mechanical engineer who had arrived at Raytheon Goleta two years after the shipwreck.

"She wants to know more about her father," Gill told the other men as they arrived.

I introduced myself. A couple of the men were around Raytheon in 1960, but didn't work with my father. These men believed they had nothing to contribute, but they didn't realize how I cherished even their indirect memories. I carried a notepad and wrote what I could. I wasn't a reporter, but I knew that I'd never remember all the details if I didn't take notes.

"It was a big event," a man named Charlie commented. "I arrived at the Goleta Building from the downtown offices and everyone was crying because they had just heard of the accident."

"You need to talk with Dr. Bob," Gill said. Gill took out his cell phone and made a few calls. Before we went our separate ways, Gill handed me a short list of names with phone numbers, including Dr. Bob's and another Bob. "Contact these guys," he told me.

****

For some reason, I was hesitant to call the top man on the list, Dr. Bob Watkins. As a warm up I called the names listed below his, introducing myself by saying, "Gill told me to call you."

While most were cautious, they also graciously shared their memories. Finally, I dialed Dr. Bob's number. No one was home, so I left a message. Throughout the day we played phone tag, but by Wednesday afternoon, Dr. Watkins and I finally connected.

"Why don't you come up to my home for coffee and biscuits tomorrow morning with my wife Rachel and me?" he said.

I hung up, elated that I had the opportunity to meet him face to face.

Dr. Bob Watkins had been at Raytheon in 1960.

SURPRISE

"I'm excited to meet Dr. Bob," I said to Uncle Al and Aunt Lynda as I sat at the kitchen table the next morning.

They smiled and said, "We have a tennis match this morning. We look forward to hearing all about it."

I arrived at Bob and Rachel Watkins' home perched on a hill top and nestled at the end of the canyon lane that they shared with three other homes.

"Welcome," said Dr. Bob, a jovial white-haired gentleman who looked strangely familiar. I shook his hand, and he ushered me into a living room filled with people. On the far side of the room, two familiar faces beamed at me.

Uncle Albert and Aunt Lynda were still wearing their crisp, white tennis outfits. Instead of a tennis match, they had gone ahead of me to their longtime friends' home.

I quickly realized why Dr. Bob looked familiar. I sat across from him just a few days earlier at AJ Spurs. Apparently, Dr. Bob had made the connection from my phone message. The Watkins' and my aunt and uncle had square-danced together for over 30 years. But until I called, they never realized that they also shared a shipwreck story.

In addition, to Al and Lynda, I was greeted by retired engineers who had worked with Dr. Bob in the infrared division at Raytheon. We took a seat. Once the last man arrived, we were a circle of seven.

"We understand that you're seeking information about your father," Dr. Bob Watkins opened the conversation after everyone first introduced themselves. "We all worked together at Building One on Hollister."

Tingles ran down my spine as I realized that these men had worked with my father.

Dr. Bob told me how the Infrared Division (IR) under his direction gave birth to the Shillelagh (pronounced shi-lay-lee) technology, and how Raytheon was successful with it because it was simple, reliable, and lethal. "This science was understood as 'talking on a beam of light,'" Dr. Bob said as he described the technology used for communicating with the Shillelagh missile system.

"I have a Shillelagh," Dr. Bob said, jumping up from his chair and walking toward his garage. Dr. Bob returned holding a wooden club and grinning.

I learned later that the club was indeed called a shillelagh, and was Dr. Bob's inspiration for one of the US Army's most effective weapon systems.

"The tests conducted from the *Marie* used similar technology; however, they were attempting *underwater* communications," Dr. Bob explained. "You must have a transmitting and receiving device." He extended his arms, one hand representing the surface device and the other the underwater device. Dr. Bob grabbed the napkin on the couch beside us, and

FIG 2: My drawing of the Shillelagh.

drew a picture, "I believe it was set up like this."

Dr. Bob continued, "Dr. Max Krasno had a clever idea for testing laser-based communications. They went up to the rooftop of Building One on Hollister, and they had a clear distance to the Santa Ynez Mountains." Dr. Bob said proudly and waved a hand toward the Santa Ynez Mountains beyond his picture windows.

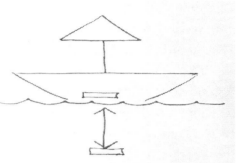

FIG 3: *Communicator usage. My recreation of Dr. Bob's napkin drawing.*

As they described the laser range that spanned Raytheon's Building One on Hollister Avenue and the Santa Ynez mountains, the retired engineers were so excited, they began finishing each other's sentences.

"We made a light beam and we shot it toward the mountains," Dr. Bob said.

"Then we had to wait for the beam to return," Don said.

"Which was $1/86,000^{th}$ of a second," Lee added.

"Remember my great idea of using a garden gazing ball?" Don said with a sparkle in his eye.

They all chuckled.

Don turned to me. "We took a glass ball, maybe the one in the garden out there," He said, pointing out the window to the Watkins garden. "But the radiation beams were *absorbed*, not reflected," Don began, "My brilliant idea verified that only a silver-backed mirror gave the amplitude and modulation needed."

"The *Marie* hit an object. That was one speculation," Lee interjected, turning the conversation back to the shipwreck. "It was common

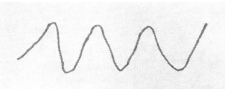

FIG 4: *My drawing of light beam "modulation" wave or signal.*

knowledge that the waters in the SB Channel were calm on the morning they went out, but the waves increased considerably by the afternoon. They could easily capsize a boat. That was another possibility."

"The *Marie* had the equipment for talking on a beam of light," Dr. Bob said. He stopped short when the doorbell rang. Opening the door, he welcomed Howie, another retired Raytheon engineer.

"Teresa is interested in what we were doing in the infrared division," said Dr. Bob.

"The US was threatened by Russian submarines," Howie said. "And the military had money to spend trying to establish a defense against the Russian submarine menace. So, the infrared department was developing communications systems to help with this."

At Howie's mention of the Russians, my mind traveled back to when the Berlin Wall was crumbling. I asked my mother, "Why do I have this wild idea that Dad might have been kidnapped by Russians, and if Russia opens up, Dad may come walking home?"

I had assumed Mother would dispel my childhood myth. She admitted that a kidnapping was one of the scenarios that had been discussed, and that she had also entertained the idea that my father could come walking home. "It's in God's hands," she said.

Howie added credibility to what I thought was little more than a family myth.

"So, the men of the *Marie* had a guy with the equipment at each point, to see what was useful to help with our National Defense," Howie said. Howie's arms outlined a horizontal use of the sending and receiving equipment.

"Very creative group... the IR Dept.," Lee said.
"Krasno hired the team," replied Dr. Bob

"Belmont equipment used for talking under water via infrared?"

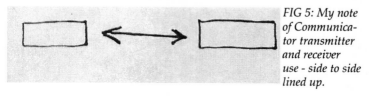

FIG 5: My note of Communicator transmitter and receiver use - side to side lined up.

Howie asked.

The others nodded.

"Russell and Terres were divers. It was a 'toy shop' under water. Russell was a good guy. Special guy." Don's voice trailed off.

"I was in the radar department," said Lee. "The infrared department was a highly innovative group." "I talked with your dad, but especially with Jim Russell. I came to Raytheon in January of '59," Don said. "The first day I came to work we played with an airplane and I went home thinking this was going to be a great place to work."

"Airplane?" Dr. Bob left the group and disappeared into his garage. We could hear him shuffling things around. He returned shortly, holding up a two-foot-long white model airplane. "Look familiar Don?"

"We weren't making money in the Infrared Department," Don said.

"In '62 an audit group came to review operations because of the financial issues," Dr. Bob added.

"Program funding was phased out and a new process began that took several phases before a project was fully funded," Lee added. "No matter how great a success you had in research, you had to sell your idea to the company." The date, 1962, raised a red flag in my mind. That was when the victims' families' lawsuit surfaced in the judicial system.

"Santa Barbara had a lot of technology. The IR Division on Hollister was a small entity," Howie said. "Some 87 other places could have been better and more advanced in IR development." Howie recounted how he started with Raytheon in 1956 with the Belmont group. "When I arrived at the Goleta site. A group at lunch asked, 'Play Bridge?'"

"'No, I said.'"

"'Willing to learn?'" asked the group.

"'Uh,'" I began.

"'Sit down,' the Bridge group demanded. They hardly missed a day. It was unusual for anyone to miss a game," Howie said.

"When Harold Mackie missed two, then three games, we were really concerned." He looked down at his hands, folded in his lap.

"I worked with optical physics at Raytheon in Chicago," Dr. Bob said. Then the company told them they were going to move to the western suburbs. "I thought they meant western Chicago. They were talking about California. Raytheon wanted to be near Lockheed.

"Folks at Raytheon like to tell the story about Santa Barbara's welcome ceremony, held on the steps of the Hollister building. The Lieutenant Governor of California hadn't done his homework and pronounced the name incorrectly: 'Ray – A – Thon,'" Dr. Bob said, mimicking the mispronunciation.

With a little homework, the welcome committee would have also learned the meaning of the company's name. "Ray" comes from "rai," an old French word that means "a beam of light," and "theon" comes from the Greek word for god. "From the gods, a beam of light."

During a lull in the conversation, Don stood up. "I need to be leaving." It was past noon and the conversation was drawing to a comfortable close.

"There is a Raytheon Retiree's Picnic, on Wednesday, September 7th. It's a potluck," Dr. Bob said. "You might find it of interest to join us."

I planned on it.

CHAPTER 9:

Imagineers

On Friday morning, I called Bob Wilke once again. He was the other Bob on the list I got at the bakery. He was reluctant at first, as he and his wife, Helen, were packing for a trip. However, we agreed to have a brief dinner date at Denny's in Goleta that evening before they headed out of town.

"It was all state of the art technology," he said.

He told me how they were experimenting to see what would happen. When they stumbled onto something they would ask, "Is it useful, and can we work with it?"

"The whole sequence began with Raytheon in Chicago developing an infrared communication system," said Bob. "I ran the optical tests."

He told me a story that overlapped with some of the details I had heard the day before at Dr. Bob Watkins' home.

"In the infrared department, we built and tested communicators."

I heard of Raytheon Chicago the previous day, but didn't understand how it fit in with the *Marie*. "After Raytheon moved to Hollister Avenue, we were right across from the Santa Barbara Airport in Goleta. Dr. Krasno had the brainstorm to go up to the rooftop. We would go up on the roof and bounce a beam off the mountain, about 3.5 miles as the crow flies."

Bob added mathematical details, a tendency I noticed was

characteristic of the engineers.

"So, then the question became, 'Can we extend this?' We had two communicators on the mountaintop attached electronically, so that we would beam our signal up to the receiver at the top of the mountain. It would then send the signal to a transmitter down into the valley towards Solvang." Wilke's arms moved to animate and recreate the activity.

He continued to pick up speed, and his delight in telling the story showed on his face. "We happened to be on the roof when we saw a missile going up from Vandenberg Air Force Base. We tried to bounce a signal off it, but the missile went too fast, so we didn't catch anything. But one day, we did."

I was familiar with Vandenberg Air Force Base, a thirty-minute drive north of Goleta. My oldest brother Jim had been a technician there, working the launch system. Bob continued, "We recorded some information on a tape with our communicator, and then we started to analyze it. We called ourselves the Imagineers because you had to imagine what might be recorded. After several missiles and after a time, we began to see some patterns that began to make sense. That is when Dr. Bob Watkins, and likely Dr. Krasno, wrote a white paper and sent it to the Air Force saying, 'Look what we can do.'

"That is how we got the contract for looking at missiles. Because of that contract, we were given the launch codes from Vandenberg. And every day at various times they would change the code for that day.

"Russian Trawlers were off the coast of Santa Barbara, they were tracking and trying to gain information from Vandenberg's launches as well," said Wilke. "We had access to special codes. So, after we were on this contract, Vandenberg informed us when they were going to do a bogus missile launch to throw off the Russians."

My heart started pounding and my palms felt sweaty. I wanted to have him stop and repeat what he just said.

"One of my family's myths is that Russian espionage may have played a part in the *Marie* tragedy," I said.

By this time, we had finished our meals. The plates clattered as the server cleared them. I ordered a fresh cup of coffee and asked, "How does this all relate to the tests underwater and the *Marie*?"

"It all goes back to communication by infrared," Wilke confirmed. "Once we were successfully transmitting back and forth through the air, somebody said, 'I wonder if we could communicate under water?'

"The idea was to take our regular communicators, encase them in waterproof containers, and try to beam infrared under water." He described the dimensions of the communicator: 12" x 8", with a black window on one end. He sketched an image for me on my notepad:

He went on to give me details I already knew from the news articles, that Raytheon had contracted a vessel for the tests. "They were setting up to run underwater tests with two communicators.

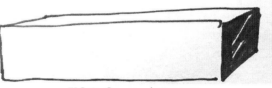

FIG 6: *Communicator note.*

"I was supposed to be on the *Marie* as an observer that day," said Bob. "but they felt it was more important to test the water samples they brought back from the previous trip. They wanted me to analyze how transparent sea water is to an infrared beam. That's what I was doing the day when the *Marie* went out. The group went out very early, and they were supposed to be back somewhere about 5:00 p.m. But when five o'clock came around, there were no sightings of the boat or anything. I assume it was Dr. Krasno who got the Coast Guard involved. That part of the story I don't know."

"What did you do when the *Marie* didn't return?" I asked.

"It was about dinner time. A lot of us went down to the wharf to stand around and wait. We stayed there until 11:00 p.m."

Like my mother, he understood the team was due back the evening that they departed. But, as I examined the details closely, it became clear that the team went out on Tuesday, June 7, and everyone went in search and down to the dock on Thursday, June 9.

"What happened on Wednesday?"

"The Coast Guard was out searching," he said. "There was no indication of what happened. It was just a wait and see type situation. It wasn't until a day or two later that they found some debris. They had no idea where the boat sank or what happened to it.

"I had a few nights where I didn't sleep very well. I could imagine a mishap and these people being in distress. Hal Mackie wasn't much of a swimmer. It was a tough experience. And I had a strange feeling, because I was supposed to be on that craft.

"The event was emotional for the entire company because we were like a family. People were crying. We felt so helpless."

We sat in silence. It was our humble way to honor the moment. I could tell that he found some peace in sharing his memories with me. I know hearing his story brought me peace. Our eyes met and we smiled at each other.

Was he aware that he didn't say what happened on Wednesday?

Finally, Bob held up a laser pointer and circled a narrow red beam on the floor. "This is an offshoot of the technology they were working on. So are devices that use IR light, like TV remotes and checkout scanners in stores."

My cup of coffee had grown cold, and it was getting late. "My father and the others must have felt honored to be working on a worthy effort," I said.

"I think the key thing," Bob Wilke continued, "was that the top brass could tell the technology was working."[17]

I returned to Al and Lynda's feeling a deep sense of peace. I was in awe of the window into my father's world the retired Raytheon engineers opened for me by sharing their stories. Dr. Watkin's words rang in my memory. "We didn't discover the science," he'd said. "We engineered expanded uses for it." I respected and admired these men and their accomplishments. And my father had briefly been one among them.

The experience of the last few days had drained me emotionally, nourished me spiritually, and frightened me. I had thought I was going to learn about a shipwreck. Instead, my mind was now juggling memories that included Chicago, California, Vandenberg AFB's Pacific Missile Range, missiles, and communicating on a beam of light. I felt like it was all spinning out of control.

I knew that only a divine hand could have orchestrated these encounters, and I had to trust in God to see His purpose for it all.

Saturday, I woke early and took a drive, somewhat aimlessly along a very familiar path.

I parked and took a second walk to the Lost at Sea Memorial. I sat on one of the benches and reviewed my notes.

Soon, two men walked on to the slab of cement. I overheard one of the men telling about his wife's experience spearheading the creation of the slab, bronzes, and benches to honor her younger brother who had been lost at sea.

I went over and introduced myself to them.

"How is it that the monument is such a perfect space, yet recognizes no individual, group, or story?" I asked.

"The city gatekeepers permitted the construction of the monument, but wouldn't allow further identifying information, not even of those who contributed funds or time or talents. My wife devoted herself to raising the necessary funds within her circle of family and friends. Another generous benefactor contributed to the monument with virtually no recognition."

The man said that he and his wife didn't know about those lost on the *Marie* until sculptor Bud Bottoms added his creative energy to the effort. "Bud sculpted the dolphin family," the man pointed toward the fountain at the base of the wharf across from where we stood.

The encounter with these two men helped me better understand what I now called the Lost at Sea Memorial. At first, I was angry that someone had created a memorial and I wasn't involved or invited. But eventually I realized that this was a blessing, because now I didn't have to build a monument to the *Marie*. A monument already existed. The Lost At Sea Memorial wasn't a perfect solution, but it was a beautiful and peaceful location.

On my last evening in town, I had supper with Laura Funkhouser at her apartment, the same apartment where my father and uncle were raised. As I sat in an armchair and she on the couch, I felt a sense of *déjà vu*. Laura's husband came up the tile staircase, and at that moment a distant memory flashed in my mind. I saw Dad and Mom holding each other's hand. I lowered my head as I caught my breath and closed my eyes.

It had been quite a week, and this memory was like a wink from heaven.

Not long before, I sat on a porch swing with a couple girlfriends, overlooking a wilderness. "I'd like your prayers," I told them. "I'm interested in knowing more about my father and the shipwreck he was lost on." This week had been a providential succession of not-so-chance meetings. Since the time I was a young girl, I had prayed to "Our Father who art in heaven." Now, I couldn't help but feel that perhaps those very prayers had led me to this week's window of opportunity, to Al and Lynda, and to these retired engineers who gave me insight into what had interested my father and changed my life.

FIG 7: Grandparents dancing at a Luau in honor of my Grandmother Terres' birthday. Held at Hollister apartment, Old Town Goleta. (cir 1950's)

CHAPTER 10:

Memories

Something inside warned that I wouldn't get a second invitation to the Raytheon Retirees Picnic. I couldn't let this opportunity slip away, so I returned to Santa Barbara two weeks later. After my first visit to Uncle Al's, I left with a photo album devoted to my father's childhood through young adulthood. I wanted to take other family photo albums, but Uncle Albert wouldn't give them to me.

"What will be left to entice you to return?" he said. The photo albums were tempting, but I had my heart set on a better treasure. On my last visit to Uncle Al's, I had asked, "Do you remember Grandma's antique record player with all the small records?"

He nodded. "It was sold along with many things after we lost her."

"I thought as much," I said. "I remember one time you put on a small black record and I heard someone singing. 'That's your dad,' you told me."

When I returned to Uncle Albert's, I found the small record, encased in brittle yellow paper, on the dresser in my room.

I was delighted. "You found it!"

"It took considerable shuffling, but I still had it," said Al. He took the record over to his record player.

My mind wandered back to that night. "That's my dad, Grandma," I cried out, but instead of being happy, she ran from the room. I was bewildered. Why would she run away?

Albert put the old record on a turntable, and once again I heard my father's voice calling out to me. My heart leaped as Dad sang a beautiful old love song about kisses, caring, and dreaming.[18]

Al took the record off the player. "Your dad goes on to sing *Slow Boat to China* with Alan Sepulveda, and then I tell a joke about the Goleta Department Store. It was a take on a popular TV routine. The record is yours if you promise to have it digitized and share copies with your brothers."

I hugged him. "I promise." I took the record from his hand and held it to my heart. "Your grandmother couldn't bear to remember your father," said Al.

A distant memory surfaced. "She visited my bedroom only once," I said.

I was seven years old, and Grandpa had died earlier that year. We had moved into a new house and I invited Grandmother to a tea party in my new blue and white bedroom. She had given me her mother's twin white crocheted bedspreads, and I had placed them proudly on my new twin beds next to the wicker bassinette that Dad and a bunch of other Terres babies had slept in. I felt like a princess in my new, blue and white room. I had arranged my collection of mini piggy banks in the cubbyholes of my tiered, white-wooden bookcase, an assortment that included a lion, a horse, a hippo, but, ironically, no pig. On the top, in a place of honor, I placed a framed photograph of my father.

When Grandma walked in, the door bumped into the bookshelf, and my dad's photo fell. Grandma picked it up and looked at my father's formal Navy portrait a moment.

"Your dad made that bookshelf in high school," said Grandma, returning the picture to its place.

"Guess that's why I like it," I said.

Without another word, she turned and left.

I was confused at the time, but now I understood.

"She couldn't bear the sight of his face," said Albert. "We had to remove all the photos. I guess she had to escape the sound of his voice, too."

It never dawned on me to ask Grandmother why she never spoke about my father. The truth was, none of us spoke about him.

****

The next day, I hopped onto the back of Uncle Albert's red, Gold-Wing motorcycle and we headed to Stow Park for the Raytheon Retirees Picnic.

In addition to my notepad and camera, I carried flyers explaining my interest in the shipwreck. Although I didn't know exactly where my efforts were leading me, I knew I needed to form a circle of communications.

It seemed reasonable to announce the upcoming 50-year milestone of the shipwreck, thus giving me a logical purpose for connecting with the retirees.

At the Raytheon retirees' picnic, I was once again face to face with Dr. Bob Watkins. Dr. Watkins introduced me to the others who had gathered in the park. I was pleased to encounter more people from Raytheon who lived through the 1960 tragedy and were willing to share their memories. I took down a few notes and contact information and hoped I would be able to touch base again.

After the picnic one person responded by letter and two by e-mail. I valued every insight.

One person wrote:

> I never did hear an official finding of the cause of the accident, but it appeared to be a combination of a less-than-seaworthy ship combined with no or inadequate onboard radio communication capability....
> (John, Letter to the author, 2007).

Another wrote:

I worked at Raytheon during the time the ship was lost. All the men who were lost from Raytheon came out of my department and one out of my section. It has been a long time.... I was an electronic technician at the time, working in the Infrared Department, and a lot of the work...was secret.

(Jerry, First e-mail).

In another e-mail, Jerry wrote:

I just remember your dad as a young engineer at the time. About my age I think, trying to support his family, like me, and the suddenness of it all. All the people lost were good guys....

P.S. I do remember that your Dad was friendly and likable.

(Jerry, Second e-mail).

CHAPTER 11:

Distress Signal

My home office occupied two rooms connected by a full bathroom. The larger room overlooked the 9th fairway and green of the nearby golf course. I could see the clubhouse in the distance through the window. The smaller room—what I called my inner office—was on the other side of the bathroom. This room had no windows and was piled high with project papers and binders. The walls were usually covered with project-related post-it notes and timelines, along with posters, artwork and family photos that fueled my imagination.

My trip to the Raytheon Retirees Picnic hadn't brought any great revelations, but I had made many contacts that would be helpful in my quest to learn more about my father. Now, back in my home office, Grandmother's scrapbook lay spread over my desk as I reviewed the contents of sympathy cards and letters in the back pages.

One letter stood out. Postmarked June 25, 1960. It was a letter from my mother to my grandmother written from our cabin shortly after dad was lost at sea.

The letter released a flood of memories.

Mother and the four of us were in the shade on the cabin's green deck. "I need your help," she said. "Let's write a letter to Grandma Terres."

I clearly remembered not wanting to write. I wanted to talk with my grandma. I wanted to ask, "Grandma, what happened? Where's Daddy?"

Long-buried feelings and confusion resurfaced as I read the collection of letters. I remembered my brothers and me, sitting on our sleeping bags as we wrote letters and drew pictures for Grandmother.

I was too young to write, so Mom told me to draw a picture of my younger brother, Donny. I didn't want to draw a picture. I wanted to talk to Grandmother. I wanted my daddy. I had cried, but mother didn't understand me.

Now, almost fifty years later, long-buried frustrations bubbled to the surface as I read my mother's words:

> I will try to come back to Santa Barbara that same week, so I thought that we might plan to have a service Friday or Saturday – that would be the 8th or 9th of July. Or maybe it would be better to have it Sunday or Monday the 10th or 11th....
>
> I think about these plans but somehow I just can't give up hope. I keep dreaming at night of them in a boat or landed at Baja California below Ensenada somewhere where they couldn't get in touch with anyone quickly. But I guess I will have to try to go on with as normal a life as possible after a month has passed....
>
> Please take care of yourselves and we will see you in a little less than 2 weeks.

"I needed to get to the cabin's safe-haven," Mom told me later. After Dad wasn't found right away, Mother moved us all to "higher ground." Mom said on one of the rare times we talked about it.

Finding this letter was yet another step in unlocking the door to my heart's unresolved issues.

****

I returned home one day to an e-mail with the subject line, "Your Dad." It was from a cousin on my mother's side. I was already familiar with most of the information she shared; however, one detail piqued my interest.

"Your dad had told your mom that if there was ever any unordinary trouble, he would turn his sweatshirt inside out. Supposedly they found a sweatshirt turned inside out."

My heart began to race. I wanted to grab the phone and call immediately. But I decided to hold off until I could do a little more investigation.

I opened the document where I had entered the news articles from Grandma's scrapbook, spanning a period from 1960 to 1969. I typed "sweatshirt" into the document's search box. I got one hit:

> Richard A. Dowse, 134 E. Alamar Ave., the owner of the *Marie*, last night positively identified a gray engine hatch cover as being from his boat. He also identified five life jackets, all of them returned to Santa Barbara Harbor by the two Coast Guard cutters involved in the search. One of the life jackets had tied to it a man's blue sweatshirt. Both the sweatshirt and the lifejacket itself were torn, as if by sharks, Coast Guardsmen said. They believed it had been worn by one of the still missing men.[19]

I picked up the phone and dialed my cousin Gayle in Hawaii. Gayle was 12 when my father was lost at sea in June 1960. She broke the news about the shipwreck to my mother's parents.

Mom's parents—Gayle's and my Nanny and Poppy—often spent time camping in the Nevada desert in their sixteen-foot trailer. They were on one of their adventures when the tragedy happened, and couldn't be easily reached.

My aunt called the Nevada Highway Patrol and they tacked notes to post office bulletin boards around where Nanny and Poppy might be, hoping they would find the message: "Call home; son lost in shipwreck."

Nanny and Poppy finally saw the note and called Gayle's home.

She was the only one home and told her grandparents about the shipwreck.

Nanny and Poppy closed their campsite and headed to Santa Barbara to help with the kids, but found an empty house. Mother had already gone to the cabin to get away from the reporters. Nanny and Poppy headed up to the cabin, too.

Gayle described the significance of the sweatshirt. "Because of the top-secret nature of the research, your mom and dad had a signal that if anything went wrong, he would turn his sweatshirt inside out and tie it to a life jacket."

Mom never mentioned this. She told me how signals were used during her years as a Navy Wave and how Dad, a jet engine mechanic, had used them on the USS Yorktown aircraft carrier to identify distant aircraft as friend or foe as well as jets preparing to land or in need of special emergency services. But if she had ever said anything to me about Dad's sweatshirt being located in the search, I had no memory of it.

I turned to the scrapbook and re-read the words "One of the life jackets had tied to it a man's blue sweatshirt…as if torn by a shark."

Uncle Albert later confirmed that Dad had talked about leaving behind a signal if anything went wrong out at sea.

After sifting through the conversations and news reports, I concluded the signal was that Dad would tie his sweatshirt right side out if he was saying goodbye; however, he would tie his sweatshirt inside out to signal an unusual threat, such as espionage.

No wonder I grew up thinking the scientist and my father were kidnapped by Russians.

Was the sweatshirt right-side out or inside out? Mother had fled the area before she learned about dad's signal. Something went terribly wrong that day, but what?

CHAPTER 12:

Dolphin Family Sculptor

A phone call from my friend Laura Funkhouser turned the tide. She had just read an LA Times Magazine article about Bud Bottoms, the sculptor who contributed to the creation of the *Lost at Sea Memorial*. The story began and ended with references to the *Marie* shipwreck.

"There's a picture of your dad and Bud Bottoms in scuba gear," she said, "The article says Bud should have been on the *Marie*."

"I'm drawn to understand the shipwreck, but I'm having no success in connecting with Raytheon's president," I said. "I'm frustrated. What else can I do."

"You started at the top. Try starting at the bottom," Laura said. She explained how to leverage the Freedom of Information Act (FOIA) as well as military and national archives and their historians. "Use the tools available to citizens."

After we said goodbye, I found the LA Times article online. Sure enough, there was a half-dressed Bud Bottoms pulling on clothes, and in front of him were two wetsuit-clad men in an open shelter of a boat.

I examined every image in the article and read James "Bud" Bottoms description of his friends lost on the *Marie*.

"[They were] most expert outdoorsmen, nervy, athletic tough guys who might one weekend whip down to Mexico to hunt panther and the next be back home to spear a basking shark, dive for lobster or bag some venison." [20]

Because I was becoming familiar with the basic story facts, I recognized that the article contained some misinformation. The number of victims reported lost and recovered was incorrect. My father was called Jim or Jimmy by his friends; yet, the article referred to him by his given name, "Diego."

I lingered on the printed words, "The nature of the underwater tests had to do with submarines; and more than one speculated a Russian submarine's involvement."[21]

At the time, I had no idea if this was true or a myth.

The article also recounted Bud's entry into the bronze sculpting world from a graphic design background. Santa Barbara selected his entry of a dolphin family leaping together for a fountain at the end of the city wharf. Bud worked with local foundries to bring his vision into being.

I e-mailed a link to the article to my brothers. My brother Don was online when my e-mail arrived in his inbox. Don lived next door to an editor with the LA Times. With her assistance, Don connected with Bud by phone. Within an hour, Don called me to tell me about his conversation with Bud Bottoms, and that he would be joining Bud at his studio the following Saturday.

His swift action confirmed what I already knew. Don, who was only one when Dad died, shared my thirst to know our father.

Don said, "Bud has an upcoming TV interview to be held at the breakwater memorial, something on why he does what he does." Don also recounted how Bud said, "Dad saved his life,"[22] but I must have missed whatever he said after that.

I envied Bud. He had a story to tell—a story that began and ended with a picture of him and my dad on the *Marie*.

These revelations would have been stressful under the best of circumstances, but with our family's ongoing struggles related to Mother's estate—especially the cabin—I was beginning to feel angry because I didn't have a story to tell about my dad.

CHAPTER 13:

Battles

I was angry because I couldn't resolve the scrapbook story and, on top of that, I had to engage in painful family battles.

As executor of my mother's trust, when she died I had to put my grief for her on hold. Now those long-buried emotions began to leak through my carefully-constructed defenses. I found it difficult to communicate with family members who had an interest in the cabin. We all shared years of good memories from there. However, by the winter of 2007 a definite chill set in. I harbored feelings of anger, abandonment, betrayal, and rejection, especially over things cabin-related.

I battled with Mom's health insurance company, which went belly up after 9/11, leaving thousands in unpaid bills. I had to travel to her home in San Francisco area to wrap up her condo and other personal effects. I grappled with local, state, and federal tax paperwork. I endured a year of preparations for the face-off with arbitrators and the man mother had married the year before she passed away. I tried to minimize his share of the estate, but couldn't get it below one third of what mother's four children inherited, excluding the cabin.

Like the heavy winter snow that blanketed the cabin, my mind was weighed down by frustration.

"I'm going to sell the cabin," I told Ken.

"You don't want to do that," he said.

"I'll give it away to a cousin, then. That's what some believe is the right thing to do." Tears flowed as I read aloud a terse e-mail.

"Use wisdom," Ken advised. "Your reactions to words are honest, but they have limited perspective. Take heart. You have come down the path by picking and tackling one low-hanging fruit at a time. Keep taking baby steps and you'll get through the cabin's remaining paperwork and surmount the issues."

Ken's words were like a life-preserver.

"Okay, I'll keep on," I said.

But it wasn't as easy as he made it sound.

****

I fought on the home front—in Arkansas—also. I didn't ask to be the leader of the Family Program, but when I was assigned the role, I took my position seriously. Nevertheless, I wasn't prepared to deal with three binders filled with national standards, regulations, expectations, and training that applied to soldiers and their families. I expected to fill the role only two years, but those two years stretched into five.

With the wars in Afghanistan and Iraq and a brilliant GED program picking up speed, PEC expanded to 450 staff and housed up to 30,000 students and attendees in any single year. Additionally, for the first time in history full-time National Guard Bureau staff were deploying from PEC, and their families were also under our nurture and care.

I felt stressed because I had no game plan, little training, and sometimes minimal patience as I juggled the complex emotions involved with serving families, volunteers, soldiers, civilian staff and Colonel Kenneth H. Newton.

I finally decided to see a counselor, who suggested I begin journaling. I found a blank journal that had a salsa dancer on the cover. That made me smile. I used this journal for all things related to the *Marie* shipwreck. I started a second journal that covered hodgepodge of issues such as the cabin and my changing body, mind, and spirit.

I also began a digital journal about the shipwreck. This one was more like a communication log where I entered dates, connections, notes, results, and actions to take.

It was in doing these journals that I made a stunning discovery.

My father had never had a funeral or memorial service.

That discovery came because of one newspaper article's sub-head: "ALL BUT ONE."[23] The article listed all the funeral services that had been held. My father's was not among them.

I searched Grandmother's scrapbook but found nothing about a service for my father. The newspaper description of my father offered little to no insight into his short life other than that he graduated from Santa Barbara High School, was a Navy vet of the Korean War, graduated from California Polytechnic University as a mechanical engineer and was lost at sea while working for Raytheon.

I asked Uncle Albert about Dad's memorial service.

"There wasn't any," he replied. "Your mother and grandmother believed they would find him in Mexico," he said. Uncle Al went on to tell me how both my grandmother and my mother had had dreams of the lifeboat holding Dad in it. Some scuba diving friends had even charted the Santa Barbara Channel currents to Santa Rita, a place in Baja California.

Al told me that he believed the lack of a memorial service contributed to my grandmother's inability to accept her son's death. No wonder I knew so little about Dad. I became angry at this, too.

I decided that because our father's short life had not been remembered or honored, I would do something for him on the 50th anniversary of the shipwreck.

****

During my battles, I often looked to Ken for support and, most of the time, he was sensitive to my situation. But sometimes he reacted like an Army staff sergeant.

He thought of it as "iron sharpening iron." But right then my iron was more like linen. I was wearing a stack of hats that I had never asked to wear, and the weight was crushing me.

One day when I came to him for support, he said, "Just get over it. I can't be your girlfriend."

His words were a gut punch.

I wanted to call my mother crying, but she was gone.

I wanted to cry with girlfriends, but they were in Hawaii.

Ken's words hurt because what he said was true.

A military command has many responsibilities, and Ken's shoulders bore the weight of PEC. I expected Ken to be my counselor, best friend, and lover, but he was as stressed as I was.

Nevertheless, his sharp words made me feel isolated, like I was treading water and desperately trying to stay afloat.

Ken was soaring high as PEC's Commander and the Commandant but I was crashing and burning. My frustration grew as I considered the shipwreck story, Grandmother's grief, Mother's letter written from the cabin's deck, sweatshirt signals from my father, and Russian trawlers.

CHAPTER 14:

Perspective

Finding myself in an emotional corner was a new experience. I no longer had a personal or professional support network, and the relationships I was building were too new.

It was a crisp winter morning. I decided to take a sunrise walk down the golf-cart path that ran by my office window. Sometimes I listen to music when I walk, but not that day. I listened. I looked around. I observed the morning sunlight as it woke up the world. Stripped of their leaves, the trees along the path looked dead. But they were very much alive, and when spring came everything would change. Everything looked bleak, but something had to be happening.

I was in a personal winter, a season that I should not fear, but honor. The bare branches around me were not dead, but awaiting their rebirth in spring. But I realized that I, too, would be reborn to enjoy springtime.

I had no idea how long it would take to be renewed, but I decided to embrace this season of life. I stretched myself by taking a variety of workshops and small group sessions. I read books and nurtured new friendships. I took three classes at PEC on facilitation, leadership, and (change) management. I reached out into the community of Little Rock and joined a businesswomen's prayer breakfast. I volunteered at a wellness center, a girls' home, and city-wide clean-up days. Because dancing brings me joy, I made space in my inner room where I could be free to take out my castanets and dance. Transformation didn't happen overnight, but as I became more open and committed to the opportunities I did have, I also became more grateful for them. With each small step, I emerged from my isolation.

Something was stirring in Ken's heart too. When our oldest child's father-in-law, Dr. Robert Rice, invited Ken to a men's group that met weekly to talk about succeeding at home and work, he went.[24] As he participated in the men's group, Ken began to change.

He began contributing around the home more. "One good deed a day," he said.

I wasn't sure what that meant.

I heard him repeating Bible verses. "And we know…God works… to the good…of those that are called…according to His purpose."

"What's up with the broken record?" I asked.

"They said it was a good verse to know. Five points, one verse, to sum up the Bible," he said as he repeated and taught me Romans 8:28.

I was touched by the changes I saw in Ken. I had feared for our future. But he was a man of character and now was choosing to spend time with a group of men who were helping him grow. He was trying to serve God. He was serving me. He was serving his nation.

One thing led to another. When Robert Rice's wife, Marion, invited me to join a women's group, I agreed to go. Then when they invited us to attend church with them one Sunday, Ken and I went. Attending Fellowship Bible Church fed our wellbeing and our marriage. It equipped us to manage our emotions, our finances, and our family. Worshiping a sovereign God became our joy and our life purpose.

One day at our small group, I found myself sitting on an old, green metal glider, overlooking a pond surrounded by a stand of pine trees. One of the other wives, Glenda Watson, sat next to me and Marion Rice, leaned against the rail.

If I trust these folks, I should be able to share one of my deepest secrets.

"My child's heart longs to know my father and understand his story, how and why he was lost in a shipwreck," I said, almost in a whisper.

"Tell me more," said Glenda.

My heart soared with her acceptance and encouragement.

"What purpose will it serve?" Marion asked. She seemed to be sincerely interested.

"I feel a calling on my heart to do so," I said feeling this response was lacking.

It was true. I could feel the two-year-old crying out within me, wanting to know her father, needing to know if he lived or died that day. I tried to hold back the tears as my throat tightened. "Will you pray for me?"

I didn't understand what was moving me forward; I just felt drawn to do it. So, on that rusty glider, I was vulnerable and transparent with a couple girlfriends whom I had come to trust.

A few weeks later, I found myself sitting with Marion, this time at a demonstration for the Mustard Tree Art Festival.[25] The festival had a different biblical theme every year. Marion had entered previous art festivals on themes of Psalms 23 and Jonah. Today's demonstration was to explain this year's theme: *The Prodigal — An Exploration of Luke 15.*

The presenter described the three parables from Luke 15: the lost coin, lost sheep, and lost son. Jesus' parables told of a search to find something of value, a humbling experience, a time of repentance, and a moment of rejoicing, all examples of the joy God takes in restoring what once was lost.

As I sat beside my friend, I visualized the *Marie* shipwreck story, realized as a work of art. I saw a cutaway of the deep, blue Pacific Ocean, with the sun setting behind Santa Cruz Island in the distance. A collage of black and white newspaper clippings in the foreground served as a frame. Front and center was a picture of Grandfather at the helm searching for one of his two sons. A stack of stones in the foreground formed a cross, echoing Santa Cruz (Holy Cross) island, each stone bearing a cameo image of one of the seven men. A heavenly light shone in from above, bathing the images and connecting the past with the present. I have a creative background, and over the years I had created quite a few photo collages. So, when I left the presentation with Marion, I was inspired to create the image I'd seen in my mind's eye as a shipwreck commemorative art piece.

Back in my inner room, I took out Grandmother's scrapbook. Flipping through the pages, I focused on the images I found. Could they be compiled, I wondered, as I closed my eyes to try and visualize it.

My inner room was perfect for a creative effort where no one would come in to bother me. However, my space had also become a dumping ground for project piles and other odds and ends.

I needed to organize the room for a new purpose—as a place of creativity.

I purchased a bookshelf and a couple of baskets and bins to hold other things. I shuffled furniture to create more desktop space. I hung three large mirrors on the walls that had been catching dust in a storeroom. I also created an open space, because I longed to exercise with dance as I had from childhood. I hung pictures that I loved to look at. I tacked up encouraging quotes. I even hung some artwork from my years toying with pen and ink, watercolor, and graphic arts. My inner space became a unique hodgepodge, a creative refuge.

The commemorative art continued to take form in my mind. I considered the various ways I could create it. I could do a pen and ink image of everything, including reproductions of the news headlines and text, and cover with a wash of watercolor. Or I could paint a background and paste copies of the news articles into place. I could attempt to create something using photo-editing software and print technology, but I hadn't used such technology beyond removing red-eye, cropping edges, and printing. I could tinker with the software, I thought, perhaps using Photoshop to place the images into a layout and design.

I'd have to give it some thought.

Ultimately, I created a piece I titled *Real-Time Luke 15.*

My artwork had seven ovals overlaid on a stack of seven stones. Each of the six ovals framed an image of one of those lost in the shipwreck. However, the bottom oval held a mirror where an image of Mr. Paul Lovette belonged.

This was because, in all the news articles with photos of the lost men, Paul Lovette's was never included—except for the photo under the headline "Six Santa Barbarans Lost at Sea; Body of 7th Found."[26] Below this headline was a picture of the Coast Guard off-loading a stretcher that held Paul Lovette's shark-torn body, covered by a tarp— Lovette was originally from the East Coast and was new to the Santa Barbara area. When his father came to recover his body, he left without a word to reporters.

Connecting the image, headline, and mirror was a spoke on the helm's wheel.

By creating an image to tell the story of the *Marie* shipwreck, I saw the tragedy in a new light. It wasn't black and white but, part of a colorful legacy.

The Fall 2008 Prodigal Art Festival's opening night came, and my art-piece was displayed in a prominent place. Below the piece, its name *Real-time Luke 15*, was printed on a small card.

As friends gathered to celebrate and view the three hundred other entries on display, I was pleased because the small card briefly described the calling on my heart and what the story depicted.

Some of the ladies I was building a connection with stopped by.

"You should be pleased. It came together well," Marion Rice said.

"You persevered," said Glenda Watson.

"You are a woman on a mission," said Linda Slaton.

Sandy Bone said, "God is revealing Himself."

I had spent many years in a man's world, and I found it interesting that the encouragement from these women meant so much to me. I was most surprised that out of the thousand plus people who stopped by, only one noticed a deliberately-designed detail.

"Body of 7th Found," Ann Parkinson said, running a finger gingerly from the newspaper headline that she read, across one spoke of the ship's wheel, over to the mirror. Then she positioned her face in such a way that her reflection filled the space. She winked at me and then moved along to the next art-piece.

The next morning at sunrise, I was up for a trek along the golf-cart path, walking and running. I felt as if a rainbow of warm colors surrounded me. I felt confident, because I knew I was moving on a path of discovery. A path that began with a scrapbook, was pulled forward by engineers' memories, and now clarified by an artwork collage, made up of news and images.

****

Whenever I hear something repeated, perhaps in a small group, then a book, then a different group or person, I try to focus on what is being revealed to me. After one such set of synchronized experiences, I wrote in my journal,

- [ ] What has God stirred up in your heart?
- [ ] What are you doing about it?
- [ ] How are you wise to the resistance that wants to derail the good you could do?

Another time, "empowering the generations" was the general theme of the repeated message. My friend Marion called me early one morning.

"I was led to call you and give you this verse," she said. "Tell the generations to come where God has been faithful. This may be your purpose," she suggested.

Another week I attended a GriefShare discussion group hosted by my church. I learned that both small and great change bring with them cycles of emotions. We usually process through little changes well. However, the big changes—or when change is piled on top of change—can overload even the strongest of people.

I learned that some folks get stuck in anger and grow bitter.

When I signed up for the GriefShare group at church, I thought I was finished grieving for my mother. I joined the class because Ken believed that I needed it, and I wanted to reassure him that I did not. But I was blindsided the night they showed a film on the grief children experience with loss. My childhood tears showed up, and I fought to keep them back. I had joined in on every other evening's discussion, but not that night. It hit too close to home. And the experience made me aware that, indeed, I had unresolved issues.

One of the small groups I attended required us to have lunch with one of the workshop facilitators. I was delighted with the lady I was matched with. Sandy Bone was a certified therapist and a great presenter—funny, insightful, deep—and she was originally from Southern California. She also was the wife of the facilitator of the GriefShare class I had just completed.

After our meal, Mrs. Bone said, "Remind me why you took the GriefShare class." This opened the door for me to tell her briefly about my mother, the shipwreck, and my personal journey.

Sandy said, "Rest in your quest." She told me that one way to know if something isn't a calling is if life becomes unbalanced.

It was a message that I had heard before on managing change. A balanced lifestyle was one with good habits with good boundaries. Thus, if a major change impacts one area, it doesn't impact everything.

I remembered the newspaper article I had found on my airline seat, about the son who had lost everything because he had searched to solve the answers to the loss of his father. His search had cost him his family, his earning power, and his emotional health. Although the CIA had been in the middle of his mystery, perhaps the son had allowed his life to become unbalanced?

Another week, I ran into the word "idol" and I had to consider what implications that word had for my life. A passage from Ken Sande's book, *The Peacemaker*, interested me:

> An idol is anything apart from God that we depend
> on to be happy, fulfilled or secure…. idols can arise
> from good desires as well as wicked desires….
> As you search your heart for idols, you will often
> encounter multiple layers of concealment, disguise,
> and justification. One of the subtlest cloaking devices
> is to argue that we want only what we legitimately
> deserve or what God himself commands….[27]

Was God trying to tell me something? Had I made my earthly father an idol? Had I come to enjoy my search into the shipwreck more than a search for my God? I knew my family virtually worshipped our cabin in the woods. Perhaps I still did, too, if I held unrealistic expectations.

Another week I found one unique message that touched my heart by C.S. Lewis. My mind kept returning to Aslan's words, "No one is told any story but their own"[28]

These words lit a fuse inside me. I understood that there were many perspectives in any single story to be told—including my story and the *Marie*.

For the first time, I felt that I could face whatever came next. I started out simply wanting to clarify the story in the scrapbook. With Uncle Albert and the retired engineers, I grew to learn more about my father. Now a larger challenge lay before me. I wanted—needed—to do my best to uncover the truth of what happened that day for future generations.

It was time to investigate the mystery of the *Marie*.

FIG 8: Above: Dad as a sailor. Mom as a Navy Wave.
Diego Terres, Jr. and Marian Terres.

FIG 9: Top: My family of origin before my youngest brother's birth.

FIG 10: Above: My family at Dad's graduation with Engineering degree from Cal Poly San Luis Obispo, CA.

FIG 11: Right: My family of origin (Jim, Rick, Don, me) with my grandparents, days after the Marie's loss. I remember the photographer giving us bubbles.

FIG 12: *Above: Dale Howell and family. Wife Dawn. Left to right: Gregory, Diana Linda, and Glenna. See Chapter 27 "For The Children" for more information.*

FIG 14: *Above: Dad, friends and shark.*

FIG 15: *Below: Cal Poly San Luis Obispo scuba-diving club suit up to go on the Marie in search of monster lobster, May 1958.*
*Appendix has pictures of this group on the Marie and bio's of the men lost on the Marie.

FIG 13: *Above: Dale Howell and Dad show off their legendary monster lobster catch.*

FIG 16: Left: Dad with Jim Russell posing in front of Raytheon Santa Barbara, June 1960.

FIG 17: Above: I'm with Dr. Bob and Rachel Watkins at the surprise breakfast. Bob and Rachel display items they played with.

FIG 18: Right: I'm between Bob and Helen Wilke in Old Town Goleta.

FIG 19: Jeannie Russell with her father James (Jim) Russell.
The story to this picture is found in chapter 42, "A Phone
Interview." Used by permission of the Russell family archives.

FIG 20: Above: Dale Howell, Jim McCaffrey, and Jim Terres, at the Channel Islands area. Three Santa Barbara Highschool Graduates. Three Veterans. Three friends.

FIG 21: Albert Terres sits on a whale tale bench at what I understand is the Lost At Sea Memorial. Located at the end of the Santa Barbara harbor breakwater. It was created to recognize no one and to honor all who are lost at sea, to include the men of the Marie.

Part-II SEARCH

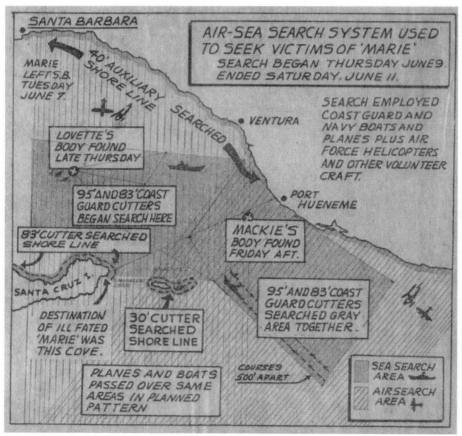

FIG 22: Above is the "Air-Sea Search System" used to seek victims of the Marie.

CHAPTER 15:

Freedom of Information

Laura Funkhouser recommended I start at the bottom. She also suggested that I use the Freedom of Information Act (FOIA) and National Archives and Records Administration (NARA) system.

So that's where I started.

I contacted the Coast Guard's historian and submitted a FOIA request for information on the *Marie.*

"We only have information dating back that far if it hit the coast-to-coast news," he said.

When I mentioned that it might have indeed been national news, my contact agreed to go look in their archives.

"Nope. Nothing," he said when he returned. "Try the National Archives. Records that were once active and possibly top-secret go through a transition in specific increments of time and are then moved into the NARA system."

The National Archives were in Washington D.C., so I began planning a visit to the area. Ken's sister would soon be graduating from the Army War College in Pennsylvania. *If I attended her graduation, I could drive three hours south to Washington D.C. and begin my research.*

****

I attended Colonel Mary Katherine "Kathy" Chamber's

graduation at the Army War College, as the Newton family representative. Ten years earlier Ken and I had lived nine months in Pennsylvania while he attended and then graduated. As I drove through the guard station at the famous Carlisle Barracks, I noticed the sign, "To Preserve Peace Not War," and I was reminded of the military and civilians that had come here from around the globe in hopes of preserving peace.

At the pre-graduation meal, I sat with Kathy and a classmate of hers. Kathy's classmate was a colonel who was also an engineer responsible for deactivating nuclear weapons and storage sites. As we chatted, I learned that his graduation project had involved collecting a selection of oral histories from senior Army Science Board members.

"Their memories stretched back into the beginning of the Cold War," said the Colonel. He was the standing President of the Army Science Board and he was pleased that he had captured and preserved a piece of history that was slipping away with the fading memories and deaths of his predecessors.

As we continued our conversation, I didn't have much understanding of how a Science Board fit into the context of the military or the *Marie's* scientist, Dr. Beardsley, but in time I would.

After the graduation, I continued to Washington D.C.

With tractor-trailers rushing past and a summer storm whipping around me, I traveled down Interstate 81 toward the next leg of my adventure. I hit the DC beltway at rush hour and as I crawled along in rush-hour traffic, I called my daughter, Dete, who lived in Arlington, Virginia. I planned to stay with her for two of the three nights I was in town.

Next, I wanted to connect with a man who worked for the National Oceanic and Atmospheric Administration (NOAA), Dr. John Cloud. Laura Funkhouser encouraged me to contact him because his PhD was from the University of California at Santa Barbara, and much of his research included the Santa Barbara Channel. I'd met him once, during an Old Town Goleta Cultural History Project activity, but I hadn't approached him. I was uncomfortable about asking anyone for help. However, I now understood that I would never solve the mystery on my own. I didn't know how to tap into what Dr. Cloud had to offer, but I knew I had to try.

Before making the call, I organized my thoughts.

By e-mail, I had established my intent at the archives.

If he only knew how much time it took to compile what I knew and didn't know.

After researching the 1960 shipwreck and search, I had noticed a 30-hour gap between the time the *Marie* was overdue and the beginning of the search. I wanted to know if such a long wait was normal. I also wanted to know why so little debris was collected. And what about the lifeboat? And was there really no radio on board the *Marie*? Also, I hoped to find info on the underwater project.

"Dr. Cloud?" I said when he answered his phone.

"John here," he said.

"Teresa Newton-Terres here. I'm heading to D.C., and if I make it to either NARA-I or II tonight, I'll have less than two hours. Any suggestions?"

It was a Friday evening and the parts of the NARA libraries were open until 9:30pm.

"Definitely." His voice was encouraging. "Since you have to jump through a couple hoops first, use your time to get a research card and familiarize yourself with the archive holdings and locations."

I was comforted by his encouragement, so I continued to make my way through rush-hour traffic to the National Archives. Would I find something of interest?

When I finally stood in front of the huge marble building on Pennsylvania Avenue, I realized that I had passed by it many times when we lived in DC, never wondering what was inside. I took a deep breath and grasped one of the two wrought-iron handles to the massive wooden doors. I pulled, but it didn't budge. I looked around as a man in a suit came by. "Excuse me," I said. "Do you know if this is the main entrance to the archive?"

"You're at the right place. They closed early, because of basement flooding," he said.

I still had daylight to burn, and I was on a mission to use my time wisely. I called a contact number for the other archive, NARA-II, and found out that their library and card-issuing center was open as scheduled. If I took a shortcut through the city, I could avoid the beltway traffic and reach NARA-II with ample time. My night's mission was still on.

NARA-II in College Park sat in the middle of a site with a lot of acreage with well-lit parking. The front of the building was glass, and the interior lights brightened the surrounding area.

After the receptionist gave me an overview of the building, she sat me down at a computer and I watched a tutorial about the responsibilities of a research cardholder. Finally, they took my picture and issued me a plastic card with my photo and name on it.

Card in hand, I scouted out the building's lower level lockers, first floor entrance, snack shop, second floor research library and third floor cartographic records and aerial photographs library.

My cell rang. The caller ID showed it was Dr. Cloud calling.

"Greetings, Dr. Cloud," I said.

"Call me John."

"I'm now a card-carrying researcher," I told him.

He had called to check on my progress, and we made plans to meet for dinner at the end of the next day at an Argentinean restaurant close to NARA-I. My daughter Dete would join us.

I found a Marriott not far from the archives and settled in for the night.

CHAPTER 16:

NARA-I

I arose early the next morning and returned to NARA-I on Pennsylvania Avenue. The Pennsylvania Avenue archives were built in 1930 to house the Charters of Freedom: The Declaration of Independence, Constitution, and the Bill of Rights. Now the archives also housed Coast Guard records.

The doors stood wide open as I entered NARA-I, research card in hand. After processing through security, I asked timidly, "Where does one begin to do research?"

"Genealogy research in there," he said pointing to a door on the left. Then the guard motioned toward an open door on the right at the far end of the lobby. "I saw someone go in there that may help you."

"Thanks," I said, smiling.

I must have looked lost as I went through the door. A man passing in front of me stopped in his tracks.

"Can I help you?" he asked.

"I was told that I could do some research on a shipwreck," I asked, smiling sheepishly.

"Sure, let's sign you in, and you can tell me more," the man said.

I noticed his nametag. His name was Mr. Peuser.

I put my bag on the floor and wrote my name on the sign-in sheet. Then I pulled out a piece of paper. On it, I had compiled a timeline of all the details of the 1960 loss of the *Marie* and the subsequent search, all taken from Grandmother's scrapbook.[29] A black box circled the gap in the timeline created by the *Marie*'s departure, expected return, and the search. Inside a box created by this timeline gap, I had written: "What happened?"

I handed the page to Mr. Peuser. "My father was lost in a 1960 shipwreck along with six other men working for a Raytheon-related project. They were engineers and scuba divers conducting underwater equipment tests off California's coastline."

"Your need is just the kind of request we long to serve," Mr. Peuser replied, obviously interested as he read the details of the timeline. "Wait here," he said, and disappeared through a doorway at the back of the room. Within minutes he returned along with another man. "Mr. Charles will get you started and Ms. Abbot will be in shortly and may offer more insights."

Mr. Peuser checked in on my progress later, and encouraged me to go to the Veterans Administration website and request my father's 214 Record. "You'll be glad you did," is all he said.

My new research helper Mr. Charles showed me how to locate source documents. He brought over a binder and we sat down together at a research table. Mr. Charles flipped through several pages and, placing a finger on a spot, he took a document request form from a pile stacked in the middle of the table. "You will be looking at documents in RG 26, and record ID, E384," he said.

RG stood for Record Group, 26 for Coast Guard, and 384 for Search-and-Rescue or SAR. After turning more pages in his binder, Mr. Charles wrote on another request form: *RG 26 and Cape Sable CG95334.* Then looking at my research card, he added my researcher's number to the sheet. After he completed the forms, Mr. Charles said, "I'll go submit these pull-slips." In one hour, you can go across the hall to the small review room and they will have the sources available for your review."

It was a long hour before I placed my personal belongings in the researchers' locker as required. Then, with pencil, paper, and laptop, I entered the resource reviewing room, a small wood-paneled, windowless library with private tables. One person sat at a table, examining a leather-bound book with calligraphy and gold-leaf decorated vellum pages. It looked like something I had seen behind glass in museums.

A woman entered the room, rolling a cart loaded with boxes. I went over to her and gave her my NARA research card. "These are yours," she said, and handed me the pull-slips that Charles had filled out. I signed a form, accepting temporary responsibility for the sources within the boxes. Then she wheeled the cart over to a desk and quickly explained the rules:

"One box off the cart, one folder out of the box, one page at a time."

The first box I brought to the table was labeled, *Cape Sable CG95334 – 1960*. When I opened it, I could smell a trace of salt water. I took out the pages for June 1960. For the most part, the legal-sized forms were filled with blue ink on both sides. My hands trembled as I held these pages that opened a window into the past.

The logs included each day's reporting of wind, temperature, visibility, seas, head-count of seamen, position, drills held, commanding officer, morning orders, and miscellaneous events that occurred. Each entry was signed by the seaman who wrote it.

These pages were out at sea. Preserved. For me!

Before I began recording details, Ms. Abbot, the Coast Guard Archivist at NARA-I, stopped by and introduced herself. "I submitted a couple more pull-slips for you, and the source-boxes should be out shortly." She told me that she had requested the 1960 Coast Guard's Port Hueneme, California, Light-station Log, the Coast Guard Collision Log, and another box of Coast Guard Search and Rescue (SAR) Reports.

"I'm going to look at every piece of paper you recommend," I said, excited. "Thank you. It's okay to type out the details into my laptop?" I asked.

"Sure," said Ms. Abbot. "You can use the copy machine, too," she said pointing to the back of the room.

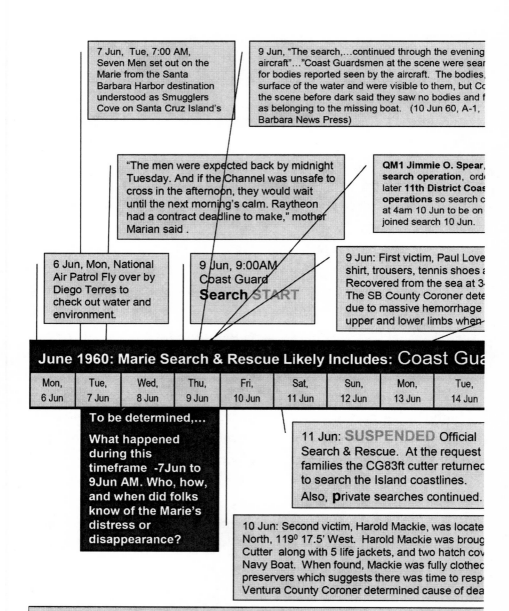

7 Jun, Tue, 7:00 AM, Seven Men set out on the Marie from the Santa Barbara Harbor destination understood as Smugglers Cove on Santa Cruz Island's

9 Jun, "The search,...continued through the evening aircraft"..."Coast Guardsmen at the scene were sear for bodies reported seen by the aircraft. The bodies, surface of the water and were visible to them, but Co the scene before dark said they saw no bodies and f as belonging to the missing boat. (10 Jun 60, A-1, Barbara News Press)

"The men were expected back by midnight Tuesday. And if the Channel was unsafe to cross in the afternoon, they would wait until the next morning's calm. Raytheon had a contract deadline to make," mother Marian said .

QM1 Jimmie O. Spear, search operation, ord later 11th District Coas operations so search c at 4am 10 Jun to be on joined search 10 Jun.

6 Jun, Mon, National Air Patrol Fly over by Diego Terres to check out water and environment.

9 Jun, 9:00AM Coast Guard **Search** START

9 Jun: First victim, Paul Love shirt, trousers, tennis shoes a Recovered from the sea at 3- The SB County Coroner dete due to massive hemorrhage upper and lower limbs when

June 1960: Marie Search & Rescue Likely Includes: Coast Gua

Mon, 6 Jun	Tue, 7 Jun	Wed, 8 Jun	Thu, 9 Jun	Fri, 10 Jun	Sat, 11 Jun	Sun, 12 Jun	Mon, 13 Jun	Tue, 14 Jun

To be determined,...

What happened during this timeframe -7Jun to 9Jun AM. Who, how, and when did folks know of the Marie's distress or disappearance?

11 Jun: SUSPENDED Official Search & Rescue. At the request families the CG83ft cutter returned to search the Island coastlines. Also, private searches continued.

10 Jun: Second victim, Harold Mackie, was locate North, 119⁰ 17.5' West. Harold Mackie was broug Cutter along with 5 life jackets, and two hatch cov Navy Boat. When found, Mackie was fully clothec preservers which suggests there was time to resp Ventura County Coroner determined cause of dea

27 July 1960: **Comdr Lionel H. deSanty,** the senior investigating officer, 11th Coast Guard occurred since the vessel's underwater body had not been inspected since 1958. The large to raise stresses for which the vessel was not designed. This of course does not preclude th

FIG 23: Above: Timeline, version one, that was hand carried to the National Archives on the first day of research at NARA-I, Washington D.C.

ng by the light of flares dropped by search
earching for any signs of the boat itself and
es, the pilots reported, were under the
Coast Guardsmen aboard the single cutter at
d found no debris which could be identified
1, 'Six Santa Barbarians Lost," Santa

ar, **Commander** of the 95ft cutter from Santa Barbara and **in command of the**
rdered boats and plane to **remain clear of the missile range area** - 9 Jun. An hour
ast Guard headquarters reported that the Navy had **agreed to suspend missile**
h could continue. The vessels stayed with the search until dark, 9 Jun. They left again
on the scene at dawn. **Two Coast Guard aircraft** and an **Air Force helicopter**

vette, was found wearing a T-
s and wearing a life preserver.
t 34⁰ 12' North, 19⁰ 35' West.
etermined Lovette's death to be
ge caused by loss of flesh on
en attacked by large fish.

13 Jun, Lionel H. de Santy, Senior Investigating
Officer, **Coast Guard's 11th District headquarters**,
started an investigation into the loss of the Marie.
Charles Adams, Raytheon's Chairman of the board
of directors, of Boston, MA due to attend
proceedings.

uard, Air Force, Navy, Marine Corps, & Civilians:

	Wed,	Thu,	Fri,	Sat,	Sun,	Mon,	Tue,
n	15 Jun	16 Jun	17 Jun	18 Jun	19 Jun	20 Jun	21 Jun

15 Jun: At about 6:00PM a third victim, Dale Howell, was found by a
Navy boat 11 miles southeast of Port Hueneme, and was fully clothed
and wearing a life preserver. The Ventura County Coroner determined
cause of death to be shock due to exposure.

21 Jun: Fourth victim, James
C. Russell, located 1 ½ miles
south of Pt. Mugu; autopsy
indicated he died of
exposure, shock, possible-
drowning.

ted at 2:10PM at approximately 34⁰ 05.5'
ught in by the Cape Sable Coast Guard
overs that were ferried to the Cutter by a
ed including two sweaters and two life
spond prior to the Marie's sinking. The
eath to be shock due to exposure.

d District Report Conclusions include: It is opined that a structural failure could have
ge concentration of weight on a small area of the cockpit and after deck would tend
the possibility of collision with a submerged object or an unidentified vessel.

For the rest of the day, I sat spellbound as I reviewed details and began to copy the information from the Cape Sable's logs into my laptop.

The archives at NARA-I held information on one of the Coast Guard cutters used in the *Marie* search, the largest of two cutters mentioned in the newspaper articles. They also held the Coast Guard station logs of Port Hueneme, a harbor for Naval ships located south of Santa Barbara. Both logs contained direct references to the *Marie* shipwreck and the subsequent search.

While these logs were valuable, I had hoped to find details about the Coast Guard Station at Santa Barbara, the Navy's Point Mugu, and the San Diego Naval Air Station, because they were mentioned in newspaper clippings in the scrapbook. In addition, I had a short list of Navy vessels that were listed as coming and going from Port Hueneme Harbor. I wondered if I'd be able to track down the ship's logs for these vessels.

I was especially interested, in Ms. Abbot's efforts to locate an official Search and Rescue report, the SAR, she called it. She had requested a box of the 1960 reports, but it held nothing on the *Marie*. When I reported back to her, "No record for the *Marie*."

Ms. Abbot came and searched the box herself. "Perhaps it got misfiled," she said, and went off to look for the missing document. Within an hour she returned. "No SAR," she said. "The record could be in the West Coast archives or NARA-II at College Park. When you go to NARA-II at College Park, connect with Mr. Zerby. If you go to the West Coast archives in San Francisco, connect with Dr. Glass."

That was the first time I realized that there were even more archives outside of the DC area.

As the day progressed, I realized that typing the details was too time consuming. To speed things up and make sure I didn't miss any details, I began to use the copy machine. I skimmed a page for relevance, then if I wanted to copy it, I folded a long scrap of paper around the page as a tab. After I had a collection of these, I went over to the copy machine and copied them. I could record the details electronically later.

Thus began my adventure as a researcher. As I left the massive marble building and returned to Pennsylvania Avenue, the warm colors of late-afternoon sun poured over the chaos of rush hour in the nation's capital.

I went across Pennsylvania Avenue to Starbucks, where I met my daughter Dete for a drink. Later we walked to the Argentinean restaurant that Dr. Cloud had selected. He offered further insights that related to the Santa Barbara Channel.

"The *Marie* was likely lost in The Channel Islands National Marine Sanctuary," he said, explaining that artifacts such as shipwrecks were jointly managed by NOAA and the National Park Service.

The Santa Barbara Channel Islands National Marine Sanctuary encompassed the waters surrounding Anacapa, Santa Rosa, San Miguel, Santa Barbara, and Santa Cruz Islands and extended six nautical miles (11 km) offshore around five of the eight islands. It was a huge area to search.

CHAPTER 17:

Logs & Change of Commands

On Monday, I returned to NARA-II at College Park, Maryland.

After stowing my purse and personal belongings in the lower level lockers, I went looking for Mr. Zerby. I found him in the *Finding Aids* resource room, a small side room on the second floor off the textual records library.

"Ms. Abbot sent me to you," I said.

I handed him my timeline of the events surrounding the shipwreck and briefly explained what I was doing. I mentioned the documents that I located at NARA-I, and the information that I was still trying to track down. "Ms. Abbot said I should look for the culminating report from the search and rescue in the Santa Barbara Channel," I added. "She called it an SAR?"

Mr. Zerby walked over to a nearby table and took a 5x7 multi-sheet carbon-copy form. Next, he reviewed the finding-aides in the room that would help me to fill in the form. Then he handed me a blue sheet of paper that outlined the hours of the library's pull-slip schedule: Mon – Fri at 10:00, 11:00, 1:30, 2:30 with an additional pull on Wed, Thu, and Fri at 3:30.

"Submit your pull-slip on time," Mr. Zerby cautioned. "Otherwise, requests will be delayed until the next pull." He was direct.

Should I tell him I'm new at this?

I looked at the clock. I didn't have much time before the first hour of pull-slip processing began. I took a deep breath and picked up a pencil.

Since log books had proven useful the previous day, I began by submitting a short stack of pull requests for more log books. I had a list of vessels and installations that were either mentioned in one of the scrapbook's newspaper articles or listed in the log books I had just reviewed. Once my first forms were completed, Mr. Zerby had to review and sign-off on them before I could officially submit them.

"Your pulls will return sources in an hour," he said. Several pull-slips throughout the day came back with "Nothing in archive" written on them. The pull-slips were for a USAF C-119, a USAF 515, a Navy Drexel #4, the Pacific Missile Range and the *Marie* Search and Rescue culminating report.

"Are these ships, airplanes, or helicopters?" I explained that the C-119, 515 and Drexel #4 were listed on the Coast Guard *Cape Sable's* log. The Drexel #4 brought the second victim from the shipwreck to the *Cape Sable.* "The Navy's Drexel #4 had to have come from somewhere," I reasoned.

"Most likely, the Navy Yard archives will have useful sources," said Mr. Zerby.

More archives?

By the time I returned my first cart of sources, my next cart was ready. This cart contained mostly submarine deck logs.

I wanted to look at submarine daily logs because of a theory that a sub might have surfaced unexpectedly and crashed into the *Marie*, sinking her. It was a scenario like an incident that occurred while Ken and I lived in Hawaii. A US submarine surfaced and accidentally sunk a Japanese educational fishing vessel.[30]

"To locate submarine logs," Mr. Zerby said, "you first need the names of the submarines." He directed me to a library computer to search the Internet to generate a list of submarine names and their numbers. One list included over 700 submarines. "How do I determine which subs were stationed off California June 1960?" I asked.

"That's another question for the Navy Yard," he said.

I already had a list of three American submarines that I presumed may be in the Pacific in 1960. I had made note of two names during a visit to the Submariners Convention in Little Rock. I had collected another name because of reading the book, *Blind Man's Bluff: The Untold Story of American Submarine Espionage.*

I filled out pull-slips requesting 1960 logs for the subs I had identified by name. On a whim, I also asked for the log for the USS *Razorback*. The *Razorback* had recently been transformed into a museum and permanently docked a few miles from my home along the Arkansas River. I thought it would be an interesting way to honor the state I lived in, not to mention humoring my husband.

When I reviewed the three submarine logs, I discovered they all were operating in the Pacific Ocean around Hawaii's Pearl Harbor. I didn't review these subs logs further, as they could not have collided with the *Marie.*

The *Razorback* was assigned to the San Diego Naval Base in 1960. However, it was moored in San Diego during the days in question. While the *Razorback* wasn't involved with the *Marie*, its daily log was helpful because it listed the subs that moored beside it daily. I requested the logs from these subs and they led me to other subs, and then others, along with their tending ships.

Before long, I had requested, reviewed, and copied pages from over a dozen submarines. In time, my interest in the USS *Razorback* would grow when I learned that one of her crew, from June 7, 1960, was later convicted of selling secrets to the Soviets.[31]

The submariners' logs seemed to have their own set of rules. Some of the logs conformed to standard nautical practices; however, once the subs submerged, the logs often read, *submerged,* and included little to no information. Other logs always read *submerged,* giving no details at all. Another variation was the log for the USS *Growler.* Many of the pages had been, "Withheld due to restricted access." [32]

The months removed from the *Growler's* log included June 1960. *Why were those months removed? What was happening?*

One submarine logging characteristic I found interesting was that the log made note of the commanding authority for each harbor that the sub entered. Usually the rank or name wasn't mentioned, just the position. One log listed "SOPA is COMNAVAIRPAC" for those subs entering the *Command of the N.A.S. North Island, Coronado, California.* (SOPA = Senior Officer Present Afloat. COMNAVAIRPAC = Commander of US Naval Air Forces, Pacific Fleet; NAS = Naval Air Station). The log entry appeared to ensure that everyone understood who held the responsibility and the chain of decision-making responsibilities.

The practice of recognizing and confirming who had the authority and responsibility interested me. It promoted clarity. People knew who was on top and in command.

Understanding chain of command, a line of authority, would prove beneficial in more than one way for me as I went forward. It would even help resolve issues with my other family mystery—the cabin.

CABIN CONFLICT

The cabin and the related family issues were never far from my mind, even when I was trying to research about submarines. I had grown frustrated with some of my "cabin family" because it was increasingly clear that they didn't recognize the position mother held. They seemed to think of Mom more like a camp counselor who could be obeyed or ignored. They failed to understand that Mother had been the sole owner of the cabin.

I understood their perspective because I had once misunderstood the issues.

Because several of my relatives were not aware who held the cabin authority, I faced increasing conflict. They didn't understand that as mother's executors and trustees, Ken and I now shouldered responsibility of the cabin. My oldest brother, Jim, was respectful and my youngest brother, Don, was seeking to understand the issues – behaviors that made the challenge bearable and gave me hope.

As trustees, Ken and I had to prepare paperwork for the IRS, the Office of Records, and even the National Forest Service. Because the cabin was on federal land, the National Forest Service were our landlords. Now that Ken and I had to make decisions for our cabin family, I hoped they would respect our position.

I had already endured one lawsuit, brought by the man whom my mother had married a year prior to her death. He sued Mom's trust, along with Ken and me personally as trustees. In the suit's aftermath, our insurance company declined to provide a protective umbrella policy for five years. As a result, I was worried about Ken's and my risk exposure. Thus, I managed estate and trust affairs conservatively.

I felt that maintaining the cabin status quo was reasonable, but other family members wanted to change the arrangement. As a result, I was butting heads with relatives often. Instead of researching the shipwreck and serving the National Guard families, I was sidetracked. I moved slowly on the cabin paperwork because I didn't want to trigger emotional land mines. At least not until all the cabin's legal ducks were in a row.

The conflict was stressing me out, and I didn't know how to handle it.

"Work on the emotionally-charged cabin issues in the afternoon so that your whole day isn't ruined," said a therapist.

"Lock the cabin door," a legal counselor recommended until issues are resolved.

Emotions were heating up, and too many of my cabin family failed to understand or respect the constraints I was under. If the paperwork wasn't correct, the next generation of cabin owners and users would be impacted.

"I'm selling the cabin," I said more than once. I had the authority to do so, and would have done if it weren't for Ken. He gently reminded me that my mother hoped her family would continue to gather at the cabin.

My youngest brother encouraged me, too. "I'll shield you," Don said. His words and actions made a difference. I was able to get through the legal paperwork because I mentally stepped back from all

I perceived to be true and reconsidered all things –myths, memories, documentation. Then, I leaned back into my responsibilities. I grew to understand the issues with more clarity as I wrestled with my immaturity.

I shook it off and returned my thoughts to the task at hand.

CHAPTER 18:

Ocean of Context

Several submarine daily logs offered useful details. Others raised a mental red flag, but I wasn't sure why. The entries that caught my eye were those that contained details and notes listing maneuvers conducted on Tuesday, June 7, 1960, and the days following.

My mind wandered as I imagined subs gliding through the cold dark blue waters off San Diego the day my father and the other men went to sea. I felt the chill of the ocean, but it was only the library's cold room, lowered to protect the archived documents.

As I read the logs, I wondered what they were describing. The USS *Salmon* was conducting laboratory experiment maneuvers. The USS *Redfish* was manning and stationing the fire control tracking party and practicing manned battle stations. The USS *Growler* was on patrol. But where? Were my father and the others testing infrared technology by trying to track the movement of these submarines? Had they hoped to detect a sub as it passed through their light beam?

I realized that I needed to pinpoint the longitude and latitude coordinates listed on the logs. On first inspection, the total distance that these subs traveled in any day suggested that they probably weren't near the *Marie*. The distance between the San Diego or San Francisco harbors and the Santa Barbara Channel was long by land or sea.

None of the submarines' logs I reviewed included a record of such extended travel occurring on or just after June 7, 1960. Nevertheless, my curiosity was piqued and I copied logs for Tuesday through Sunday, June 7-13, 1960.

As I reviewed all the submarine logs, I remembered the submariners whom Ken worked with in Hawaii or at the Pentagon. Their special insignia was a dolphin.

During one of Mr. Zerby's breaks, I spoke with one of his colleagues.

"Have you checked out the technical reports?" he asked. "As a government contractor, Raytheon would be responsible for submitting regular technical reports. These would be transferred to the archives and in due process be de-classified."

"Brilliant," I said. With his help, I completed a pull-slip requesting the "Technical Library Reports generated by Raytheon 1958-1960."

Soon I was reviewing a selection of reports. Most of the documents were old contracts.

The retired engineers had said that their project was funded by new money that was being put toward helping with the Soviet submarine nuisance, I thought.

I also found it interesting that the archives had technical reports listed that were not available for my review because they were still classified. "Anything dealing with nuclear technology is still classified," said the archivist. "It's all of your advanced weapons used in the Korean War and the Polaris Program."

Only one technical report drew my interest. It appeared to be within the right time frame, initiated in 1959, the year my father was hired. It was labeled the *AN/BQC-2 (XN-1) SONAR Set Sonar Communication System (SESCO)* project. I wasn't convinced of its relevance, because the report mentioned SONAR. I didn't know the difference between SONAR and INFRARED other than that they were spelled differently, but the report didn't appear to encompass the project testing equipment from the *Marie*. Nevertheless, when I read some details, my heart began to race. The pages were from a report submitted just after the shipwreck.

"Electrical System was tested in accordance with the submitted Test Procedures/Report." I held my breath when I read, "Difficulty was encountered." I continued to read, "...stability of the clock's crystal...test results were not included." Was this the contract that the device and test from the *Marie* served? I scanned the "Summary of Test Results" and the statement, "test was complete...with the exception of a transducer array...results invalid due to the instrumentation."

I flipped through the report reading what looked like a routine status report, the kind of report that measures a project's heartbeat. Looking at more pages, I found that the words that had caught my attention were repeated in reports filed before the shipwreck – Jan 1960 and Dec 1959.

My heart sank as I began to realize that, given the report before me, nothing unusual had occurred in June 1960. My intuition urged me to copy the pages anyway. I pressed on, but I continued to think about the report and the brief mention of a "difficulty." I realized how foolish it would have been to lift a statement like this from the report's context and miss the truth by not digging deeper. Thus, I continued to ponder the statement, "The AN/BQC-2 (XN-1) tested was complete, with the exception of a transducer array."

What is a transducer? An array?

I knew that the men on the *Marie* used equipment to "communicate over a beam of light." While the technical report focused on SONAR not infrared, it was still of interest to me because of the intersection between Raytheon, the government, communication technology, submarines and the dates of interest June 1960.

COLD WAR CONTEXT

The light shining in through the floor-to-ceiling windows was growing dim. My legs were stiff from hours of sitting and I shivered from the air conditioning. I got up and returned the cart of resources that I had reviewed. I decided to stand while I waited for my next cart to arrive. As I did, I noticed that I was leaning against a bookshelf of sources compiled and bound together in a collection. *Foreign Relations of the United States, 1958–1960*, was embossed in gold letters on a red leather binding. Together they looked like a set of encyclopedias. The volume *United Nations and General International Matters* caught my attention. Then, my eyes were drawn to the volume labeled *Laws of the Sea.*[33]

I was curious to know more about the international waters. I remembered the Russian trawler that a retired Raytheon engineer had mentioned. It was spying on the missile launches. In addition, I had repeatedly read in the ship and submarine logs reference to entering international waters. In time, I'd learn of the waters that began and ended off the California coast and ran through the center of the Santa Barbara Channel.

Dr. Cloud had said, "The *Marie* sunk, most likely, in NOAA's sanctuary or national territorial waters."

Were the sanctuary and territorial waters the same?

At the time, I had no knowledge of water boundaries. I was following any relevant trail. Thus, I opened the book titled, *Law of the Sea.* [34]

During the spring of 1960, the United Nations held a convention on the laws of the sea ("UNCLOS II"). At the convention, the Department of State advised the US Delegates to seek out an agreement for narrow territorial rights—three miles. Although this would serve the Navy's national security interests, it was a problem for local fishermen. A three-mile boundary was pushed, but there was also a willingness to recognize a six-plus-six as the legitimate law of the sea.

As I read about the convention, it appeared that the countries of the world who participated were either allies of United States or the Soviet Union. During the six-week gathering, a number of memoranda, telegrams, and phone calls were exchanged between the Geneva Convention Delegates and the Department of State in Washington D.C. But the conference resulted in no new agreements." [35] I made a note to myself to check on the current international water boundary as well as for 1960.

I thought of my father who fed his young family from the sea.

Mother used to say, "In an hour of scuba diving, your father would have enough fish to feed the family for the week."

Dad was attending engineering school at the California Poly Technical University when he began fishing for food. Once he chartered the *Marie* for the Cal Poly Dive Club for a day of scuba diving. They were looking for legendary, monster-sized lobsters he encountered out at the Santa Barbara Channel Islands. Unfortunately, the *Marie*'s engine stopped in the shipping channel and not even Dad could repair it.

I returned the *Law of the Sea*, and picked out three other volumes from the same period, relating to national security. Unfortunately, there was no mention of the Marie shipwreck in any of the books, but one topic surfaced repeatedly: The U-2 shoot-down. At the time, I didn't notice that a discussion of satellites and photographic reconnaissance often accompanied the U-2 references.

I learned from reading Kenneth Sewell's book *Red Star Rogue* that the days around the *Marie* tragedy were framed by the U-2 incident. I also discovered that to understand the *Marie*, I must understand the U-2 incident and its relationship to the Cold War.[36]

The first time I saw a reference to a U-2, was in Grandmother's scrapbook.

In a letter to the editor, Markham Field MacLin wrote:

> I consider [the crew of the *Marie*] as being as worthy of hero stature as the pilot of the U-2 planes, because even though they did not know that their lives were in danger, they did die while undertaking a project to help insure the safety of the free world.[37]

When I read Mr. MacLin's words, I was humbled, inspired and proud to think that someone believed that the men lost in the shipwreck were heroes. I had always thought of my father as my hero and a guardian angel. But these words had likened the men to the pilots of U-2 planes.

I was slow to learn about the top-secret CIA photographic

reconnaissance with U-2 airplanes. However, I was quick to grasp the significance of the date, May 1, 1960. That was when Russia shot down one of our U-2 spy planes and captured its pilot, Francis Gary Powers.

The incident occurred one month before the *Marie* disappeared.

Early on, I had little interest in photographic reconnaissance. I was looking for information from the archives to shed light on the facts that were in Grandmother's scrapbook. I understood that, given the lapse in time and the top-secret nature of the tests, any files about the shipwrecked *Marie* should be open, if I could just find them.

I didn't see how global events related to the loss of the *Marie*.

That all changed when I began to learn about the U-2 shoot-down. All at once my eyes opened to the Cold War. One way or another, the *Marie* tragedy was related to the Cold War, and could only be understood in that light.

Reading the chronological pages of the foreign relations books, I realized how the U-2 incident eventually permeated every political and national initiative. But, I still didn't understand why a letter to the editor in a local newspaper would identify the U-2 pilot and the men from the *Marie* as heroes.

My mind circled around the items I had read and wrestled with, and those I continued to search for. I wanted to close the gap in the timeline between when the *Marie's* departure and the search alert. I also needed to understand the Cold War context and any connections with the *Marie*. But I'd found all that could be found at NARA-I and II.

The archivists pointed me to the West Coast and the Navy Yard, a place I envisioned as a graveyard for ships.

Mom used to pick me up at Travis Air Force Base when I flew in from Hawaii, and we'd head to her home and then the cabin. On the way, she would point out the mothballed Navy ships in San Francisco Bay. So, for me the term Navy Yard conjured images of rusting, decaying vessels.

CHAPTER 19:

Reporting to the Commandant

Ken returned home from PEC just after I did and I couldn't wait to show him my treasures. I was so excited I almost told him everything in one breath.

"I got to hold actual Coast Guard logs. One set of logs was from a Coast Guard ship that was involved in the search. I can see exactly when the ship was first alerted while moored in the Santa Barbara and exactly the hour it departed to join the search. I also saw logs from a small Coast Guard station, mostly passing along communications from a location at Port Hueneme.

"I couldn't find a record of the first call coming in to the Coast Guard about the missing *Marie*. The logs show Port Hueneme being alerted at 10 AM, Thursday, June 9th. And the search began with another vessel. The logs are a key to that map in the scrapbook diagraming the extensive search."

When I paused to catch my breath, Ken broke in. "What did the Coast Guard station at Santa Barbara list as the first call," he asked.

"There weren't any records for the Santa Barbara Coast Guard station in the D.C. archives."

"So, you'll need to go to the West Coast?"

"Apparently," I said. My throat tightened a little. I followed up in a feeble voice. "And there's another archive in D.C."

Ken raised an eyebrow. "I thought this was the research trip to end all research."

I felt the two-year-old's heart beating. I wanted to cry.

Why does it have to be so hard? Why won't someone make it easy on me? Just give me a fact sheet. A press release. A simple outline. Anything. I just want to know what happened!

Out of the corner of my eye, I saw Ken pause. Then he came near and drew me to him. "Poor baby," he said patting my back.

I melted in his arms and the tears came. He held me tighter and rocked me back and forth without saying a word.

We had both listened to Pastor Parkinson as he gave a sermon about wise moves. And he told the men in the audience a few good words about living with a woman.

"Moses said at times like this to not try to solve the problem, just hold your woman and not say a word." Moses was Ken's nickname for Pastor Parkinson. "Is it helping?"

"Yes."

"Wise man. Now can I say a word?"

"Is there any stopping you?" I said returning my attention to gather up my treasure-trove.

"You are going out West for Fiesta, just tag on some research."

I kissed him. "Brilliant idea."

And just like that, I had the Commandant's clearance to take flight on another mission.

CHAPTER 20:

Detection and Deterrence

"I will look at every scrap of archived paper if that's what I have to do."

A spark ignited inside me as I attempted to unravel the *Marie* tragedy. I wanted to uncover everything available. I also wanted to understand what my father and the others were doing out there, and why. During my brief initiation to the archives, I learned that there were limitations and gaps in the records.

I made plans to visit the other archives.

****

From the book *Shadow Divers*,[38] I learned that a museum display had helped some scuba divers in their research into a German U-boat submarine mystery.[39] I hoped I might have similar success when I travelled to Chicago for the annual National Guard Family Program Conference.

After the conference, and before catching a flight to San Francisco, I visited the Museum of Science and Industry.[40] At the museum, I found a helpful display about how the Navy leveraged science and technology in ships and submarines, not to mention their challenges with anti-submarine warfare (ASW) during WWII and the Cold War.

The Navy's openness in sharing information with the public intrigued me. Here, for the public's benefit, the Navy told the story of their challenges and countermeasures. When the Raytheon engineers told me their stories, I didn't know whether they were secrets that should be held in confidence. This display helped me put the Raytheon engineers' testimonies into perspective.

I learned that today's submarines have the same basic mission: "Stalk the depths to attack and defend against the enemy." But now, subs also conduct "electronic eavesdropping in areas where surface ships and airplanes can't reach." Another display gave insight into battles fought in the "electromagnetic spectrum."

The display described electronic sensors that can gather *electronic intelligence* (ELINT) by detecting the type of electronic equipment being used by the enemy. "This information helps the battle group to make decisions and protect its own frequencies from enemy jamming attempts." Because of the Navy's increased capabilities in detecting targets with radar, infrared sensors, and sonar, today's subs are far less vulnerable than their WWII counterparts. One display, *Finding an Enemy Submarine*, caught my eye.

The display described "sub-hunter" helicopters. The helicopter's tools included: sonobuoys, dipping sonar, and radar. The display showed how devices that used the science of *magnetic anomaly detection* (MAD) could find hidden submarines by sensing the faint magnetism of their metal hulls.

From my earlier research, I recalled reading about something identified as a "515," that joined the search for the shipwreck victims and debris on Friday, June 10, 1960.

Was it a helicopter? With sensing tools?

****

When I left the museum, a storm was threatening. I returned to the hotel to pick up my luggage and catch a shuttle to the airport. Although my flight was delayed two hours, the rest of the evening and my flight to San Francisco was uneventful.

I arrived in California, rented a car, and drove to the San Bruno area on the southwest side of the San Francisco. It was late when I arrived at my hotel, so I decided to wait until the next day to begin the next phase of my research.

NARA SAN FRANCISCO IN SAN BRUNO

The next morning, I headed out to locate the NARA San Francisco located in nearby San Bruno. I had connected with NARA archivist, Dr. Glass, and offered him a list of what I hoped to locate. He had only a few comments and no suggestions for me prior to my arrival.

I wasn't sure what to expect when I finally located the low-profile building nestled in a secluded area among tall eucalyptus trees a few blocks from a busy boulevard.

The security was easy to pass through, but it didn't matter that I had a research card from my Washington D.C. efforts. They had their own process that required I present my driver's license. After signing in, I was directed to the archive library.

I approached a counter where a library assistant sat.

She didn't smile at me.

"Where can I find Dr. Glass?" I asked. "We connected via e-mail and he should be expecting me."

"I'll let him know," she replied. "You can wait over there." She pointed to a table near the entrance of the small library.

I was eager to get started, and it seemed like forever before Dr. Glass showed up. I reviewed my growing list of questions, about SAR, technical reports, daily log books, etc. Then, I flipped through a few sources that occupied the shelves around me.

Once Dr. Glass came to sit at the table with me, he was devoted to my project. He told me about the boxes of sources that he had pulled in advance. "They may or may not offer you answers."

With Dr. Glass's help, I learned that California's coastline was divided by both the Navy and Coast Guard into the 11th (South) and the 12th (North) districts, and that the county of Santa Barbara straddled these districts. Thus, sources I might be interested in could be archived either in San Francisco or Los Angeles. I also learned that there could be gaps in the records. The Coast Guard, being a smaller national service entity, devoted itself to its main mission. Thus, it didn't devote a great deal of time trying to preserve what it considered outdated records.

"I didn't locate the sources you asked about, but that doesn't mean that you won't find them," said Dr. Glass. "Many people start by reading the command histories. These are documents intended by military officers to provide an annual commentary about the status of their command."

"I'll review anything you recommend," I said. I was eager to dive into the documents he had pulled for me.

"I'll have the cart brought out. You will need to keep all the records in there," he said and pointed to a small, glass-enclosed library behind us.

The glass-enclosed library had a desk space where a library assistant kept watch on people reviewing the archive's source files. Although Dr. Glass had tried to temper my high hopes, when I heard wheels squeaking and saw someone rolling a cart of boxes across the outside library space and toward the glass enclosed review room, I felt like a child ready to open her Christmas gifts.

COMMAND HISTORIES

Although there were many different documents, the command histories caught and held my interest. They offered me a bird's-eye view of what was going on in the general area of the *Marie* shipwreck, including a listing of incidents and accidents. According to Mother, my father had been hired in 1959 to serve a new project. Therefore, I carefully reviewed 1959 and 1960 documents.

Although the precise organizational structure didn't become clear for a long time, I was intrigued as I reviewed each box, file, and document. Narrowing my focus, I searched for dates (June 7, 1960), contractors (Raytheon or Lockheed), location (Santa Barbara Channel), and technology (Infrared). My search focused on command histories from the U.S. Pacific Fleet Air Alameda, the Naval Air Station of Alameda (NAS), the San Francisco Naval Shipyard, Staff Headquarters, and the Naval Weapons Representative of Special Projects.

Falling in to my familiar routine, I began to review and tab pages to copy. But at the same time, I began to create mental threads that I hoped one day to weave together.

****

By the end of the day, I'd found enough interesting material to make my visit worthwhile, but I finished without locating the shipwreck's culminating *Search and Rescue* report.

"It must be down in the Los Angeles holdings," said Dr. Glass.

CHAPTER 21:

Old Spanish Days

The following day, I caught a flight to Santa Barbara, to celebrate the Old Spanish Days Fiesta. After a week of festivities, I planned to continue to NARA Los Angeles.

As I flew in I could see the airport's red-tile roofs, white stucco, and blue accents. Looking toward the mountains, I saw the Raytheon Santa Barbara headquarters. And in the other direction was Goleta's beach, with its deep green ocean with cobalt blue sparkling water, brought back good childhood memories. I shivered as I remembered swimming in the cold water.

"Your father told about thick globs of tar that seeped up from the ocean floor, because tar pockets were so close to the surface," Mom used to tell us.

Tar stuck to our skin too, but we never complained.

Ken met me at the airport. From the plane, I could see him waving.

I was eager to tell him everything I found—and didn't find.

We embraced, but he must have known what was on my mind. Placing a finger over my lips, he said, "We can debrief later. This is *our* fiesta time."

This was Ken's first Fiesta. Old Spanish Days Fiesta was something Mother and I enjoyed together, and I had spared Ken in the past. I had always participated in the Fiesta either as a performer (when I was young) or as an escort to a performer (when my daughter, Dete, danced). In recent years, I'd served as a stage manager.

In Grandmother's scrapbook was a letter to "*Los Bailadores* Dance Group," a volunteer dancing group that my family participated in. "Because of the untimely loss of Jimmy Terres, the dance practice…has been cancelled." There was also a handwritten note to my grandparents, "…we didn't mail one to Marian. Our hearts are with you all.[41]"

At the last Fiesta mother and I attended together, she told me, "Because I was not from Santa Barbara, I never got to dance."

Mother was raised in the San Francisco Bay area. After they married, she and Dad remained in San Francisco, where they were both stationed with the Navy. After they were discharged, they moved two hours north of Santa Barbara in San Luis Obispo to go to school. When Raytheon hired my dad late in 1959, they moved to Goleta. Grandmother told me how well my grandfather danced, but she never spoke of my father dancing. I never realized that my father also enjoyed dancing until my journey of discovery into his life. Apparently, Mother and Father joined my grandparents in the dance group destined to perform at the Fiesta, "Noches de Ronda." After the shipwreck, the group performed without my parents. But the sad memories never prevented Mom from enjoying the Santa Barbara Fiesta.

I remember Grandmother trying to encourage me to dance when I was little. She said that children in Spain would jump up and dance for no reason other than simple enjoyment. But I had no desire to dance or do much of anything. From the time I lost my father when I was two, it was as if I were in a trance. The shipwreck so deeply affected me, I had no way to process my grief.

At least not until I was five.

One day when I was five, I saw another child dancing, swirling, clapping, and stomping uninhibitedly, and it was like someone snapped me out of my trance. A spark ignited in me and I caught a glimpse of what grandmother had been trying to tell me.

I remember admiring the girl's beautiful flowing dress. "I want to do that," I thought.

Grandmother must have noticed something in my eye, and she whisked me backstage. There I met a friend of hers, along with her granddaughter. Soon I was dancing and experiencing a joy I'd never imagined.

From that time on, dancing became my refuge from the stresses and sadness of life. And the Old Spanish Days Fiesta was always a highlight.

This Fiesta would be special, as it was the first time I'd shared the festival with Ken, Uncle Albert, or Aunt Lynda. And for the first time, I was not going to be serving in some way as a volunteer.

This year, I was a Fiesta *tourist*.

I missed the familiar timeline of activities and traditions, but I was nevertheless captivated by my home town.

Even though I was now a tourist, Uncle Albert, Aunt Lynda, Ken—who had come out on a different flight—and I found a variety of activities to enjoy at the Fiesta. We picnicked on the lawn and watched the rehearsals at the Santa Barbara Mission. The actual performances were too crowded.

We all dressed up in Fiesta costumes and enjoyed a delightful luncheon at the Woman's Center where Lynda was a board member. Later, we sat on folding chairs and watched the parade.

Dressed in the traditional white shirt, black pants, black jacket, black hat and red sash costume, Uncle Albert looked even more like my grandfather. And Lynda had an array of Fiesta skirts, flowers, and shawls to share with me. I enjoyed sharing her treasures as much as if she were my mother.

Like my mother, Lynda wasn't from a Spanish lineage; however, she was raised in Santa Barbara and graduated with my uncle from Santa Barbara High School. Over the years, she had participated in many Fiestas. I couldn't have been happier if I had been attending with my own parents.

****

The last day of festivities, Ken returned to PEC in Arkansas. I stayed behind and ventured to the Santa Barbara Recorder's Office, hoping to find records from the lawsuit filed by the victims' families after the shipwreck. The court case awards had enabled me to attend a college preparatory high school during my junior and senior years, but I was too young to remember anything about the actual case.

"It was the boat's fault," was what I understood. Grandmother's scrapbook supported that conclusion. A small newspaper article repeated some shipwreck details along with the case's final verdict.

The County Records Office was located on the second floor of the Santa Barbara County House, one of the most photographed buildings in the world because of its awe-inspiring architectural beauty. Its massive white stucco walls and red tile roof were fashioned after a Mediterranean palace. The courthouse had expansive sunken gardens and was the site where Fiesta's evening performances were held. The performances were known as Las Noches de Ronda, "Nights of Gaiety" a name originated by my Grandmother Terres. [42]

At the front desk I completed a form, paid a small fee, and soon held a copy of the records I was seeking. I sat down on a nearby chair and fumbled through thirty pages of material.

A timeline log on top read: "Estate of Hugh James McCaffrey." Hugh James (Jim) McCaffrey was the captain of the *Marie*. Like my father and Dr. Beardsley, his body was never recovered. McCaffrey, I understood, owned a sporting goods store and rented the *Marie* to Raytheon.

In her first filing, on July 1, 1960, Constance E. McCaffrey, listed three children. However, later documents listed four children.

I found a document my mother filed.[43] The widows of James Russell (Helen T.), Hal Mackie (Betty Lou), and Dale Howell (Dawn Darlene) filed claims similar to Mom's. In addition, Dale Howell's widow, filed an order with the Industrial Accident Commission of the State of California. However, she took the case off the calendar a year later.

Strangely, I could find no filings from the widows or families of Paul Lovette or Dr. Beardsley. I asked the assistant if he could shed any light on the subject.

"Call the State of California Office in Sacramento," he suggested.

Returning to Al and Lynda's, I phoned the State of California and requested information on Case No 61 SBA 2330, but again found nothing.

I knew there had been a court case, but finding out about it was proving more difficult than I had imagined.

****

Just before I left Santa Barbara I asked Uncle Albert, "Can I help you get rid of a few of those old bullfight posters?"

I gave him one of my "Southern Belle" smiles. I had my eye on taking home the old movie projector too, but I couldn't fit it into my suitcase. Instead, I asked for the posters, a family treasure I'd wanted as soon as I saw them. I knew they would look fabulous on the walls in my home.

"We have a bag check policy before you can leave," Uncle Albert said as he brought me the stack of posters. "I've got to make sure you leave stuff here for a return trip."

I chose three posters with colors and designs that pleased me.

"That leaves you several for your sons," I said. "I'll share these with my brothers," I added, although I wasn't sure I wanted to. My child's heart cried out, "Mine, mine, mine!" With certain things, I struggled with possessiveness, and these posters may be one of those. The next day, I gave Uncle Albert a hug and turned to Aunt Lynda. "Thank you for all the fresh roses in my room and warm muffins with berries each morning. I love you," I said as I waved good-bye.

Uncle Al took me to the Santa Barbara airport, and I flew 160 miles south. I was planning to stay with my brother Don and his family while I did research. I would visit with them in the evenings, and continue my search for the truth about the *Marie* tragedy by day.

FIG 24: Left: My grandparents dancing at Noches de Ronda at Santa Barbara Old Spanish Days (cir 1950's).

FIG 25: Below left: My parents at mom's first Old Spanish Days, (cir. 1951)

FIG 26: Below: I'm preparing my daughter, Dete, for the Old Spanish Days Children's Parade, (cir. 1986).

FIG 27: Above: Ken, I, Aunt Lynda and Uncle Albert at Noches de Ronda for Old Spanish Days, Santa Barbara, CA. I'm wearing treasures of my great-grandmother's, grandmother's, and mom's.
FIG 28: Below: Ken and I are with Bob and Helen Wilke meeting at the fund-raiser for the Kiwanas Club, pancake breakfast at Old Spanish Days.

CHAPTER 22:

A Real Researcher

"You're a real researcher," said the desk assistant when I showed up at NARA Los Angeles at Laguna Niguel the next morning.[44] I smiled at their reaction when I pulled out my plastic ID card from NARA-II in College Park. I didn't know what a "real researcher" was, but I appreciated the compliment.

"Mr. Wormser should be expecting me," I replied.

A few minutes later, Mr. Wormser, a tall and lanky man, drew up a chair next to me. He brought with him the list of the sources I was interested in. "You have enough to keep you busy for weeks," he said.

We reviewed my wish list and together laid out a plan to prioritize my three days of research. He went to the assistant's desk and returned with a stack of the familiar NARA pull-slips.

"These are already prepared and I'll have the first cart of boxes brought down." Mr. Wormser then left me in the hands of his assistants, who led me into the glassed-in reviewing room. The room contained six tables neatly arranged with a seventh table at the head, where the assistants sat guard.

I wanted to review every document the archives held that was in any way related to "the shipwreck thing" as Ken had begun calling it. But I also had to be realistic with the time I had. So, I sifted through the boxes, files, and source documents, applying my newly-acquired skill of scanning for relevant dates (June 1960), government contractors (Raytheon at Santa Barbara; Lockheed), topics (submarine tracking; missile tracking), technology (Infrared), and staff (Dr. Beardsley).

I went quickly into a robot-like approach of sifting through documents as if panning for gold.

After a long day of reviewing I drove ten minutes to stay with my younger brother Don and his family in nearby Irvine. The next morning, I was up early and out the door to arrive at NARA when the doors opened.

The three librarians made my daily researching interesting, and sometimes a bit comical. Although they shuffled papers and processed folders, their main task was to sit in the research room and watch me.

Over the next three days, two men and one woman rotated in and out of the room. Never was I left alone. There were the usual overhead cameras, but these people were like watchdogs. The three librarians each had unique ways of protecting the archive holdings. One, a sallow-complexioned man, coughed if I lifted a page from the table as I reviewed it. "Keep the papers flat on the table," he said ever so gently and without a smile. He cleared his throat if the tip of my pencil's eraser touched the paper.

When it came to making copies, one watcher wanted me to keep the papers to be copied near me, and then he would come to me to remove staples before I could copy. Another preferred that I bring the source documents to her desk for the same purpose. The third let me go about my research of reviewing, copying, piling, and replacing sources box by box without having to bring the documents to him. However, all three required that the sources copied have a heading that showed up on every copied sheet: "Reproduced from the holdings of the National Archives and Records Administration Pacific Region (Laguna Niguel)." I grew to appreciate that detail, as I always knew which documents came from their holdings.

Although I found each librarian's quirks amusing, I understood they had an important job to do. Their mission was to protect the source documents. During my research, I learned that someone had recently stolen a historic document and placed it on the Internet for sale. Considering this, I was thankful that these guards were alert.

****

I wrapped up my third and final day of research an hour before the archives were to close. After calling it quits, I sought out Mr. Wormser to thank him and his staff for all their assistance. I commended him on having the most diligent staff that I had encountered. Mr. Wormser shared with me the heartache they had endured in losing a source to greedy hands.

I was leaving NARA Los Angeles at Laguna Niguel with some golden nuggets. And, although I was generally pleased with the three long days of research, I was disappointed that the holdings of the NARA Los Angeles at Laguna Niguel offered me no final Search and Rescue report.

The SAR report wasn't in the NARA holdings at Washington D.C., San Francisco, or Los Angeles. Yet, the archivists all seemed to believe that such a summary report existed, a sentiment echoed by an article in grandmother's scrapbook.

Maybe the shipwreck and search weren't important enough to preserve the summary document.

Or, maybe it's located at the Navy Yard in Washington, D.C.

CHAPTER 23:

Debrief

I was pleased with the status of my life. I had intentional flexibility in my life that allowed me to devote myself to special interests such as my family, the PEC Family Program, and my shipwreck project. It wouldn't have been possible, if I hadn't first embraced my purpose as a supporting spouse and set work-as-usual on hold. I grew to enjoy the space to be a wife, mother, grandmother and researcher.

Ken had yet to obstruct my adventures into shipwreck research. However, with my journeys to the East and West archives, I was at a point where I couldn't see an end to this tunnel. Now I faced the need to return to DC.

I was discouraged that my pursuit of knowledge was so time intensive. Still, I was trying to stay positive and grateful for any pearl of information I could uncover.

I couldn't lose Ken's support. Not now.

Back in Santa Barbara, he didn't want to hear about my research and he had requested a briefing upon my return. And a briefing is what he would get. I carefully compiled the records that traced my expenditures on the East and West Coasts including flight expenses. I'd even tried to mitigate costs by combining my archive visits with other, planned trips.

Our household's available funds were not limitless. We were trying to get out of debt and save in preparations for our mandatory Army retirement and the decreased income that would come with it. Thus, alignment of expenses served my shipwreck interests and our household strategies, because I didn't want to undermine either front.

I drafted up a spreadsheet with an overview of my expenses. Another handout would give Ken an overview of what I'd reviewed and found interesting to my efforts. Although I knew he'd be most interested in my bottom-line numbers, I was exciting about sharing what I'd discovered.

Before I left, Ken reminded me, "Don't chase after missiles. Red herring. Focus, focus, focus."

I knew he was trying to be helpful. I was looking forward to sharing with him that my little shipwreck research was leading me down many paths that were boggling my mind: submarines, ASW, missiles, Pacific Missile Range, foreign nations, and programs like the POLARIS and Guided Missile Data Exchange Program.

Thus, despite Ken's attempts to narrow my focus, I felt drawn to missiles.

One reason was that the retired Raytheon engineers told me they were tracking missiles. They also said that the technology at sea was like that used with the Shillelagh Missile System. Another reason was because of what I'd read about the, USS *Norton Sound*.

The *Norton Sound* was in the Pacific Missile Range the afternoon of Monday, June 6, 1960, going out past Anacapa Island to San Nicolas Island (west of Santa Cruz Island) to "blow its tubes" and conduct a "tracking operation." The sequence was repeated four more times on Tuesday June 7, 1960, the same day that the *Marie* set out from the harbor toward Santa Cruz Island.

Folks must think it weird that someone my age is investigating an almost 50-year-old shipwreck where her daddy was lost.

Ken was skeptical, but deep down my heart told me I was doing what I was supposed to do. Among all the information, I believed I would be led to something that would piece together the *Marie* mystery.

Preparing for the briefing to Ken, I was creating a flip chart with a rainbow of colors emphasizing key points, the biggest point being the Pacific MISSILE Range. Given what I thought I knew, everything happened in and around that expansive area.

WEST COAST ARCHIVES

(1) Coast Guard Scrapbook with no mention of the *Marie*

(2) Anti-Submarine Warfare article points to infrared of interest to Aerospace

(3) Lockheed's Special Project's Office and flow of VIP tours *(Including a Rear Admiral Beardsley)*

(4) Ordinance Lab at Corona (Memos of TERRIERS and POLARIS missiles.)

(5) Santa Cruz Island Assets

(6) Pacific "**MISSILE**" Range

I have yet to locate the SAR as it remains a mystery. Thus, the Navy Yard may be my last hope.

Just as I was ready to present my information to him, Ken called to me as he bounded up the stairs and toward the garage. "I'm heading out."

I dropped my marker and followed him.

"I thought we had a debriefing!"

"I trust you," Ken said. "You put thought into understanding your expenses and your findings. I support your concerted efforts."

"But, I was looking forward to telling you what I'd learned."

"I'm off to hunt and gather at the hunt club. My son's coming down." He gathered me up and swung me around once then planted a kiss on my lips.

I shook my head as I watched him drive off.

What's a girl to do? Perhaps he peeked at my flipchart with an arrow pointing to missiles?

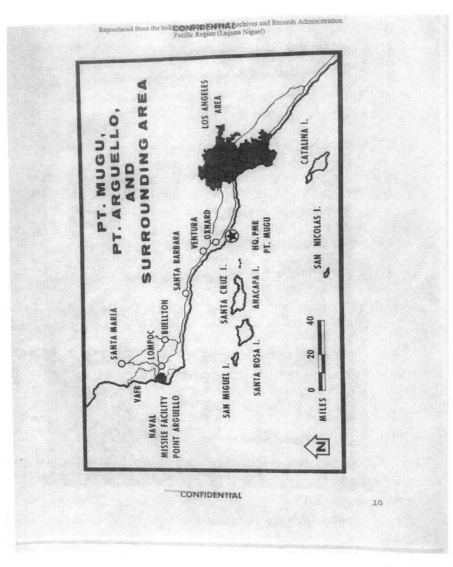

FIG 29: A page from the Command History of the Pacific Missile Range, 1960. Reproduced from the holdings of the National Archives, Pacific (Laguna Niguel).

CHAPTER 24:

The Navy Yard

After returning from California, I began making plans for my next journey to Washington D.C. to see what the Navy Yard had to offer. Fortunately, Ken had an upcoming workweek at the National Guard Bureau headquarters in Washington D.C. to select those soldiers who would be offered the opportunity to attend the prestigious Army War College. I decided to tag along.

Ken reserved a hotel room located across the street from Dete's apartment in Arlington, Virginia. Dete had to work that week, so I would be able to focus on my shipwreck research during the day.

In preparation for my trip, I connected with Ms. Lloyd, of the Naval History Center by e-mail and then over the phone. What do you have at the Navy Yard that might help me?" I asked.

"The command histories are good," said Ms. Lloyd. "You might want to also check out what the Ships' Histories Center has to offer."

****

Once in Washington D.C., I took the metro to the Navy Yard. "Head toward the sun," Ms. Lloyd had told me, "and the Navy Yard gates should be on your right side."

Sure enough, I found the gate at Parsons Avenue, off M Street. I showed my military ID, and was permitted to move past the guards.

As I entered I saw what the book, *Shadow Divers*, described as, "...an ancient-looking complex of trolley tracks, cobblestone roads, libraries, and classrooms."[45]

I had printed a map I'd found online. I wanted to start at Building 200, the smaller of the two archives. That building was next to a snack bar where I could get a cup of coffee and catch my breath before launching into my research.

SHIPS HISTORY CENTER

The entrance to the Ships History Center was a small doorway at the far end of a dark hallway. An intercom was placed next to the locked door. I pressed the button and said, "Hello," I said. "I'm here to do research. A Dr. Cressman should be expecting me. My name is Teresa Newton-Terres."

No one answered.

I waited, hoping someone would come in or out, but nothing happened. I checked the time on my cell to confirm that I was within their hours of operation.

"Hello," I said, pressing the button again.

Maybe there's another entrance?

"Good morning," a voice bellowed out from the intercom.

I repeated myself, "I'm here to do research and a Dr. Cressman should be expecting me," I said.

"Hang on," the voice said.

A few seconds later the door opened.

"Good morning," the man said. "Cressman hasn't arrived, but you can hang with me until he does."

I followed Mr. Wilbur, the art director of *Aviation News* magazine, into his office off a central corridor near the front.

Mr. Wilbur offered to get me a cup of coffee and scurried out of sight, leaving me to admire his creative space: a small artist's easel, a big computer monitor, and many objects from which to draw inspiration.

When he returned with my coffee, Mr. Wilbur pointed to the magazine I was flipping through, a recent issue of *Naval Aviation News*.

"That's what I put together," he said.

The cover text read, "The Legacy of the F-14 Tomcat." I had been reading a spread on safety that used a comic figure, Grampaw Pettibone. After recounting a recent incident where a jet didn't land on the ball approaching a dark aircraft carrier's landing strip and plunged into the ocean on the other side. Luckily the pilot bailed out safely. Grampaw cautioned, "We're all in this together – aviators, LSO's, seniors in chain, everybody. Ego, pride, and fast boarding rates shouldn't get in the way of safely bringin' the troops back aboard, 'specially when it's dark out."

"Is Grampaw Pettibone your creation?" I asked. I had noticed that the art and colloquist credited was Ted Wilbur.

"That's my father," Mr. Wilbur said.

"This is fabulous." I spread out its centerfold, a photo of two Tomcats soaring against a deep blue sky. "Makes my heart beat, and I'm not an aviator," I said.

He handed me a folded map. "Maybe this will be of interest to you. I just put it together."

I unfolded a poster-sized listing of the U.S. Navy Support and Tactical Land-Based Squadron patches.

"Thanks. I hope I have an opportunity to look at more of your handiwork," I said as Dr. Cressman entered the office.

"The majority of past issues are available online," Mr. Wilbur said. "So, you can do just that."

"Thanks for babysitting me," I said smiling.

"Good morning," said Dr. Cressman. He had a kind face and a casual, gracious manner. I could tell he was both knowledgeable and enjoyed what he was doing, and that he could probably retire at any time if he desired.

After initial pleasantries, I followed Dr. Cressman down the hall, trying to catch a glimpse of all the framed Grampaw Pettibone illustrations. At the opposite end of the hallway was an open space with some tables.

Before arriving at the Navy Yard and its Ships History Center, I had learned that Robert J. Cressman had written *That Gallant Ship: USS*

Yorktown (CV-5). My father had served on the Yorktown. I mentioned that my father had served on the Yorktown, but Dr. Cressman explained that the USS *Yorktown* he wrote about was lost in the battle at Midway in WWII. The USS *Yorktown* my father served on was a newer ship, the CV-10, and was now on permanent display at Patriot's Point outside Charleston, South Carolina.

I found it confusing that new ships shared old ships' names, but this was part of my awakening to the importance of knowing both a vessel's name and its number.

"When did your father serve?" Cressman asked.

"If I remember correctly, it was Jan 1951 to Nov 1954."

Dr. Cressman disappeared down the hall without a word. The area that he had brought me to looked like an employees' lounge: three tables, a couch on one end, and at the other end a sink, microwave, and copy machine. I placed my things on the table next to the couch. Shortly, Dr. Cressman returned and handed me a ledger where I wrote my name and contact information.

"While I pull what I can from the list that you e-mailed me, you can look through these," he said, handing me an archive box.

"That works for me."

The first thing I pulled from the box was a ship's history of the USS *Yorktown* (CV-10) – two pages that covered 1951-1954. I made myself comfortable as I began to read about the ship that my father had served on during the Korean War.

I respected Dad's work as a jet engine mechanic. But after reading his handwritten memoir, recounting his family's trip to Spain in 1950, I saw him less as a mechanic and more as a storyteller.

The *Yorktown* history immediately drew me in. I looked for a specific mention of Dad, but the history focused only on generalities such as destinations and missions. The introduction mentioned that the ship was commissioned in January 1947 but remained idle until "… ominous overtures by the Communists threatened world peace." After a modernization at the Puget Sound Naval Shipyard, in April 1953 she powered from Alameda to San Diego and by August 1953, over to Pearl

Harbor.

Most likely, Dad boarded the USS *Yorktown* at Alameda harbor across from San Francisco. Mom and Dad would have been married by this time. My oldest brother Jim would have been eight days old when deployed.

I had always thought that Dad went to the Far East before he married Mom.

I touched the small pearl that hung from a delicate chain around my neck. Dad bought the pearl in Japan, picking it out using the advice he got from the jeweler who leased space in the Old Town Goleta properties. Mom had it set in her wedding ring. I knew that much. Now I understood that Mom had married Dad using a simple gold band. Her pearl ring came upon his return and in celebration of the family they had begun in their marriage.

This thought lead to another memory. Mother once told me she spent time at the cabin and worked every day cleaning cabins and rooms at the Strawberry Inn. "I earned the money to have my second baby," she said. She liked to tell me of her cabin days cleaning. "Your dad was away, your brother Jim was young, so Grandmother Streeter watched him."

I guess Dad was at sea.

Within two years, my other older brother Rick was born. By that time, the Korean War was over and Dad was out of the Navy and learning to become a mechanical engineer at California Polytechnic University at San Luis Obispo.

The *Yorktown* ship's history summarized its activities from 1947 to 1955 in two succinct pages. "After the usual shakedown cruise and post shakedown repair period, the *Yorktown* was proclaimed fit and ready for sea duty." Another resource—movement cards—listed every port entered: Alameda, San Francisco, San Diego, back to Alameda, Bango, Bremerton, Seattle, Seal Beach, San Diego, Long Beach, San Diego, and back to Alameda, and finally San Francisco. By August 27, 1953 the Yorktown was safe at Pearl Harbor. Then, it was off to Yokosuka, Sasebo, Hong Kong, East China Sea, and back to Yokosuka.

Then it went back to Pearl Harbor and returned to Alameda and San Francisco by March 3, 1954.

On July 8, 1953, the *Yorktown* set sail for Pearl Harbor, followed by a tour of Manila and then returned to its home-port of Alameda. Upon its return, on March 3, 1954 the carrier returned with a $25,000.00 cash gift to the Shriners' Hospital for crippled children. It was reported to be the largest single donation ever collected aboard a Navy ship for charity. I wondered what part my father may have had. He would have understood the importance of the Shriners' work because his brother, my Uncle Albert, had battled polio as a youth. "The Shriner's hospital made the difference," Uncle Albert said of his recovery.

The ship's history also mentioned that the *Yorktown* was in the movie, *Jet Carrier*. I would try and find the film to see if I might see my father in it. I remember seeing some photos of Dad with a jet and its pilot.

"That's a famous jet," Mom had said.

Was that jet in the movie?

I had read the USS *Yorktown's* ship's history and movement cards, more than once by the time Dr. Cressman returned with additional resources.

When Dr. Cressman returned with additional resources, pointed to the *Yorktown* ship history. "This warmed my heart," I said. "To think my father had a part in these activities."

"If you know your father's squadron number, I will have even more details," said Dr. Cressman.

"I may be able to do just that after I get home," I said, thinking of the discharge papers that Mr. Peuser, the NARA 1 archivist had encouraged me to obtain. As Mr. Peuser had said, I was indeed delighted because with my request I not only received a copy of Dad's military record, they also sent me all the medals Dad had earned.

I had not yet shared the medals with my brothers. I was saving them for an appropriate time or event.

"Nothing on the Drexel #4 you asked about," said Dr. Cressman. He explained that it was probably a smaller, surface vessel that wouldn't document movement and history. But he brought me ship's histories for the USS *Norton Sound* and USS *King County*.

Dr. Cressman also handed me a thick document. "You can have this," he said.

Historical Report Covering the Pacific Missile Range and the Naval Missile Center at Point Mugu from 1-November-1945 to 30-June-1959.

"Wow. Free of charge?"

"It's an extra copy and just taking up space," he replied. "No one's looked at this stuff." He brought other files on the Pacific Missile Range, including news releases and the Comptroller's Annual Report on Funding.

When I was out on the West Coast, I obtained a copy of portions of the 1960 Pacific Missile Range history. I couldn't remember if I'd seen an overview of the range's prior history, but the PMR had been a thick file.

"The copy machine is over there," Dr. Cressman pointed to the right corner, "Copy all you want and we'll count them all up at the end before you leave. "I'll check on you in a little while. Otherwise, I'll be in my office if you need me," he said with a smile and left me to my research.

I sat down and arranged the sources. I placed the Pacific Missile Range information to one side to read later. I had finished reading the *Yorktown's* ship's history, and began flipping through the histories of the USS *Norton Sound* and the USS *King County*. Eventually, I focused in on the *Norton Sound*, the ship that had been just beyond the Santa Barbara Channel and Santa Cruz Island, "blowing tubes" and "conducting tracking operations" on Monday and Tuesday, June 6 and 7, 1960.

Were the Norton Sound and the Marie part of an orchestrated operation?

The history told about the *Norton Sound's* involvement in the launch of SKYHOOK balloons in 1949. Balloons "carrying over 100 pounds of instrumentation, were tracked for as long as sixteen hours by the ship's radar while they telemetered (radioed) information concerning cosmic radiation from a position high above the earth."[46]

I remembered a picture of my mother in her Navy Wave uniform holding up what she said was a weather balloon. She was in the Navy 1947 to 1953, but back then, pregnancy was reason for discharge.

"The picture was in a Navy publication," Mom told me.

I made a note to ask Dr. Cressman for help looking for the publication.

Given the USS *Norton Sound's* history and the memos I'd already read in the archives, I surmised that the blowing tubes and tracking from June 6-8 was related to TERRIER missile experiments.

I closed the *Norton Sound's* history and opened the USS *King County's*. This ship was moored on Tue, June 7, 1960. However, the log indicated that it was doing something unusual in the Santa Barbara Channel on Friday, June 10, 1960.

This vessel wasn't listed as one of those assisting with the *Marie* SAR.

What was it up to?

Apparently, the *King County* was attached to Submarine Squadron Five until June 1959. After that, she operated as a unit of the Eleventh Naval District under Pacific Missile Range orders. Her service included participation in the Discoverer XII Satellite Launch, data capsule recovery operations, and Corvus Missile Launches. Interestingly, the *King County* was retired July 19, 1960 and her name stricken from the Navy List of Ships on August 1, 1960.

Why? Should I be curious that she was taken out of service soon after the Marie shipwreck?

I was pleased when Dr. Cressman came to check in on me. I needed a break. I had begun shuffling and flipping through the other documents, trying to determine where to begin.

"How's the research?" Cressman asked. He told me that he would be out for a couple hours, but he could make a run into the archives before he left. A man about the same height and build tagged along behind him.

"Do you have any media files from 1960?" I asked.

"Yes, I've got just the thing," Dr. Cressman said. "Why don't you tell my colleague, Mr. Curtis, about your research while I go retrieve something for you. Mr. Curtis is the Navy Yard's Head of the Naval Aviation History Office. He may be able to help you."

"I'd love to," I said. I gave Mr. Curtis a quick summary of my quest to locate information on the *Marie* shipwreck.

"Follow the money," Mr. Curtis replied. "It's what my father taught me."

As he said this, my eye caught sight of the coin drawn on the cover of the Pacific Missile Range comptroller's report.

Follow the money.

That was the best advice I'd received in a while.

I had been following a lot of threads as I tried to weave together details, but instead of a beautiful tapestry, my mind was becoming a tangled rat's nest.

"I'm looking into a rendezvous between the USS *King County* and an Air Force C-119. The C-119 somehow picks up data from the *King County*." It didn't register that I had just read the *King County* ship's history, where it participated in data recovery missions, because I was distracted by this aviator and his dad's wisdom. "Do you know what a C-119 is?" I asked.

"Sorry. Off hand, I'm not sure," he said.

"It was a long shot. Thanks anyway. I'm not even sure if the ship and airplane are connected to my shipwreck."

Dr. Cressman returned with a few media files. One even briefly mentioned a C-119.

My stomach growled, but I wasn't going anywhere. I had stowed an apple in my purse. That, along with coffee, would have to hold me until I was finished. I was eager to wrap up this archive and head to the larger archive, The Naval History Center.

FOLLOW THE MONEY

Follow the money.

Mr. Curtis's words echoed in my thoughts. To track the money, I turned my attention to, the *Pacific Missile Range Comptroller Annual Report: The Effective Use of Money, Material, Manpower, Year Ending*

30 June 1960. It would have helped if I knew the program's name or number, but I wasn't going to let a detail like that stop me.

The comptroller's history was approximately 50 pages. Several pages had a graphic of a big coin divided like a pie, with pieces that represented the various budget expenses and categories. Since I had reviewed the PMR Command History, I recognized many of the program expenditures (SPARROW III, CORVUS, Research, Dev. & Installation, Assist Others).

I noticed once again that some program names were in capitals and others were not. Later I learned that those in all capitals were code names. As mentioned in the command history, there were several Infrared Guidance and Control System programs in development.

When I had reviewed most of the document, I came to a page labeled "Boat Operations." One line stood out: "...various unscheduled research operations as well as *providing local sea rescues in the area*" [emphasis added]. The Pacific Missile Range Command History I had also mentioned dates of civilian sea rescues, but nothing in June or about the *Marie*. The page also listed and described the costs of 13 boats that ranged in size from 45 to 125 feet. However, a Drexel #4 wasn't listed.

If the *Marie* and its crew were simply working on a civilian operation, it seemed reasonable to believe that search and rescue activities would be recorded somewhere. Were the Raytheon team members on the *Marie* civilians testing equipment? Or were they working on a secret project? If secret, whom were they serving?

These were questions I needed answers to.

I turned to the next page, labeled Ship Operations. This page simply listed four vessels, one of which was the USS *King County*. The *King County* was on my mental radar, because it was in the Santa Barbara Channel conducting a "data pick-up" with the C-119 during the active search for the *Marie*. [47]

As I scanned the page, I noticed one ship's name was conspicuously absent.

I quickly flipped back one page, then forward. The USS *Norton*

Sound wasn't listed. I had already read that the Norton Sound was in the Pacific Missile Range "blowing its tubes" and "tracking" several times on Tuesday June 7, 1960. I assumed the *Norton Sound* was a PMR asset, but perhaps it was under a different command. If so, whose?

The ship's histories, came to mind. I shuffled through files until I located the USS *Norton Sound's* history. Skimming quickly through the file, I confirmed "TERRIER and TARTAR experimental firing" under the authority of the "Commander Naval Air Force, US Pacific Fleet."[48] The ship's daily logs would also confirm who was in charge, but I couldn't check these until I returned home. However, it would be a while before I connected the *Norton Sound*, TERRIER, and memos from the Naval Ordnance Laboratory in Corona California.

****

I turned my attention from the Pacific Missile Range to the new files that Dr. Cressman had brought. One file held copies of *ALL HANDS: The Bureau of Naval Personnel Career Publication*. I flipped through the stack, my eyes skimming material and moving quickly over dates and details. When I saw a 1965 article that included the date, July 20, 1960, I slowed to read the words in context.

"The most dramatic moment in the development of Polaris took place on 20 Jul 1960, when the launching of a test missile from *George Washington* proved the workability of the system. This was the first time a Polaris was launched from a submerged submarine, and the successful launch was repeated less than three hours later."[49] When I saw the reference to Polaris, I thought of the archives in California and a book that still collected dust *on my shelf, half read.*

The date was significant to me, not because of the Polaris accomplishment or because it was 43 days after my father was last seen. July 20th was my birthday. I turned three that day, and I was crying and screaming while clawing at the kitchen back door that led into the garage. Mother and grandmother sat in the dark at the kitchen table, ignoring me. I wanted my remote-controlled white dog that walked and barked. It had broken only minutes after they gave it to me.

Mother put the broken dog quickly in the garage, out of sight.

"I'll replace it tomorrow," she said. I wanted to hug the broken dog. Grandma brought it to me, but mother took it away. Now, years later, I understood that Mom and Grandma were talking about my father who went missing six weeks earlier. We must have only recently returned from the cabin. In their grief, they apparently didn't realize that my heart was broken, too. I wanted to hug the broken doggie to let it know that it was loved. Tears welled as long-buried emotions tried to resurface.

I returned my attention to the article. "During her first deployment, *George Washington* carried A-1 missiles. Polaris is a deterrent, and the best part is – it works so well it may never have to be fired."[50] A photo at the bottom of the article showed a circle of buoys on a calm ocean surrounded by support vessels, and a missile shooting straight up out of the water and into the sky. The caption read: "POLARIS test missile is launched from a controlled area in missile range during first underwater test shots." The "pop-up" test was conducted off San Clemente Island.

Another question stirred in my mind, as I considered the July 20, 1960 test launch. Had the team on the *Marie* been testing technology destined for this dramatic moment?

"They had a deadline to meet," Mom had said about the tests they were conducting.

Apparently, the results were due the following day. She thought something had to be sent to Washington D.C., but wasn't sure.

****

Dr. Cressman returned from lunch and checked in on me. When I described the difficulty I was having in finding information about the *Marie* shipwreck, he replied. "Civilians lost at sea serving the Navy do not get very much attention."

I respected his comment, but I was uncomfortable with it. I didn't know if the men on the *Marie* were fulfilling a contract task for the military, or if they simply got in the way.

When I finished copying files, I stopped by Dr. Cressman's office to tell him how much I appreciated his help. It was late and I was exhausted; however, the archives would remain open for another hour. So, I walked the three blocks to the Naval History Center's Operational Archives.

I introduced myself to the staff at the front desk. "I've spent a great day at the Ships History Center," I said. I told them that I intended to be in all day tomorrow, and I confirmed their hours and research regulations. Ken had taught me the value of doing "reconnaissance." After scoping out the site, I left the Navy Yard as the sun was setting.

THE NAVAL HISTORY CENTER

The next morning, I retraced my steps to the Navy Yard and, once inside the gate, I went directly to The Naval History Center. Ms. Lloyd came from an office and welcomed me to the operational archives. "I'm looking for the culminating report about the *Marie* shipwreck and the search and rescue report. In addition, I'm looking for information on submarine activity along the West Coast in June 1960, foreign or domestic, and anything else you can tell me about what was going on from June 7-11 in the Santa Barbara Channel."

Ms. Lloyd introduced me to Mr. Hodges. Mr. Hodges, a civilian, looked like a physician. He wore a cotton lab coat, but his coat was blue rather than white.

"Please do what you can to ensure Ms. Newton-Terres' requests for sources are served," Ms. Lloyd told him.

Mr. Hodges led me into the resource library, a bright room with a large window, but only a few tables. I reviewed once more my list of objectives and hopes for the day's research.

"It will take me a little while," Mr. Hodges said as he left the room.

I took out and began reading material I had collected the previous day.

Soon, Mr. Hodges returned with a cart with boxes and left them with me.

A lady sat at the only other table, reviewing a stack of materials. She was so focused on her work she didn't appear to notice us.

"She's writing a book on women in the military," Hodges whispered.

I had been keeping a handwritten journal as well as an electronic log so that I could retrace my steps, if need be. My grandmother had created several scrapbooks in her lifetime and the *Marie* shipwreck's scrapbook was the most incomplete. I didn't know if I could complete her scrapbook's story, but I was going to try my best.

I turned my attention to the records Mr. Hodges had brought me, and reviewed a selection of news releases and press coverage of the Pacific Missile Range that summarized the 1960 achievements. I reviewed a one-page *Command History of the Naval Air Force, U.S. Pacific Fleet.* Eventually, I would learn that this was the command to which the vessel the USS *Norton Sound* was attached when it blew its tubes in the Pacific Missile Range at the same time as the *Marie* search and rescue. Of the command history's five brief paragraphs, one caught my interest.

> Increased emphasis on anti-submarine warfare was reflected in the commissioning of four Carrier Anti-Submarine Air Groups and one ASW Patrol Squadron, and in the shifting of certain existing patrol squadrons to more strategic points on the West Coast and in the Western Pacific. Additionally, various [anti-submarine warfare] exercises were conducted, including the first major joint Canadian-American exercise for defense against submarine-launched missile attack on the North American continent.[51]

Was the Marie somehow involved in this?

Nothing in this Command History identified the role or mission of the USS *Norton Sound*. I was so focused on my research I was aware of little else. I began reading the 1960 command history of the Western Sea Frontier. This history included two supplements that bore security stamps. One was stamped CONFIDENTIAL and the other SECRET. I began with my usual quick skim of its details and dates, but stopped dead when I read that 50 unidentified submarines were spotted in the Western Sea Frontier area of responsibility. A visual sighting of a Russian submarine had been confirmed mid-year, and the sub was followed for two weeks.

Was this connected to the Marie? Perhaps the USS Growler was on this sub's trail?

"Ms. Newton-Terres?" a voice broke in. "It's closing time."

"Huh?" I said engrossed in the records and reports. I looked up and noticed Mr. Hodges standing by my table. The sun was setting outside the windows. I had skipped lunch, instead popping peppermints in my mouth all day and taking a drink from the water fountain when I needed to stretch my legs.

"Before you leave, I need to make sure your copied documents are reviewed, dated, and stamped as declassified," he said.

****

On our last evening in Washington D.C., Ken, Dete, and I decided to take in the Spy Museum. We had all heard that it was an experience not to miss and none of us had ever been there. That evening, I learned about the deadly serious world of espionage between the U.S.A. and closed societies like Russia. The insights I gained reminded me that the *Marie* tragedy occurred at the height of the Cold War.

I knew that I needed to track and trail further into the depths of 1960 espionage.

I left Washington D.C. somewhat disappointed. Once again, my research uncovered no Search and Rescue (SAR) report, no insight into the Drexel #4 ship, and only a brief mention of a C-119 that, two months after the *Marie* incident, missed catching something that fell from space. However, I was pleased because I had a wealth of material to sift through at a more convenient time as I looked for more threads of information to weave together.

Without the final SAR report, I was left to piece together the shipwreck based only on the news reports in Grandmother's scrapbook. From my very first day of research, at the NARA-I on Pennsylvania Avenue in Washington D.C., I had hoped to locate the final SAR report within one of the nation's archives. If I had that report, I hoped to find who made the first call for help, and the exact hour and day. Also, the contract number and the technical reports that the *Marie* tests produced.

Without this information, I might have to approach Raytheon again.

CHAPTER 25:

Coast Guard Connections

I'd wrestled alone with the Coast Guard's source documents long enough. I believed an understanding of the details on the *Cape Sable's* deck log would enable me to decode the shipwreck and the subsequent search, but reading the log was like trying to read Chinese. None of it made sense to me.

I had come to a point in my research where I needed insight into the material I'd collected.

"Why don't you e-mail Sutter Fox?" Ken suggested. Sutter, now a retired Coast Guard captain, had shared an office with Ken at the Joint Pacific Command Headquarters at Camp Smith in Hawaii. Sutter and his wife, Bonnie, now lived south of Los Angeles.

I sent him a short e-mail. "I'm visiting Santa Barbara for the Fiesta. I'm also working on my 1960 shipwreck project. I'm researching the shipwreck where my dad was lost, and I have a few questions to put to someone with Coast Guard knowledge. Can I afford your consulting fees?"[52]

His response was encouraging. "Shipwreck? Well, as far as my consulting fees go, free advice is worth what you pay for it! I'm intrigued and would be glad to talk with you about all of this."[53]

Encouraged, I sent a longer e-mail saying, "I seek to gain insight on the entries below," and I attached the ship's log that had generated them.

Sutter replied within minutes. "Do you have the SAR case file? I'm not sure how long we hold onto those. I remember paperwork management laws that required us to forward certain things, shred others after so long."[54]

I sighed, thinking of the effort I had devoted to looking for the elusive SAR. With that report, I would be able to identify many things, including when the first call to the Coast Guard was made. I could verify the amount of time that passed between the *Marie's* expected return (Midnight, Tuesday, June 7) and the newspaper's account of when the Coast Guard was first contacted (Thursday, June 9, shortly after 9:00 AM).

Why was there a 33-hour gap between the Marie's failure to return and the start of a search?

By midnight, a more detailed e-mail arrived from Sutter. To it he attached a decoded copy of the *Cape Sable* Deck Log I had originally sent him.

"I really enjoyed going through the ship's log," Sutter wrote. "Thanks for the memory jogger. I haven't thought about these kinds of things in quite a long time. I searched in the Santa Barbara Channel a number of times while I was CO of the Coast Guard Air Station in Los Angeles from 1991-1993, so the area is familiar to me."

As I'd hoped, Sutter's insights into the log were truly helpful. My child's heart and mind wanted to exaggerate the importance of details. On the other hand, my adult heart and mind sought the truth.

One phrase in the report that had confused me was *secured search*.

What does that mean? Is it referring to an area being kept secure or guarded?

Sutter explained that the phrase, *secured search* meant that they stopped searching. "Secure in the naval services can mean several things, but this usage means to stand down from whatever the unit was doing," he added.

Commenting on the Deck Log, he clarified an entry that had

originally set my mind spinning: "Papa Secure (Sierra) Search." Sutter explained that it referred to a type of search pattern used in a large area when position of distress is unknown.

I recalled the line drawing in one of the Santa Barbara News Press maps of the search pasted in Grandmother's scrapbook.

One entry baffled Sutter at first: *CGUFig1294*. He hadn't heard of a Coast Guard term, *Fig*. "Except for *your* Fig," Sutter wrote. (Fig Newton is what my husband's friends called him.) But after Sutter reviewed the original source document I sent, he laughed. Apparently, my handwritten entry was a transcription error.

"It should be U*F-1G*1294," Sutter informed me.[55] The reference was to a Grumman Albatross airplane with the number 1294.

I wondered if the Albatross was among the first on the scene and if it was the plane mentioned in the Santa Barbara News Press and Los Angeles Times reports:

> Coast Guardsmen at the scene were searching for any signs of the boat itself and for bodies reported seen by the aircraft. The bodies, the pilots reported, were under the surface of the water and were visible to them, but Coast Guardsmen aboard the single cutter at the scene before dark said they saw no bodies and found no debris which could be identified as belonging to the missing boat.[56]
>
> Coast Guard plane crews reported sighting three bodies. But this discovery occurred just before dusk and several hours later two cutters were still on the difficult job of finding the bodies in the vast, dark ocean.[57]

I also wanted to understand how the Coast Guard estimated coordinates for the *Marie*.[58] The scrapbook news clips said that the *Marie* didn't have a radio. If this was true, then they couldn't have gotten a position from a mayday call. I had been told that no one knew where the *Marie* went down. So, how did they come up with search coordinates?

I asked Sutter, "How was this position set?"

Sutter responded, "ISP or *Initial Search Positions* are established a number of ways. The best is oil on the water or debris or eyewitnesses or mayday or LKP (last known position) reports. Computer programs and local knowledge give us ideas on which way to orient searches based on winds, tides, currents, etc. If we are searching and find something, it is not unusual to reorient a search to take advantage of new information."

Frustration welled up within me as I read the e-mail and document. I was delighted that Sutter was eager to help me. At the same time, I felt agitated and I didn't understand why. I had emotions churning in me that I couldn't understand. It was dark outside, but the August heat and humidity radiated through my glass windows. I felt like I was drowning in perspiration.

I just wanted to solve the shipwreck mystery.

CONNECTING WITH JOHN STITES

Sutter mentioned in his initial response that he looked through a Coastie's website named *Fred's Place*, for the people listed on the *Cape Sable* Deck Log.

"I found one person from the log: Stites, John BMCM."

It was the name of the Coastie who had entered many of the Cape Sable's Deck Log entries during the SAR for the *Marie*.

"If you wish, I'll send him an e-mail," wrote Sutter.

"Please do," I replied. "Let him know I'd like to connect with him too, if that is agreeable."

****

When Sutter's next e-mail arrived, I was at my computer looking out across the ninth fairway and green to the golfers around the clubhouse. I had a clear view of the lush landscape. I enjoyed the view from my large office windows under the shade of tall pine trees. Although it was cool inside, the late August sun was heating up outside.

Ken and I were preparing to leave for the National Guard Association of the United States (NGAUS) in Puerto Rico.

Sutter's next e-mail said he had contacted John Stites, and that John was looking forward to hearing from me.

Before flying to Puerto Rico, I sent a greeting to Mr. Stites.[59] It was a simple introduction. I attached copies of three news clippings to jog his memory: the photo of the Coast Guard moving a shark-eaten body from the cutter to the pier, Coast Guard and Raytheon leaders looking at the recovered hatch cover, and the map with a line drawing of the SAR area.

When I returned from Puerto Rico, John's response was waiting for me.[60] I could hardly believe it. I had connected with someone who had participated in the search for the *Marie*.

John shared what he remembered:

"I will always remember that case because of the tragic loss of so many lives. I had never before or since been on a case involving that many people where none were rescued, and that is something I won't forget.

"Because of the good weather that night, calm seas and warm water, I thought we would be picking up survivors but it was not to be. QM1 Jimmie Spear was our cutter's Acting C.O. and was designated On Scene Commander. We had learned the *Marie* along with crewmen had been hired by Raytheon Corp. to take their people out to a point off Santa Cruz Island for the purpose of testing a classified underwater piece of equipment, possibly some sort of Sonar.

"We arrived on scene and found nothing, not even debris. A long and thorough search was conducted by multiple units including aircraft. Some debris was found but not as much as expected from a boat sinking. Since we were the largest boat and OSC, the other craft brought recovered debris to us. I don't remember much about the debris other than the hatch and a life jacket.

"With all the boats and aircraft searching a relatively small area we realized early on that chances of finding anyone alive were slim. We continued the search, hoping for a sighting that never happened. I don't recall if the *Marie* was later refloated or inspected by divers but it was believed the bow ramp on that old landing craft worked loose resulting in uncontrollable flooding. One of the bodies was recovered by another unit which we took aboard and another as I recall was brought into Santa Barbara.... Two bodies were later located off Port Hueneme."[61]

Good weather, calm seas. John's words echoed in my mind.

FIG 30: *Above: The Coast Guards Cape Sable, CG#95334. John Stites (BMCM) stands on deck, in the middle.*

CHAPTER 26:

Anti-Submarine Warfare

Between Sutter and John, I continued to learn about the Coast Guard and grew more comfortable with the jargon.

For example, in Coast Guard lingo, "Status Bravo Two," means "ready to go…in two hours." So, the status told how soon the *Cape Sable* could be heading out to sea on a mission. I learned that "Status Charlie" meant the ship was out of service for maintenance.

Apparently, the *Cape Sable*, was placed on "Status Charlie" before 9:00 AM on Wednesday, June 8, 1960, the morning after the *Marie*'s departure from the harbor. John Stites remembered that they tore the engines apart for maintenance. An entry on the following day, Thursday, June 9, 1960, led Sutter and me to believe that the Commanding Officer (CO) went on leave while the SAR was in progress. But John clarified that the CO's leave began in the morning at 0700 (7:00 AM) as the entry indicated, but that the entry was placed at the bottom of the log page because someone had neglected to enter it at the proper location. This delayed entry showed me the CG desired an accurate recording of events.

DEBRIS

As I reviewed John's e-mails, I recalled something he had said about the debris: "Found nothing, not even debris." Later he wrote "Some debris…not as much as expected from a boat sinking." He went on to describe the protocol used at sea, "Since we were the largest boat and OSC, the other craft brought recovered debris to us. I don't remember much about the debris other than the hatch and a life jacket."

John concluded that possibly the *Marie* was tidied up for its paying guests. I remembered one article in Grandmother's scrapbook described the *Marie* as a "…clumsy-looking craft, its decks loaded with skin-diving equipment and with experimental equipment."[62]

If it was loaded with equipment, shouldn't there have been more debris?

As the search for the *Marie* progressed, the news reports offered images of the recovered hatch covers. The photos showed the covers surrounded by a throng of friends and family dockside, and later by Coast Guard and Raytheon officials privately. But no other debris, such as life jackets, was depicted.

I wanted to look through John Stites' eyes and see what he remembered, because in his mind's eye he still saw the debris.

I e-mailed John, asking him if he remembered seeing a life jacket with a sweatshirt tied to it. If so, was it tied right-side-out or inside-out. In the e-mail, I didn't mention why the sweatshirt was important to me, but I included the Santa Barbara News Press reference:

> "One of the life jackets had tied to it a man's blue sweatshirt. Both the sweatshirt and the lifejacket itself were torn, as if by sharks, Coast Guardsmen said. They believed it had been worn by one of the still missing men."

John Stites e-mail response was quick:

> "I recall the life jacket but not the blue sweatshirt…I do remember it appeared sharks had ripped it. A fishing boat recovered and brought in a body. One of his legs had been chewed by a shark and is the reason I suspected there were no survivors

when the weather was so good. Sorry I couldn't help with the sweatshirt."[63]

The meaning of the secret signal my father tried to give with his sweatshirt—whether farewell or alert—would remain a mystery.

TROPICAL STORM

One of my original questions remained unanswered, so I repeated myself and asked specifically what they could tell me about the tropical storm alerts listed in the Port Hueneme Light Station log.

"Should I take these tropical storm alerts to be general weather warnings? Or, are the entries a code for a storm of another nature (Coast Guard, Navy, Air-Force) that was swooping into the area?"

I mentioned that when the tropical storm alerts caught my attention, I reviewed the entire year of Station Logs, to consider if the alerts were normal or unusual. I also mentioned that I located a couple "tropical storm" alerts, in May 1960. But the concentration and quantity of alerts in June appeared unique to me, especially because they occurred during the days of the *Marie* SAR.

Sutter's response continued to show his propensity for being an educator.

"Message traffic has four priorities: Flash, Immediate, Priority, and Routine. The abbreviations are Z O P R (don't know why)." Sutter went on to say, "Flash are the highest and must be done in 10min."

Sutter interpreted the first message, received at 2141 (9:41PM):

Wed, Jun 8, 1960 Received OP-090415Z. Tropical Storm Warning.

"OP-090415Z", for instance...it is immediate to any addresses in the TO: block, and priority to any in the INFO: block. The rest of the message is 9th day of the month at 0415 Zulu time (Greenwich Mean Time)."

He also deciphered another received at 0350 (3:50AM):

Fri, Jun 10, 1960, 0350 Received Oper. Immed. 100900Z Tropical Storm Advisory.

"In this one... [there is a] common error. When reading O, most people would [understand it to mean] OPERATIONAL... O means IMMEDIATE."

Finally, regarding a message on Fri, 10 Jun '60, 1050: *Received Gov. Priority 101500Z,* Sutter wrote, "Don't know how Gov. priority came out on this one. It would be PRIORITY for the P in the line... Lots of little things like this to remember in communications."[64]

If I understood Sutter correctly, the first alert warned of something happening on, "9th day of the month at 0415 Zulu" (June 9, 4:15AM).

Curiously, the alerts on the Light Station log spoke of storms, but the other weather details I was compiling, didn't point to a storm. I reconfirmed the entries in the Port Hueneme Light Station logs. For the most part, June listed wind "calm" and sea "calm" with an occasional entry of a slight SW swell or wind. These facts aligned to the Alameda weather log and to John Stites' memory of, "calm weather...calm seas."

I had lived in a variety of locations (Washington D.C., Pennsylvania, Kansas, and Arkansas) where storms could strike quickly. I had lived in Hawaii and experienced the thrashing rains of a tropical storm. But in over thirty years living in the Santa Barbara area, I couldn't remember ever experiencing a tropical storm.

All things being equal, I was convinced there had been a storm in the SB Channel June 1960, but, I didn't know exactly where or when.

CONSPIRACY

I asked my Coastie friends, "What might a Navy ship be doing in the Santa Barbara Channel?" I also asked about the Navy Drexel #4 that ferried debris and a body to the Cape Sable. "Where did this Navy boat come from?"

Sutter wrote, "Many ships are in that channel.... We used to call San Nicolas Island our stationary aircraft carrier. I had one crew fly out there, refuel, fly out to a Navy ship, land, refuel and run toward a ship waaaaay [sic] out. They launched when in range, flew to the ship, hoisted an injured seaman, flew back to the Navy ship where the corpsman worked on him and the helo refueled. When in range, back to San Nicolas for more fuel and then to the hospital. We couldn't have done the case as efficiently or perhaps at all without the Navy at San Nick."

John Stites responded, "I don't recall hearing the term 'Drexel' boat. I thought the Navy boats, because of the close proximity to Point Magu, were requested by the CG to assist in the search."

I checked the original source and noted that John didn't make the log entries about the Drexel.

Later, I shared with Sutter my family's myth of the possible Russian kidnapping of the scientist, dad, and the captain. I also mentioned to Sutter my suspicions about a special operation that the Navy's *King County* was conducting, but I had yet to connect with the *Marie* SAR. "Could the CG have been a front for a Navy-controlled operation?" I asked.

"Conspiracy theory allows for almost anything," wrote Sutter. "The truth is usually a simple explanation, and it is our desires and imaginations that make things complicated." He went on, "From what I've seen, this was a typical case and I don't detect any Navy attempt to control. Think of the Ehime Maru when we were in Hawaii. The USN sub surfaced and hit the Japanese training ship, sending it to the bottom. The SAR case itself was all run by the USCG even though it was near the entrance to Pearl Harbor."[65] Sutter also pointed out that in the *Marie* search mission, the Navy ferried debris to the Coast Guard.

"Desire without knowledge is not good" (Proverbs 19:2 NIV), came to mind. I hoped my internal compass would direct me to wisdom and not to wild imaginings or baseless conspiracy theories.

CLOSURE

I had expected these Coasties to help me understand the documents and the search for the *Marie*. However, I never expected to gain insight that impacted my heart.

John Stites wrote, "You can live a long time off a good rescue; by the same token, missing someone is a drag on the heart. Even if there was no chance of saving someone it is very hard to deal with the disappointment that comes with coming home empty-handed."[66]

Sutter mentioned a case that still tugged at his heart and soul.

"One time we had three people missing. One stayed with the boat and was found by a passing boat the next day. That is the only way we knew a boat was missing and that two others had tried to swim ashore.

"One of our units recovered another person, leaving only one.

"I was flying a helicopter out of CGAS Chicago so it must have been around 1975. I was in my first tour and must have been a new aircraft commander. CGAS Traverse City had a Goat (Albatross) overhead searching and they found the third person.

"I was right down near the water and couldn't see him.

"I went into a hover and the Goat crew vectored me to the man.

"He was a foot or more underwater so I couldn't have seen him, but the Goat crew could from high overhead. Anyway, we put the platform out and my crewman was gung ho to bring him aboard. My little voice said to wait for the 40-footer (cutter). Anyway, youth and full trust in my crewman told me to go ahead, I put the helo into the water and taxied over (we had boat hulls on the HH-52A helicopter).

"The man was floating with his arm hooked over a torn life jacket. My crewman was standing out on the platform and as soon as his boat hook touched the man his arm slipped off the jacket and he went straight down.

"This really bothered me because if we had waited the boat crew may have had a better chance to recover the man. I kept thinking I blew a chance to return him to his family so there would be some closure…. Many lessons that day for me. I guess you can see how this has really stayed with me even after more than 30 years. I couldn't have saved this man, but I could have given some peace of mind to his family.

"It was really tough knowing we never found him even though it was good but cold weather, light winds, and good location. There were other cases but that was probably the first loss of life and hit me pretty hard.

"Anyway, it is much more pleasant to consider the lives saved.[67]

I understood Sutter's story from the perspective of a family member who never got the closure he spoke of. Because my father's body wasn't recovered, even now there remains a flicker of hope that somewhere he might still be alive.

Sutter's story also reminded me of the news reports that I had previously found difficult to accept:

> Coast Guardsmen at the scene were searching for any signs of the boat itself and for bodies reported seen by the aircraft. The bodies, the pilots reported, were under the surface of the water and were visible to them, but Coast Guardsmen aboard the single cutter at the scene before dark said they saw no bodies and found no debris...[68]

Now I understood how the bodies could be seen from an airplane but not from a boat. Thus, my question changed. Were the bodies mentioned in the news report the same ones later recovered from the sea (Lovette, Mackie, Howell, Russell)? Or were they the victims who were never recovered (Beardsley, McCaffrey, Terres)?

CHAPTER 27:

For The Children

I awoke from a dream with the phrase, "All but one," lingering in my mind. I considered waiting until morning to write the dream down, but I didn't want to forget it. I rolled out of bed and went to write it down.

In the dream, I was at a conference center and I came to a banquet room where all the tables but one was set.

I have to call someone about that table.

I went to a different room and rummaged through closets and doors in search of table settings. When I tried to leave the room, something, buzzed around my face like a bee. I shook my head, trying to avoid it.

It wants to control me. I didn't know what it was, but I knew I needed to flee from it, and so I left the room.

Next, I found myself in front of an old-fashioned London type red phone booth. It stood in the middle of a sun-drenched, grassy hillside. I stepped inside. As I dialed a number, I looked from where I was, in the clear sunlight, to below the hill where a haze of fog encircled. Through the gray mist, I saw a train winding its way toward me.

I was afraid.

The train will not harm me, if I stay on the hilltop.

Beyond the haze and train, I saw Santa Barbara and its channel and its Channel Islands just beyond. I awoke with the lingering thought echoing in my mind, "All but one. Don't fear. Stay in the light, and it will pass you by."[69]

As I thought about it later, the significance of the dream became clear. First there was the newspaper headline in the scrapbook: "All but One." Now a dream echoed that same thought. When I understood how recognizing my father's short life would help us find closure, I convinced my brothers to gather at the 50-year milestone of Dad's loss. "Let's sing a hymn, remember our father, and enjoy a beachside BBQ," I told them. In the meantime, I planned to poke around and learn what I could about our father and the shipwreck in preparation for the family gathering.

As my effort evolved, I realized that God might have other plans.

As 2007 began, I was emotionally strong. I had taken decisive steps to resolve my battle-related frustrations. And as I faced the upcoming year, I anticipated opportunities to resolve the question of what happened to the *Marie*. But I had also realized that, even if I never solved the mystery, my search could bring comfort to my family.

To gather information prior to the 50-year anniversary of the shipwreck, I had set up a simple webpage with my name and contact information. I originally set up the page to give the retired Raytheon engineers a way to contact me. I also hoped the webpage would serve as a hook to connect me with others interested in the shipwreck. When an e-mail with the subject line, *Marie*, showed up in my inbox one day, I wasted no time in opening it. The e-mail was from Eric Maulhardt, grandson of Dale Howell, one of the men on the *Marie*. Eric found the *Marie* website when he was doing a genealogy search.

Dale Howell's body was recovered on June 15, 1960. He left behind a widow and four children about the same ages as my brothers and me. Uncle Albert had told me that Dale Howell grew up with Dad in Goleta and that they were childhood friends. Dale Howell's obit had recounted other details of his life such as his being a highly-trained survival expert serving in the Army during the Korean War.[70]

I didn't realize it when I first opened the e-mail, but the entire focus of my research was about to change.

Teresa,

My grandfather is Dale Howell. Although I never knew him, my family says I look more like him than any of my other family members. My whole family is very interested as to what happened. My family has endured much hardship after the death of Dale. My grandmother was left a young single mother with four young children to support. Her disappointment with the "explanations" consumed her life for many years. I would love to get some real answers for her before her time is over.

Any information you have would be greatly appreciated.

Eric Maulhardt

I felt hot. I couldn't breathe. For the first time, I felt the weight of someone else's expectations and responsibilities. This young man believed I could give him answers to share with his grandmother. Ironically, his grandmother probably knew more than I did. I believed, I was the one who should be asking her what happened.

I got up and went for a walk around the golf course. "Action cures anxiety," was one of Ken's personal phrases that inspired my workouts and perspective. I walked, pulling my jacket sleeves down around my fingers to fight the cold air and continued to think of what I had done thus far.

After my walk, I wrote a concise reply summarizing what I knew to be true. Seven men left June 7, 1960 just after 7:00AM never to return alive. The Raytheon project team was conducting infrared tests underwater. They were using a technology to "communicate over a beam of light."

I included a copy of the one-page timeline that I had compiled from the basic details. I also attached a list of all the news articles that I had found in Grandmother's Scrapbook, mentioning that they were likely available at the University of California at Santa Barbara library. I also confessed that his grandmother likely knew more than I did, and that my intention was to poke around the archives of original source documents until the 2010 milestone. I also mentioned my plan to have an intimate family gathering to give my father's life the honor and recognition he never received.

Eric responded to my e-mail, "My grandmother and aunt are very excited about the commemoration in 2010. I will definitely be there along with my family."[71]

When I read Eric's response, I began to realize that maybe my plans for a small, family gathering in 2010 needed to expand.

****

I planned to meet the Howell family face to face when I went to Santa Barbara for the Fiesta. I e-mailed Eric after I arrived in July 2007. However, I had second thoughts when Eric told me that his grandmother did not live near Santa Barbara, but near his aunt Glenna, in Vacaville, near San Francisco. I wanted to talk to her, but Vacaville was a seven-hour drive north of Santa Barbara, and a three-hour drive west of our cabin in the Sierra Nevada mountains. I decided to try another time.

Had I known that Mrs. Howell had less than a year to live, I would not have put off making a connection.

VICTORY TOUR

In June of 2008, it was time to retire for both Ken and me.

Although I had been reluctant to take on the responsibility of leading the PEC Family Program, now I was sad to leave it. Leading the Family Program taught me the art and science of service. I learned it's all about relationships; not perfect plans, regulations, or data. Together, the PEC people and I accomplished great things and enjoyed things that mattered. I discovered the key to getting things done is having an awareness of what is important and who is the leader. This knowledge would serve me well as I moved forward on my journey of discovery.

After the PEC change in command ceremony and Ken's retirement ceremony, Ken and I began a military retirement "victory tour."

Once we were in California, I was eager to stay a few nights with Uncle Albert and Aunt Lynda. I chuckled when I saw that Albert had put photos of my dad, grandparents and himself on top of the dresser with their eyes facing the bed. Albert had draped washcloths over his mother's eyes that faced the guest bed when he and Lynda visited us in Arkansas for Ken's retirement. Albert continued to delight me with his youthful and joyful spirit.

We treated Uncle Al and Aunt Lynda to a boat ride on the Condor Express, a high-speed whale watching tour, that crossed the Santa Barbara Channel and skirted the coastline of Santa Cruz Island. The tour briefly explored Painted Cave, the world's largest sea entrance cavern.

As we cruised I saw whales, and dolphins following along with the boat, and I had an idea. Because the Condor Express followed a path similar to what the *Marie* traveled in 1960, I thought this trip might be worth repeating at the 50-year anniversary.

Before leaving Al and Lynda's, I placed sticky notes over the eyes of our family photos, hoping to give Al a chuckle as he had for me.

The next leg on our victory tour called for R&R at the cabin, before returning to Arkansas. Before heading out, I made a quick call to the Howell family.

GLENNA HOWELL-GRIFFIN

I called the number that Eric had given me. A woman answered on the third ring.

"Hello?"

"Hi, this is Teresa Newton-Terres," I said timidly. "My father was lost on the *Marie* shipwreck."

"Oh, my god!"

I'd expected a less gracious response. Something like, "Yeah? What do you want? That was a long time ago, kiddo. Are you stuck in the past?"

Instead, this total stranger welcomed me like a long-lost relative.

Glenna Howell-Griffin couldn't have been more endearing. When she learned that I was going to be in the area, she insisted that I come over.

"I only have an hour," I said, knowing that Ken might mutiny if I took much longer than that. I knew that we could continue the dialog by phone and e-mail. I promised Ken that I would limit our face-to-face meeting to a brief introduction.

As I pulled into her driveway, it was obvious that Glenna kept a tight ship. Her home was immaculate.

Glenna, a vivacious redhead, opened the door and we embraced as though we had known each other for years.

"I wasn't surprised by your call," Glenna said. "A couple days ago I took out this album of photos and organized this file," she pointed to a binder and folder. "Then I tried to find the *Marie* shipwreck website, because I wanted to make contact with you."

Glenna proudly showed me the photos she had of her Dad. It was a small collection, about the same as I had when I started on my quest. She also shared the tidbits of information that she knew about the people in the photos.

"The Goleta motorcycle gang. This blonde is my Mom on one of her visits into town. And look who's seated here." Glenna said she pointed to my father. Glenna shared stories about her father that her mother had told her. "You know your dad was the brave white hunter and diver." Glenna mimicked her mother's voice.

She told me that her mother had died earlier that year. I wondered if she had been as spunky as her daughter.

"Dad always said that he would die one of two ways, either in the mountains hunting or in the ocean scuba diving. So, one of his two predictions came true. From what my mom said, he loved to hunt and he loved the ocean" Glenna said.

I could tell Glenna wished she knew more about her father.

I told her some stories that my Uncle Albert had told me about when our dads were kids. One had to do with exploding a bomb at the Marine Corps Base down the street, now the home of the Santa Barbara Airport. Al told another story about Glenna's father, Dale, when he came over as a teen to our family's apartment above the Goleta stores.

"Got any smokes? I'm all out!" Dale asked in a tone loud enough for my grandparents to hear. Apparently, my dad cringed and Albert snickered.

"Do you have any memories of the lobsters our dads caught?"

I asked. My computer had a photo of her father holding a huge lobster in the yard in front of my grandparent's Goleta store.

"I do remember standing in the front yard and lobsters were everywhere on the ground," Glenna said. "We used to poke at them. And I remember my mother smashing a big one with a spoon into a pot."[72]

"What do you remember about the *Marie*?" I asked.

"I was five when Dad died," Glenna said as if that gave her an excuse not to remember much.

I had learned from my own experience that, although I was young, I remembered more than I originally gave myself credit for.

I knew that the shipwreck changed my life. As a result, I tried to value every day, knowing my father had given his life so that I could live mine. And from a young age, I was keenly aware that decisions had consequences. I knew wisdom came at a price, and I hoped that the price my father paid was not lost on me.

"Did your mother tell you anything about her experience?" I asked.

"I remember Mother saying how Dad would tell them, 'If a ship goes down you grab anything, anything that floats, life jacket, ice chest, anything that floats!' Mother said lots of equipment floated, yet nothing like that was found at sea or near Dad."

I could sense a struggle inside her, as if she were wondering what prevented her father from grabbing debris and following his own safety practice.

"I remember there was a lawsuit, and I remember sitting in court," she added. "We had Social Security from Dad. And when mother had little money left to take care of us, she went to court to gain access to some of the lawsuit's funds. When we turned 18, I could access the balance of my account to pay off bills and buy a few things," said Glenna.

I mentioned that our experience was similar, funds from Social Security and the lawsuit. But Mom didn't take us to a courtroom.

Glenna told about a vision her mother, Dawn, had. "It was

around the time they found Dad's body. Mother was in a living room, and Dad came through the front door dressed in his wetsuit, the one in the picture in the LA Times article, all dripping wet. Dad told her, 'Everything will be okay.' After he said these words, the vision disappeared. She got up examined the floor where he had appeared. The floor was wet.

Wow! I sat in silence a moment to honor the memory.

Glenna directed my attention to two large reels of 16mm film, labeled Dale Howell. "My sister had these films compiled and I believe they hold hunting and scuba diving memories," she said. "They are compiled on the VHS. It's broken, but I'll get it digitized."

"I look forward to seeing it."

"The big question is what happened?" Glenna said. She had already mentioned it more than once.

Glenna handed me a large envelope. The grin on her face told me she believed the contents would be helpful.

I opened the envelope and pulled out three documents.

The first document had darkened with age. I would need a magnifying glass and photo enhancement to decipher it.

"I wonder what tale the dark one tells," Glenna said.

The next document was a page filled with type, but nothing jumped out.

The third document stopped me dead.

"UNITED STATES COAST GUARD – From: Senior Investigating Officer, Long Beach"

Was it possible that I held the Coast Guard's Search and Rescue (SAR) or possibly the Court of Inquiry Report?[73]   Had the Howell family archives held all along what had eluded me and the archive authorities in Washington D.C. and California? Later, I would take time to decipher the details of all three documents: The Coast Guard report, the transcript of Dawn Howell's testimony, and the document darkened with age—which turned out to be an initial summary written by a private investigator hired by Glenna's mother.

"What did you think when I called you?" I asked her.

"Wow. I'm the last," Glenna said. She told me about losing her three siblings. Diana and Gregory, the oldest and youngest, died in an auto accident at the hands of a drunk driver. She lost her sister, Linda, to cancer a few years back. She told me how Eric was Diana's son and now lives in Ojai.

"Everyone is gone. Now to have someone who wants to talk about my dad?"

Glenna didn't have to say another word. I understood her joy in talking about our fathers. My emotions and confidence were bolstered by her childlike enthusiasm and trust that I would do the right thing.

I scolded myself for hesitating to connect with the Howell family and for fearing they would judge me for wanting to look into my father's loss. I had feared that I was supposed to have all the answers. That was the beginning of my realization that the Howell family also had questions, and that they held a piece of the story puzzle.

That day a faint voice began echoing: *For the children.*

It was like a heartbeat as I drove away, and I recognized it as an inner voice to listen to.

The newspaper headline, *All but One*,[74] in Grandmother's scrapbook had led me to plan a small family ceremony to honor my father at the 50-year milestone. In my brief encounter with the Howell family, I began to realize that they, too, wanted and needed to mark the memory of a father lost in a shipwreck. As I drove away from Glenna Howell's home, I prayed to hear and do God's will for this effort. I was keenly aware that the intimate commemoration I was planning for my brothers and myself might be changing. My father never had his life summarized and our family needed to honor Dad at the fiftieth anniversary of his disappearance. I felt a deep need to know and honor my Father. However, given the interest from the Howell family, I began to consider ways to honor my father and still meet the needs of others at the June 2010 milestone.

"Maybe I'll hook another family of the shipwreck," I thought.

CHAPTER 28:

Cabin Courage

After I said farewell to Glenna Howell-Griffin, Ken and I left Vacaville and embarked on our three-hour drive into the Gold Country foothills and up into the Sierra Nevada mountains to the cabin. My oldest brother, Diego "Jim" III, planned to join us for the weekend, so Ken and I drove to the cabin a few days early to enjoy some time to ourselves. We went there for rest and relaxation; however, I found it impossible to ignore the documents Glenna had given me. Whenever I could, I stole away to a quiet spot to focus in on every word. At night, we slept on the deck under flannel sheets and down comforters, with an ocean of stars above us.

On the third night, another dream woke me up. In this dream, I was driving down a freeway. Two huge tractor-trailers came up on either side of me and our three vehicles locked together. Soon we were in a tailspin. I heard a voice say, "Trust me. Let go of the steering wheel." The next thing I knew I was walking down the highway off-ramp. Debris littered the road. In the debris, I found two perfectly shaped seashells, but they were imitation. I spotted another shell in a mud puddle. I put my hand into the water and picked up the shell. It was yellow with age, and I could see a crab inside its hollow. Along the shell's edges were microscopic sea life.

"This one's real. There is life in it," I thought, and I returned it to the puddle.

When I looked up, I saw more people walking down the exit ramp. I followed them to a door where a person with a clipboard stood.

When I got to the clipboard holder, he said, blocking my passage "No other girl understands guys like you." I began to explain that I grew up with brothers, but I awoke before I finished my sentence.[75]

Now fully awake, I looked up into the sky, brightened by the Milky Way. A shooting star streaked across the darkness. Then I saw a pinpoint of light trace slowly across the sky, and I recognized it as a satellite.

I fell back to sleep, listening to Ken's rhythmic breathing.

In the morning, I discovered that my brother Jim had arrived during the night and had placed his sleeping pad and bag on the far side of the deck.

I told Ken and Jim about my dream.

"Life is just one mud puddle after another," Ken said with a smirk.

"I don't dream. Or, I don't remember dreams." Jim said. He went on to tell me that he didn't like to dream because one time he saw our father in a dream. Jim also made it clear that he didn't want to talk about my dreams, either.

Why he wouldn't want to see our father, I couldn't imagine. But, I considered it a sign of his own unhealed wounds. I changed the subject.

I told Jim about meeting Glenna Howell. And I mentioned what I knew about her father. I tried to tell Albert's stories about our Dad, Dale Howell, and the Goleta gang. They didn't laugh.

Jim shared one of his memories. "Dad left me with his binoculars to play with and said, 'Don't move from that rock.'" Jim said that Dad then went scuba diving. He said it as if he was pointing out our father's parenting irresponsibility at the beach.

I assumed that Dad was diving to hunt for food for us. Mother had told me that Dad could get the week's meat within an hour underwater. It was a different time, I thought. As a child, I sat in a parent or grandparent's lap while in the car without a car seat. Today, the law would call this irresponsible.

"What else do you remember?" I asked.

"Nothing," Jim said. "I don't remember anything. If there was something, I've blocked it."

It wasn't the first time I had heard him say that. But I continued to ask and he continued to come up with new story tidbits. And whenever he did, I jotted down his bits and pieces. Jim had just turned seven when we lost Dad. I felt he had many memories that hadn't yet surfaced.

I felt a growing sense of urgency to collect and record whatever stories I could. I missed the opportunity to speak to Glenna's mother, and I began to be concerned that I may lose other folks.

Jim asked me about my research into the shipwreck. He knew I had traveled all over in search of answers.

I envisioned the pile of paperwork that I had gathered but had yet to organize and dissect. And I had to confess that, although I had devoted time to the discovery, but that I couldn't explain exactly what happened—yet. I showed him the documents that I got from Glenna Howell. "This Coast Guard Report," I said, "is a great summary of facts."

Jim flipped through its pages and came to the last page, titled *Conclusions*.

I reached a finger and pointed to a concluding point and he read, "It is opinioned that a structural failure could have occurred since the vessel's underwater body had not been inspected since 1958. The large concentration of weight on a small area of the cockpit and after deck would tend to raise stresses for which the vessel was not designed. This of course does not preclude the possibility of collision with a submerged object or an unidentified vessel."

"Submarine?" Jim asked.

"Submarine," I said.

"I have yet to confirm or disprove the possibility of submarine involvement," I said as he returned the documents to the envelope.

Jim changed the subject and asked what he must have believed an innocent and reasonable question. "What's the status of the Trust and the cabin?"

I sighed inwardly. The Trust. The cabin. I knew the subject was unavoidable. For the most part, the cabin was an amazingly harmonious experience for our family. We shared most of the expenses for the cabin's upkeep. However, when Mother was alive, we were not fully aware of what she owned, did, and was responsible for. As the trustee of her estate, I now had a clear perspective, and it wasn't in line with what most of the family understood. What the legal documentation showed and what the family believed were two different things entirely.

I wanted to do the right thing and to know that it was the right thing. But it was taking forever, and I'd failed in getting my brothers to understand the complexities of the issues involved. I wanted to arrive at a win-win solution for the whole family, but I wasn't making much progress. I mumbled out a response to Jim, and hoped he was happy. I didn't want the Trust or shipwreck to ruin our plans to relax.

That night, I woke up from a deep sleep, troubled. My thoughts were cloudy as I thought about the cabin. I wanted to do what was right, but there were legal rights, moral rights, ethical rights, and then there was what kids believe was right. I had been advised that, ideally, the trustees and executors of my mother's trust (Ken and I) should oversee operations; however, our main responsibility was in distributing the Trust's assets.

For the cabin family, I was seeking to create an owner-document and user-agreement, because I believed that was my responsibility. But I was beginning to understand that a user document would need to be renegotiated. As trustees, Ken and I were passing on ownership. And that would be a trigger to cause change.

I remembered reading agreements in the archives that seemed to clarify issues and required all signing parties to understand and respect various rights, responsibilities, and chain of authority.

"Follow the money" came to mind because money is always

involved.

Again, I thought about the agreement between Raytheon and the owners of the Marie.

How did it identify rights, responsibilities, and authority?

Did that agreement reference the contract served?

I had delayed taking the final closing steps for transferring the cabin from mother's Trust. I feared signing the paperwork, because I knew it had to be filed in the county records for generations. And I took this responsibility seriously.

Grabbing my Bible, I went and found a quiet spot. "Save me from my tormenting thoughts," I silently cried out to God. My Bible had flopped open in my lap, and I began to read from the book of Joshua:

> Be strong and courageous, for you shall give this people possession of the land which I swore to their fathers to give them. Only be strong and very courageous; be careful to do according to all the law which Moses My servant commanded you; do not turn from it to the right or to the left, so that you may have success wherever you go. This book of the law shall not depart from your mouth, but you shall meditate on it day and night, so that you may be careful to do according to all that is written in it; for then you will make your way prosperous, and then you will have success. Have I not commanded you? Be strong and courageous! Do not tremble or be dismayed, for the LORD your God is with you wherever you go," (Joshua 1:6-9 NASB).

I was wonderstruck. It wasn't the first time I found comfort, courage, and guidance in the Scriptures, but it always amazed me when I found a message that spoke right to what I wrestled with. I re-read the verses and it dawned on me. Everything belonged to God, and I can only be a responsible steward of my talents, treasures, and trials.

I sat under the glow of the light bulb and considered what I had read. Then, I put away the Good Book, went back to bed and fell asleep.

****

Our victory tour's final lap came as we drove along highway 50, sometimes called "The Loneliest Road in America,[76]" and journeyed through Northern Nevada and Utah. Stunning beauty surrounded us in vast warm shades of layered stones and shapes within nature. As we returned to Arkansas, we knew that the next phase of Ken's and my life together was about to begin. And I hoped he would be in support of what I wanted to devote myself to: a *Marie* remembrance.

I had come to believe my family needed an intimate gathering at the 50-year anniversary. But as things evolved, I began hearing the faint whisper, *For the children,* and I believed it to be the Holy Spirit.

I didn't know if this referred to my father's four children, all the children of the shipwreck, or all children of God. But I was aware that God had plans in the making.

CHAPTER 29:

Telling Timeline

As fall 2008 approached, I planned to devote myself to a path of discovery leading up to a June 2010 anniversary. I would decide later if the activity was for my family only or all the *Marie* families. Now it was time to assess where I was so I could decide where I needed to go next.

I had examined all the details in Grandmother's scrapbook along with several human-interest stories surrounding the shipwreck. A stack of supporting documents confirmed that a few details were still buried. My list of books and articles offering insight into the historical context of the Cold War was lengthening. And, like living and breathing creatures, my mind maps and timelines were growing and developing.

"The timeline made the difference in our investigations," Ken said, referring to his assignment to the Pentagon's staff of the Investigative General (IG) for the National Guard Bureau. The offices he had once occupied on the IG staff and later as the Executive Officer for the Chief of the National Guard Bureau were among those destroyed in the 9/11 terrorist attacks. Thankfully, by that time Ken had moved on to his Hawaii assignment.

I welcomed Ken's wisdom about the benefit of a timeline because I was naturally drawn to organizing information this way. To make sense of Grandmother's scrapbook, I mapped out the basic details on a one-page flow chart that assigned events to corresponding dates. This timeline established a framework so that I could quickly understand how the *Marie* tragedy unfolded, for example: when the men set out from the harbor, when the Coast Guard search and rescue began, when each victim was recovered, and so on.

The timeline covering my wall quickly expanded to include pictures, Post-it notes, and documents. My windowless office morphed from a simple creativity space to a project war room. I sought a trail through the details, a path to help me understand what happened. When I proudly showed Ken my colorful wall, he smiled and said, "A beautiful mind."

He had recently seen the movie *A Beautiful Mind*, which told of the life of John Forbes Nash, Jr., a mathematical genius who made a discovery early in his career and gained international acclaim. While struggling with schizophrenia he experienced the heights of notoriety and the depths of depravity, and ultimately received the Nobel Prize.

Ken insisted I was losing my mind in the room he regarded as my "black hole."

I gave Ken all the credit for my devotion to timelines, so whenever he kidded me about my project's war room, I reminded him that I got the idea from him. As for his ambivalence toward my project, I brushed that off as simply the difference between men and women, Ken and me.

What Ken didn't understand was that by sorting out the chaotic details of the *Marie* tragedy and placing them in a proper place on a timeline, I found peace.

MY SLUICE PILE

I faced a mountain of paperwork. My inner office, filled with stacks of documents created by my research looked like something out of the reality TV show, *Hoarders*. I had briefly reviewed the documents in the archives, but still needed to sift through, organize, and file the details.

As I sorted the documents, I regarded the process as similar to what my grandparents on my mother's side had experienced as gold prospectors. Nanny and Poppy were the grandparents who had built the cabin as a summer home. They were prospecting for gold when the authorities located them and informed them that my father was lost at sea.

Panning for gold was their wintertime hobby. They would set up a campsite and then pan all winter, returning home in spring with some gold and a few buckets of "sluice" dirt that still needed to be processed. Poppy would then process the sluice back at their home in the San Francisco Bay area, carefully sifting through it in search of gold.

My sluice pile was from the National Archives.

I approached the pile of papers where I hoped to discover golden nuggets of information about the shipwreck, mindful of the adage, "Gold is where you find it." I wanted to locate an "X" that marked the spot of my treasure, but I feared I was losing the battle as I sifted, sorted, and stacked documents.

THE HOWELL ARCHIVE

I didn't have to add the three documents Glenna Howell gave me to my sluice pile. I had already sorted through them up at the cabin. As I typed every word from the three sources into my computer, I also tried to understand what insights they offered.

I identified the first of these documents as a Coast Guard report. I originally assumed it was the official Search and Rescue document, but the Coast Guard historian in D.C. told me, "It's not a Search and Rescue Report. This report has more information than the usual SAR."[77]

Although it wasn't the SAR, the eight-page report held a motherlode of facts. The document described the *Marie*, the onboard life-saving gear, and the contract between Raytheon and McCaffrey's Sporting Goods, which operated the *Marie*. McCaffrey's provided four sets of scuba diving equipment and two of the four divers. The document went on to describe the equipment Raytheon loaded onto the *Marie*, and the mission, "To conduct underwater infra-red experiments."

The report also included details such as the presence of a wooden lifeboat, and that there was no radio transmitter on board. I had assumed that the news reports must be wrong. Surely a vessel with high tech communication equipment must have low tech communication back up.

Apparently not.

The report also included a short list of the people from Raytheon, the harbor, and the community who were interviewed after the tragedy.

The Coast Guard report made it easy to organize the details that I had compiled from the news reports, the scrapbook, the ship's log, and the light station log. I also began identifying what I would eventually recognize as the generally accepted "public" story.

On the last page of the report I noted one speculation that, "... an unidentified object or vessel caused the shipwreck."

This statement reflected the persistent, Russian submarine theory.

The second of the three Howell family archive documents, contained the recollections of Glenna's mother, Dawn Darlene Howell. It was Mrs. Howell's statement of what she knew, understood, and experienced leading up to the shipwreck. The document was dated June 13, 1960, five days after the men set out for Santa Cruz Island and two days before Dale Howell's body was recovered from the sea.

I regretted that I had hesitated to talk to Mrs. Howell, thus losing the opportunity to hear her story in person. A black and white text document failed to capture the colors of the story. I had enjoyed talking with her daughter, Glenna, and now I wished it were possible to hear her story in her own words and emotions.

In her statement, Mrs. Howell described the last time she saw her husband on June 5, 1960. She recounted how he worked evenings at Vic Tanny's gym and, because they were legally separated at the time, she went there "...for the purpose of him seeing the children." During the day, he worked as a sheet metal man for Churchill Sheet Metal Shop on Haley Street in Santa Barbara.

According to Mrs. Howell, "...he lived with a roommate here

in Santa Barbara. His name was Paul Timothy Lovette and the two of them lived at 220 East Pueblo Street, Santa Barbara." She also explained that, "…he was going to be able to send me some money because he had completed a dive a few days before and he had money coming from Raytheon Corporation by June 10th." She added, "He didn't tell me who the dive would be for or what he was to be paid, but merely that he had some more dives coming up." She included that Dale told her that she shouldn't worry.

At the bottom, a couple of sentences had been added. They were difficult to read, but it looked like "I would like to make it clear…. He might have mentioned Raytheon Co. and then again, he may not have told me from whom he was expecting the money. I just don't know."

The third document from the Howell family archives had darkened with age. Glenna Howell had been intrigued by this document's condition, as if its very appearance cloaked secrets. It turned out to be an initial report created for Mrs. Howell by a private investigator she had hired. The document began,

> Our first step was to determine what investigation had been made and by whom. We found the US Coast Guard had made an investigation, arrangement and held an inquiry, and that they were preparing a report. We ordered copies of their investigation, deferring an on-the-spot investigation of our own pending receipt of the Coast Guard report. We contacted the Safe Practices Division, and the Division of Industrial Relations of the State of California to learn that they had both made a tentative stab at starting investigations which were not carried out. We had a preliminary conversation with Coast Guard Lieutenant Lusk of the Department of Marine Inspection, 1105 Times Bldg., Long Beach.

An addendum read: "COAST GUARD REPORT: This report has been received by your office, together with the summary and recommendations."

The investigator's report continued, "We spoke to the harbor master who showed us the record card of the *Marie*. The card shows the *Marie* to have sunk at anchor in May 1958. It was raised the next day. Mr. Dowse bought the *Marie* from Mr. Murray on July 31, 1958."

I had believed that the McCaffreys owned and operated the *Marie*, but I was now learning that the vessel had a long list of previous owners since its glory days in WWII service.

The investigator added, "We should probably mock-up some sort of model of the *Marie*. This would be useful in eliciting testimony from a landing or boating expert, probably Frankel (boat business owner) as to the … manner in which the Raytheon cargo was loaded."

A list for "Future Investigations" included looking into the earning power of Dale Howell and Paul Timothy Lovette. The report mentioned the need to gain "some figures of income from their places of employment for Dale Howell and Timothy Lovette, which included Vic Tanny Gyms: "We are writing the local and SB Gyms for a resume of his income during the past couple of years."

The investigation included a detail about Paul Timothy Lovette: "Interesting, this chap (Lovette) has had a number of…arrests, and apparently spent 60 days in jail in 1957 and about 30 days in 1959." and the report continued, "His employment prior to 1958 was in various sheet metal shops in the Los Angeles area."

I knew I would be rolling the details of these three documents over in my mind for quite a while. These pages moved the Howell family to initiate, "The Big Lawsuit" as Glenna called it.

THE SHIPWRECKED *MARIE*

The Coast Guard Report in the Howell family archives attempted to address the burning question: "Where did the *Marie* sink?" I had spent countless hours walking the coastal shoreline, gazing toward sea, considering the same question, and knowing that my father was lost somewhere in the Pacific Ocean's vastness. The report concluded that the "…sinking occurred in the vicinity of 34° 12' North latitude, 119° 35'

West longitude or to the eastward therefore."

That comment, however, only raised other questions in my mind, because it didn't reveal how they obtained the coordinates. The coordinates differed from those listed in the *Cape Sable*, CG95334, ship's log as an approximate location of the *Marie* sinking. Why?

I took out the two Santa Barbara Channel charts that I had picked up recently on a trip across the channel to the waters off Santa Cruz Island. The placemat-size laminated charts listed the longitude, latitude, and ocean depths, with notes on the back. One chart offered a birds-eye view of the Santa Barbara Channel with four islands and the California coastline. The other chart showed only Santa Cruz Island and its surrounding waters, including the *Marie's* supposed destination: Smugglers Cove.

As I thought about where the *Marie* sank, I considered all the sources that might hold clues: the scrapbook, the *Cape Sable* ship log, and the July 29, 1960 Coast Guard Report. Did these sources point to the same location or different sites?

First, I reviewed the scrapbook. "Coast Guardsmen at the scene were searching for any signs of the boat itself and for bodies reported seen by the aircraft…. The bodies, the pilots reported, were under the surface of the water and were visible to them, but Coast Guardsmen aboard the single cutter at the scene before dark said they saw no bodies and found no debris."[78]

This led me to wonder, if pilots could spot bodies, couldn't they also estimate an approximate location below them? I searched for airplane logs similar to the ship logs, but found nothing. Where were the bodies the pilots saw? Were they close to California's shoreline? Or the Santa Cruz Island shoreline? Or were they in the middle of the Channel? Why didn't they clarify this important detail? And a wooden vessel like the *Marie* should have left debris, but very little debris was found.

Why?

I continued to review the scrapbook articles and turned to one that was added in 1969. The article told about the discovery of a sunken vessel. "Two abalone scuba divers believed they found the *Marie* at an estimated location 2.5 miles from the shoreward side of Santa Cruz Island and 1.5 miles east of Big Cave (Painted Cave)." The divers said, 'It was 200 yards beyond the rocky floor where divers usually find abalone.'

"McMillan, the diver, was not aware that he had apparently unlocked a mystery of the sea until he radioed to Dick Pierce late this morning that he was coming ashore. 'That sounds like the *Marie*,' the diver quoted Pierce as saying."[79]

The article showed a picture of the divers with the wreckage they had found: encrusted main and reverse rudders, rudder support and keel. A seven-inch hole had been torn through one of the rudders. The divers estimated the age of the sunken vessel by the pink abalone that had attached to the wreckage.

I found this 1969 article interesting as it gave a nice summary of the shipwreck, but contained factual errors. First, the boat was listed as the '*Maria*' and not the '*Marie*.' Second, the *Marie* operator and scuba diver, Hugh James "Jim" McCaffrey, was referred to in the article; however, a listing of the victims didn't include Jim McCaffrey. Most of the information was correct, but when someone has become intimate with the truth, errors stand out.

As I considered other scrapbook sources, I came to a map. It was a hand drawing of the *Air and Sea Search System* which offered a birds-eye view of the systematic search conducted by the Coast Guard.[80] Comparing this map with my Channel Island chart, I noticed that the search area didn't include the area where the sunken vessel was discovered in 1969.[81] The Coast Guard searched the Santa Cruz Island coast-line but not beyond the coastline – a 2.5-mile expanse.

Why?

If the 1969 shipwreck location was the *Marie*, then at the time of the shipwreck in 1960, debris should have originated at that spot. The debris would have moved with the currents, and would have drifted into the search area, as Lovette's and Mackie's bodies had.

Why, then, weren't the search efforts in 1960 successful?   What happened to prevent more victims and debris from being located and recovered?

I had to assume that the *Marie* and her crew had said they were headed to Smuggler's Cove on the east end of Santa Cruz Island; however, Painted Cave is on the coast side close to the west end. Assuming the 1969 shipwreck find was the *Marie*, why was she near Painted Cave?

Maybe they finished their work and decided to go hunting for abalone and lobster?

Taking out the Cape Sable ship's log, I located the entry for Friday, June 10, 1960 and checked the coordinates listed there. Sutter Fox and John Stites had helped me to understand that, given the known information, these coordinates were likely determined by the discovery of Lovette's body the previous evening, factoring in the ocean currents, winds, and tides. I had hoped to find a source that confirmed a mayday or airplane sighting, but it wasn't to be.

On my Santa Barbara Channel Chart, I placed a star at the location of the coordinates.

Interesting.

The star floated in the middle of the Channel at an ocean buoy: *Grace.*

I returned to the Coast Guard's Report of July 27, 1960. This document listed coordinates for where Lovette's and Mackie's bodies were recovered. I placed a star on the chart at these locations. Lovette was west of Grace and Mackie was east, but both were in the middle of the Channel. Next, I turned to the last page where the report conclusion stated, "It is submitted that the M/B *Marie* sank on or about 7 or 8 June 1960 in Santa Barbara Channel between Anacapa passage and Santa Barbara Harbor.

I began to place another star at these coordinates, but stopped. They marked where Lovette's body was located. I read the conclusion again, and I understood that the final Coast Guard report went with a known coordinate. I understood that the Coast Guard's approximate coordinates, Grace, also included the detail that Lovette had apparently been dragged by sharks.

Why did they choose Lovette's location over Mackie's?

I placed a fourth star on the chart where the shipwreck was found in 1969 by the abalone divers.

The stars were clues, but of exactly what I wasn't sure. Three stars were in the middle of the channel between the islands and the coastline. One star was in 55-foot waters off Santa Cruz Island. One thing was certain: I was grateful for the Howell family archives, because the three documents shed more light on the search.

CHAPTER 30:

Eureka?

I returned to my sluice pile and took the top document. I recognized it as one I had brought from the archives at the Washington D. C. Navy Yard. Its label across the top page was in all capitals: COMMANDER WESTERN SEA FRONTIER HISTORY, 1 JANUARY THROUGH 31 DECEMBER 1960. It was a command history from the headquarters at Treasure Island, San Francisco, California.

Every document in the pile had at least one detail that was mind-candy. I was drawn to this original source because the Navy Yard had de-classified its pages along with its two attachments, labeled "CONFIDENTIAL SUPPLEMENT" and "SECRET SUPPLEMENT." I flipped the pages, hoping to learn about the Naval Command that covered the West Coast from Alaska to the southern tip of Panama, Central America and extended from the coastline out to sea, but didn't include Hawaii.

When I originally scanned the supplements, I had recognized activities related to submarines and anti-submarine warfare (ASW), so I copied it and added it to my Navy Yard bounty. I failed to recognize at that time that the document was like an "X" on the sand marking a treasure to uncover.

I began reading the 60-plus page document from the beginning,

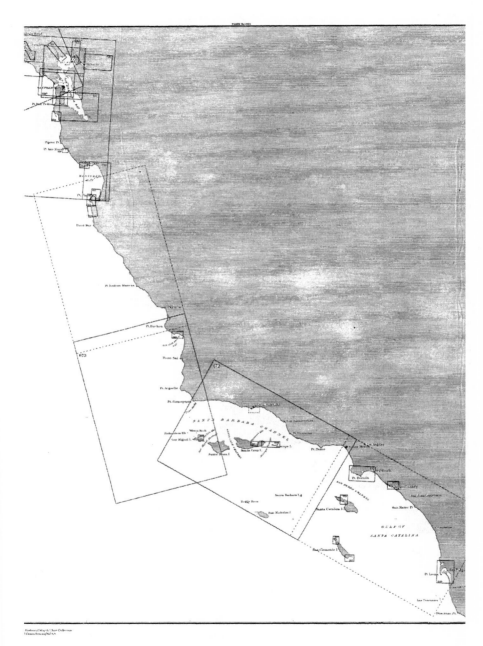

FIG 31: *The Western Sea Frontier from the Command History of the Western Sea Frontier, 1960. Reproduced from the holdings of the Navy Yard, Washington D.D..*

and this time I read every word. From the outset, the writer's ability to tell the Command's story enthralled me.

> Throughout the year 1960...preparation for defense of the area remained paramount with Western Sea Frontier activities coordinated with the other services in plans and exercise...special stewardship is outlined...In this year of technical peace but of cold war tensions, the activities of the Command were carried on in the serious realization that the Command's every action was a movement of a shield of freedom. The manner of cooperative dedication of the officers and men was similar to that which normally exists only in time of war. The personnel of the Command seemed to have gained a realization that they had responsibilities in the "battle for men's minds" just as they had duties to be prepared for military actions.[82]

As I continued to read, I was attentive to any references to submarines, but ignored other topics, including anything to do with the space age. After June 2010 activities, some of the references I had ignored would become a mother lode of important information. At the moment, however, I was interested in the Intelligence Division, introduced in the first section of the history along with the notation: "Further activities of the Intelligence Division are included in the Secret Supplement." Then my eye caught a statement that indicated an organizational change on June 10, 1960. It apparently had something to do with the Communications Division's plans for efficient handling of present and future communications.

June 10, 1960 was the Friday after the *Marie* was last seen and the day that Hal Mackie's body was recovered from the sea. Soon I would learn that Hal Mackie's widow believed if the Coast Guard had started searching just a few hours earlier, her husband would have been found alive. Also, on June 10th there was a special operation in the Santa Barbara Channel that occupied the Navy's USS *King County*.

The *King County* ship's log didn't reveal its coordinates on this operation as it had for previous PMR missions. The log reported that the *King County* was "rubber docking" and conducting a "rendezvous with a C-119" for a "data pick-up" all of which interested me. But, I couldn't tell if these activities were routine or unusual. It appeared that the ship was on a separate mission and not serving in the *Marie* SAR.

But what was its mission?

CONFIDENTIAL AND SECRET SUPPLEMENTS

I continued reading the Western Sea Frontier's CONFIDENTIAL SUPPLEMENT. As I did so, I realized that these pages summarized aspects from the commanders' histories that I had read in the archives on the West Coast, 11th and 12th Districts, which fell under the Western Sea Frontier's umbrella of authority.

> The year 1960 was a period in which over fifty unidentified submarine sightings (QUEBEC) occurred in the Western Sea Frontier area of responsibility. The sources of these reports varied from sightings by untrained civilians ashore to sightings by highly trained anti-submarine warfare (ASW) personnel aboard ships and in aircraft. A large majority of the reports proved to be invalid; however, several were on probable submarines and one (QUEBEC 34) was a visual sighting of a Russian submarine. Contact with this submarine was maintained for several weeks and was finally lost primarily due to a severe storm that moved into the area. The effort expended in investigating these sightings provided excellent training and resulted in improved ASW techniques and procedures for protecting the West Coast from the seaborne threat.[83]

"Over fifty submarine sightings" and "confirmed Russian submarine" and "maintained for several weeks." I didn't understand the meaning of Quebec and Quebec-34.

I brought the document over to Ken. "What do you think Quebec means?"

"Probably each sub identified they called a Quebec, and the 34ᵗʰ sub was tracked and confirmed to be a Russian submarine," he said.

"Brilliant," I said, and kissed him.

I had hoped to put my family's submarine/kidnapping theory to rest, but details such as these kept the theory alive.

The report didn't give specific dates to clarify when the Russian submarine was sighted, identified, tracked, and "lost primarily due to a severe storm." All I knew was that one sighting mid-year was a confirmed Russian submarine in the Western Sea Frontier.

But when and where?

The confidential supplement went on to describe the SOund SUrveillance System (SOSUS) Grid which: "provided a means to transmit secret SOSUS information in an unclassified format for the first time." The supplement described the SOSUS format as essentially the same as that used in the US Atlantic Fleet, covering a smaller surveillance area in the Pacific.

Would that include a deep-sea passage between California's coastline and its Channel Islands?

I remembered that Jim said that he and Mom talked about the SOSUS system. I made a mental note to ask him.

I scanned the next clump of text and latched onto the word STORM[84].

Was this "STORM concept" related to the "Tropical Storm" alerts that were listed in the Coast Guard's Port Hueneme Station logs?

I wanted to jump to a conclusion that there was a link; however, I knew better. I couldn't assume a direct link between what I was reading and the alerts that I sought to understand on the Coast Guard Station logs.

I didn't want to waste time and effort following rabbit trails. I had been trying to walk in wisdom, which meant gathering the facts and letting them shine light on the correct path to follow. Nevertheless, I couldn't deny that this potential clue intrigued me. I flagged the page and made entries in my notes about what I still needed to investigate at the Navy Yard.

I sat in my larger office space, overlooking my "ocean of green." Things were changing now. Beyond the windowpane, churning winds removed scarlet, orange, and yellow leaves from trees, exposing barren branches.

I needed to finish reading the command history's confidential and secret supplements before delving into other documents. Reading the supplement was tedious work, but I knew there might be more golden nuggets to discover. So, I refocused my attention and continued reading.

Next, I turned to the SECRET SUPPLEMENT. Every page was branded with the label: SECRET.

The Secret Supplement included more information about SOSUS activities in the Pacific. Apparently, by July, SOSUS had detected and correlated hundreds of ships.

I couldn't help but wonder, would June SOSUS reports show what happened to the *Marie*? Did the reports still exist? If so, where?

Looking back through the Western Sea Frontier documents, I knew that they provided a key summary of West Coast activities. Although I didn't understand every detail, I knew that I would return and reconsider them.

DECODED TIMELINE

Next, I reviewed all my timelines. I checked the timeline that had details which might or might not be related to the *Marie* mystery. I looked at my notes about the fifty submarines that were spotted and the confirmed sighting and tracking of the Russian sub (Quebec 34). And then I reviewed my other timeline, which contained details that were related in some way to the *Marie* SAR. To this I added a note about the Tropical Storm alerts: "Ask Navy Yard people about the STORM Concept within the West Sea Frontier History and determine relevance."

As I reviewed my timelines, it dawned on me that these timelines were timeline chunks, groupings of details. I had a group listing the Port Hueneme Coast Guard Station days, times, activities. I had similar listings for each of the Navy ships and submarines, as well as for the Coast Guard's *Cape Sable*.

I had the *Cape Sable's* timeline. As the On-Scene Commander (OSC) of the *Marie* search and rescue (SAR), the *Cape Sable* coordinated and documented all of the SAR resources: helicopters, airplanes, and surface vessels, as they came on scene and left. But even this was a timeline chunk, because the *Cape Sable* didn't join the search until Lovette's body was found.

I assessed the various timeline details and concluded that I needed to combine them. So, I created a master timeline. I copied and pasted the various portions, color coding each for visual recognition. Then I shuffled the details into a top-to-bottom time flow. Soon the master timeline offered a seamless flow of events and activities. Although I loved the birds-eye view, I also feared the sheer volume of detail might overwhelm me.

My master timeline confirmed that there was a lot of activity in the Santa Barbara Channel on Friday, June 10th. Some activities were directly related to the *Marie* SAR: airplanes, helicopters, and ships. The operation involving the USS *King County* was another. I included the tropical storm alerts from the Coast Guard station in the master timeline.

Although I wasn't clear what the tropical storm alerts were announcing, or to whom, they were ongoing communications over the Coast Guard frequencies. I found it curious that these storm alerts sandwiched the front and back ends of the *Marie* SAR and were dispersed in between, as well. I didn't know whether there was a connection, but I wanted to find out.

Another intriguing tidbit was that one specific minute—1528 (3:28 PM)—was listed in multiple reports (ships' logs and station logs). I didn't think much about it at the time. I was focused on creating my timeline. But, of all the assets and times recorded, this was the only minute that overlapped.

After I had arranged all the details, I returned to the minute where two log entries coincided, at 1528 (3:28pm) on Friday, June 10, 1960. That day and minute were also of interest, because the *Marie* SAR gained momentum when Paul Lovette's body was recovered the preceding evening. This specific minute, 3:28 pm, Friday, June 10, 1960, was at the peak of the *Marie* SAR. Two activities occurred simultaneously somewhere in the Santa Barbara Channel, but I had no idea where.

> ☐   1528: "Navy Drexel #4 alongside to port – transferred body and engine hatch cover," (Coast Guard's #CG95334 entry).
> ☐   1528: "Completed practice DATA pickup," (Navy's USS *King County* entry).

The Coast Guard entry was part of the *Marie* SAR. It reported on the transfer of Hal Mackie's body to the *Cape Sable*, by the Navy Drexel #4.

The USS *King County* entry was apparently part of an unrelated Navy operation. Nevertheless, the log entry remained on my radar for several reasons. For one thing, the operation occurred on the dates of interest for what was listed as a "...local operation in Santa Barbara channel..." where "...four Lockheed personnel embarked" while the ship was underway – heading out to sea.

What were the Lockheed personnel doing? Were they engineers and scuba divers like my father?

Second, the sequence of events seemed strange, given the apparent precision of the mission. Two hours out from the harbor, the ship is described as "rubber docking." Within thirty minutes of that time they are "secured from rubber docking." Inside three minutes the ship is "rendezvousing with a US Air Force C-119 to participate in a *practice data pick up*" [emphasis added]. After this, the ship repeats the same sequence, "...steering various courses at various speeds during practice data pick-up."

A Navy vessel? An Air Force C-119? A data pick-up? How is that possible while at sea? Perhaps the C-119 is a helicopter?

The next log entry is the specific minute that I had focused on, "1528 Completed practice data pick-up," (3:28 pm).

Curiously, other *King County* ship's log entries included coordinates for longitude and latitude. For this mission, the log simply states that it's in the Santa Barbara Channel.

Why?

The Channel is a large body of water. I didn't realize how large until Uncle Albert, Aunt Lynda, Ken and I cruised across it on the Condor Express. For them, it was a whale-watching tour. For me, it was a reconnaissance trip to see for myself the expanse of water, the rugged cliffs of Santa Cruz Island, and the largest sea entrance cave (Painted Cave). I could see how difficult it would have been to locate a shipwreck survivor bobbing among the dark depths of the waves, particularly if the harsh glint of sunlight hindered the searchers.

I needed to go back to working through my huge sluice pile of resources, but I remained captivated by the single minute that aligned in both logs: 1528 (3:28 pm).

"Return to the original sources," I reminded myself.

Although the digitized documents were useful, it was a wise habit to return to the original sources. First, to appreciate the originals, but also to make sure details were not overlooked in the transcription process.

I lifted and shuffled crates that were filled with files. I pulled out the Friday, June 10, 1960 CG log and then the Navy log. Locating the minute in question on each, I lay the logs side by side.

As I reviewed the Navy log, I didn't see any new insights. Setting it aside, I considered the CG log. It didn't take long to find an interesting entry that I had ignored in my transcription. It didn't seem important at the time. It was a short entry that was crossed off as if it were a recorded error.

My mind circled around the entry – what I believed had been

an error– trying to see if this shed any light on the minute.

I tried to sense what Jimmy Spears, the Coastie who wrote the report, might have been experiencing. As I did, I considered how he had been focused on the *Marie* Search and Rescue for almost twenty-four hours. All night, Spears and the men of the Cape Sable endured the cold damp air cutting through their thick jackets. The search dragged on with little to show. His dedication to detail was part of his duty to acknowledge, correct, and move on as he recorded the SAR in the ship's log, no matter how tired or how long a search dragged on.

My mind lingered again on the entry at 1528. Again, I wondered "why would the "#4" be entered in the first place, and why would it then be crossed out?"

I decided to conduct a discovery process by imagining myself to be Jimmy Spears on June 10, 1960.

I closed my eyes and tried to see myself on the deck of the Cape Sable. I'm tired, but I know six men have yet to be located – dead or alive.

A call comes in from across the airwaves to the Cape Sable.

Someone picks up the handset receiver. Maybe it's me, Jimmy Spears, maybe not.

The caller on the other end announces that a body had been located. I'm excited with the news, albeit I want to locate men alive. The voice on the other line continues to say that Naval Drexel Boat #4 would meet them to transfer the body at a location 5 miles southwest of Port Hueneme.

I, Jimmy Spears, acknowledge the dialogue, "Roger that!" I say, then I repeat the exchange of information as I write out the log entry, "US Navy Drexel Boat #4, located body (5) five miles southwest of Port Hueneme."

Maybe there is a hesitation on the other line before a response clarifies, "Stop," the voice orders. And I stop writing. The voice continues to clarify. "#4 didn't locate the body. Drexel #4 will meet you," the voice corrects.

I, Jimmy Spears, hesitate, then I cross out the #4 and I continue the 1528 entry.

So, it was possible that crossing out the #4 was a small detail. What it confirmed for me was that the Drexel #4 didn't locate the body, but was only transferring it. Did the Navy entity that recovered the body also make the call? If so, who was it? And who found Hal Mackie's body?

It was another mystery of the *Marie* search, that minute of alignment between a Navy Drexel #4 and the Coast Guard's Cape Sable.

Was it by coincidence? By design?

Either way, it coincided with the exact time that Hal Mackie's body was passed from a Navy vessel to the Coast Guard's On-Scene-Commander of the *Marie* Search and Rescue operation. I still couldn't prove that the Cape's and King's activities were linked. To do that, I needed more facts. But it at least offered a hint that something was up.

I considered everything I had recently reviewed and wondered if the *King County* activities were somehow linked with what the Western Sea Frontier said was part of its operation serving the "shield of freedom."

What was the "data" the King County was out there picking up? What if it was a recovery operation to retrieve the top-secret equipment on the Marie? Or could they have been retrieving men in a lifeboat?

At that thought, I was tempted to cry out, "Eureka!"

CHAPTER 31:

Myths And Memories

On Valentine's Day, when I returned to my desk, I found an e-mail with an interesting subject line, "*Marie* Shipwreck off Santa Cruz Island." I opened it and was surprised to find that it was from Harold Mackie's widow.

In large, bold letters, the e-mail read:

Harold Mackie was my husband

I am Betty Lou

I Hope this reaches Teresa Newton-Terres

Teresa,

Good for you! It's wonderful that you are pursuing this haunting story that has changed our lives.

The memories of that [sic] few days in June 1960 are still sharp and painful. Each day Hal and I were together was better than the last. I still want to know what happened to him and the *Marie*. We hear stories of side-looking sonar, the Navy deep-sea vehicles, etc., and wonder if there could be enough left of the *Marie* to find. I think you were pretty young when this accident happened and may not remember that a Russian sub was sighted in the Channel shortly before the *Marie* sailed to test the new Raytheon equipment. I've thought *Marie* carried something that may have been interesting to lots of people.

Hal's immediate boss. He took me through the lab after Hal died, and so my request to see where Hal worked was granted. I marvel today at the infra-red pictures from space and think that your father and my husband had something to do with that when infra-red was a new idea.

I remember that your mother, Marian, I believe, planned to go back to college after the accident and I have wondered if she did.

I met my second husband, now deceased, in Australia, went to live on a ranch, and became a registered Quarter Horse Breeder… It was necessary for me to become a different person after I lost Hal. (I was a pianist then.)

I hope you get this and find it to be of interest.
Sincerely yours,
Betty Lou

Betty Lou also wanted to know what happened to the *Marie* and its men. I also found it interesting that she entertained espionage theories. Perhaps my family was not the only one with a submarine myth.

Betty Lou's reference to "pictures from space" confused me. My understanding was that the *Marie*'s focus was underwater, tracking submarines. I ignored the statement, assuming Betty Lou's comment came from an appreciation of the noteworthy advances in infrared technology.

****

When I started investigating the *Marie* shipwreck, I believed the facts behind the tragedy were all that I needed to seek out. However, my perspective was changing. As I connected with other families who lost loved ones on the *Marie*, I began to realize that people, their personal beliefs, and emotions, held a key to the heartbeat of the *Marie* story.

I missed connecting with Mrs. Howell because I let my

insecurities get in the way. I wouldn't let that happen again. I couldn't let another member of the *Marie* family leave this world without contacting them and understanding their experience. A burning desire welled up within me. I wanted—needed—to capture every family's story.

The wisdom echoed in my mind. *It's all about relationships.*

I wanted to sit beside Mrs. Mackie and share a cup of tea. I wanted to preserve her story before it disappeared. And so I began to develop a friendship with Betty Lou. Betty Lou had a story to tell, and I had ears to hear. She had many questions. I had a few answers. But I also had questions of my own, and she had insights. I encouraged her to share her memories, including the lessons she had learned. Once a concert pianist, Betty Lou had captivated audiences with her music. Now she captivated me with personal accounts of the *Marie* shipwreck. I filled a binder with our e-mails.

Although Betty Lou and I shared information liberally, we also respected each other's boundaries. She needed privacy, and I respected that. My unspoken boundary was that I would share what I had gathered from public sources such as newspapers. I was, however, reluctant to share what I learned beyond the public record because at that point I was waiting for somebody in authority to confirm my speculations.

Over the next few weeks it seemed as if we were e-mailing each other constantly. We were like two sister birds soaring, the wings of our fingers stretching out across cyberspace.

We were more than sisters; we were sleuths.

My speculations wouldn't change Betty Lou's situation. She knew the Navy had recovered her husband's body and returned it to the Coast Guard. I believed it wise to be cautious with the information I was gathering about the USS *King County* because I was still verifying it.

ORAL HISTORIES

On my next trip to California I planned to preserve oral histories of the *Marie* tragedy. I was nervous. It was one thing to talk with someone about a shipwreck. It was something else to ask permission to record that person's story without being able to give them a specific reason other than a fifty-year anniversary. I was apprehensive because all I could tell people was that I wanted to preserve the stories before they were lost.

My thumb shot up to my Terres tooth and I pressed on it, something I always did when I was nervous.

First, I needed to get up to speed on how to conduct oral histories. I reviewed the process that the University of California Santa Barbara professor used for the oral histories taken in the Old Town Goleta Cultural History Project. Next, I called my friend Laura Funkhouser and asked her for some of the lessons she had learned while conducting the oral histories relating to the same project. I read *The Smithsonian Folklore and Oral History Interviewing Guide*, a pamphlet Laura recommended.

My next step was to outline a general plan. This included developing a list of general questions, as well as forming a short list of specific stories that I knew about and hoped to capture on video. I also needed to decide whom I would ask to interview.

I decided to begin with Uncle Albert because I knew he wouldn't refuse. In addition, if I blew the first try, I knew he would agree to a redo. I planned to capture Bob Wilke's story next, because I had been building a relationship with him and his wife. Also, Bob was a good communicator with an important thread to the story. These two men would be my guinea pigs. After I completed those interviews, I would be prepared for others, like Bud Bottoms and Betty Lou Mackie.

Although capturing oral histories was a recognized practice for preserving myths and memories, I still wasn't clear why I was doing it other than that I was seizing the opportunity, and that my gut was telling me that the effort may serve in the upcoming fifty-year anniversary.

****

Uncle Albert didn't get advance notice or a list of questions to review, but on previous visits I had told him that I needed to record him. So, it wasn't a complete surprise when I asked if he would allow me to interview him.

The next time I was in Santa Barbara I conducted his interview. I tried to act as if I knew what I was doing. Uncle Albert played his part, acting like he knew how to be interviewed.

First, I set up my video camera and tripod and placed Uncle Albert in a comfortable chair near a window so we could take advantage of the natural light. Once I was happy with the arrangement, I clipped a wireless mic to his collar and began the interview.

Before I knew it, he had answered all my questions and I was running out of things to ask. Albert had shared an array of stories that revealed a variety of emotions, stories only he could tell. I was pleased.

Trying to sound professional, I announced, "I got what I need. It's a wrap."

"Phew," he said. "I was running out of things to say."

"I doubt that will ever happen," We both chuckled, letting the last of the tension dissolve. The last part of the interview had ventured into more serious topics. Not long ago, I would never have discussed the shipwreck with Uncle Albert. My interest in the shipwreck had opened up a path to discuss our family.

"Thanks Albert," I said. I drew close and gave him a big hug. Like a father, he went along with all my shipwreck antics. His kindness and humor helped calm my insecurities. It wasn't natural of me to ask someone to sit and let me capture their memories. Uncle Albert's oral history preserved a puzzle piece of my father's life for me, my brothers, and anyone else who was interested.

With one successful interview under my belt, I confidently stepped out to preserve more memories before they were lost forever.

The next day I met with Bob and Helen Wilke. I had visited with them every year that I came into town, and I had a fair sense of the stories that I hoped Bob would allow me to record.

After arriving at their Goleta home, I went through a similar routine, setting up my equipment after determining a visually pleasing site with good lighting and comfortable seating.

Once everything was ready, I pressed the record button and began to run through my list of questions. Bob needed no prompting to tell his story.

"The sequence began with Raytheon in Chicago. In Chicago, we were just beginning to build...an infrared communication system. There's a galvanometer..." He motioned with his arms as if he were holding the device and opening it up.

"The galvanometer is nothing more than a mirror that wiggles back and forth. And you shine a light on that mirror and...there is a point where the mirror will show directly on you and into your eyes. Then it will turn off. So, it is on and off. That sets up the frequency, which is very similar to a speaker receiving the frequencies from a transmitter.... By translating that flashing light into an amplifier, you can make it into sound. And so, that is how we started our first communication system."

Bob continued with a story line that had become all too familiar to me. Night tests on a long stretch of road. Dr. Max's brainstorm to go up to Raytheon's rooftop. Seeing a "bird" go up from Vandenberg Air Force Base and grabbing their equipment. Top brass recognizes the technology was working. Somebody brings up the question, "I wonder if we could communicate under water." The plan to take their communicators, encased in waterproof containers, and beam infrared under water.

Bob's story ended on a somber note. "I was supposed to be on the *Marie*. It was a tough experience...because I was supposed to be on that craft. We felt so helpless."

****

James "Bud" Bottoms was next on my list. When I spoke with Bud on the phone, it was obvious that he was experienced in talking about his friends lost on the *Marie*. He seemed experienced at being interviewed. And so, I took the chance and asked Bud if he would mind if I taped our conversation, "...because my pencil doesn't work as fast as I'd like."

We met at the marina in front of what in 1960 had been the Coast

Guard Headquarters. Now the building housed the Santa Barbara Maritime Museum. I arrived early and waited on a bench.

When Bud arrived, he looked younger than I had imagined. We greeted like old friends, and then walked along the breakwater toward the Lost at Sea Memorial. Bud had been instrumental in the memorial's creation, and it seemed like a perfect setting for our interview. After setting up the equipment, we sat down together on one of the two whale's tail benches. Then, on cue, Bud Bottoms painted a picture of my father and his friends.

I soon found myself mesmerized by his memories. Then, just when Bud's story was building, the sound of a jackhammer startled us both. We jumped and looked around. A crew of construction workers had begun refurbishing a section of the walkway leading to the memorial and were breaking up the asphalt. We smiled at each other, picked up our things and started walking back in the direction we had come.

Bud stopped at the halfway point, leaned on the breakwater wall, and pointed out toward the sea. "That's a fantastic picture," he said. "There's the boat, the dolphins, and the pelicans."

I looked over Bud's shoulder and saw the sparkling blue ocean. In the distance, I could see a fishing boat and Santa Cruz Island on the horizon. The only sounds were the ocean waves gently breaking against the breakwater. Bud's experienced eye had quickly recognized the image provided an echo of the story I was attempting to capture from him. "That boat anchored off the breakwater looks like the *Marie*, in sight of Santa Cruz Island," he said.

Recognizing the opportunity, I said, "Let's set up here."

I set down the tripod and motioned for Bud to remain where he was, leaning against the breakwater wall.

I positioned the camera and zoomed in to capture a view of the scene over Bud's shoulder, where the boat, dolphins, and pelicans were captured in the sunlight.

"That's about the size of it," he said, waving a hand toward the fishing boat.

I knew Bud was referring to the *Marie*. Bud continued to share his memories. He was comfortable in front of a camera and I was grateful because it put me at ease. At the next lull in the story, I understood it was time to stop recording.

We moved on, meandering back from the breakwater and over to the marinas. Bud began looking for a boat that looked like the *Marie*.

Bud pointed out one vessel and said, "Not ugly enough." Referring to another, he said, "Not old enough."

I had printed out a picture of the *Marie*, taken before it had been converted from a WWII landing craft. On a corner of the paper, Bud made a couple sketches to show what he remembered. "I drew sketches of the *Marie* for the court case," he said. "It seems like they would be in a case file somewhere."

Unfortunately, at that point I hadn't found the case file.

"Follow me," Bud said.

He led me over to an electric car.

"Appropriate color," I said smiling at the grass-green vehicle that was about the size of a golf cart.

Bud pulled out a roll of paper. "This is for you".

I unrolled it and read, "The Rainbow Bridge: A Chumash Legend." I saw a picture of Bud's iconic Dolphin Family fountain that was located nearby at the foot of the Wharf. The piece told of the Chumash Indian families who traveled from Santa Cruz Island to the mainland on the Rainbow Bridge and fell off into the ocean to become dolphins. The image was the same as the bronze medallion inlaid in the center flooring of the Lost at Sea Memorial.

"Tell me about this," I asked pointing to the symbol.

"This symbol represents the Chumash Native American Indian. It shows Polaris, the North Star."

"Polaris?" I blurted out. I was confused. I had seen the word POLARIS used before but in a much different context. It was a word used in some of the archive documents.

"The symbol shows four dolphins going around the North Star," Bud said. "And the Chumash Indians call the dolphin a *lul quoy*, which means to go around, to protect, and go in peace. There are four dolphins, a *lul quoy,* circling the Polaris," he said, pointing to each of the dolphins and the point they encircled. "The Chumash believe there are celestial dolphins in the sky that circle the North Star."

Polaris. My mind circled with the dolphins.

We made our way back to the front of the Santa Barbara Maritime Museum. I was pleased that I had stepped out in faith and stretched myself beyond my comfort zone to capture this interview. Bud had offered me insights into the character and integrity of my father as well as Dale Howell and James "Jim" McCaffrey. It was bringing to light and preserving memories that I hoped would benefit more people than me.

****

Hoping to score another interview, I touched base with Bob Bryant over the phone. He had always been supportive and welcoming. I won't be in town," he told me. "I'll be off on an anniversary celebration with my wife, scuba diving in the far South Pacific."

"My testimony is likely on record somewhere," he suggested.

If I knew where the record was archived, I would be all over it.

But the location of his testimony as well as the other testimonies given as part of "The Big Trial" as Glenna called it, eluded me.

"Can I have a rain check?" I asked. "I've searched for the records that the trial generated. But, I've had little luck so far."

"Sure, the next time you are in town," Bob promised.

While in Santa Barbara, I searched phone books and the Internet for contact information for the family of James Russell. I made countless phone calls from a long list of folks who lived up and down California, looking for either James's widow, Helen, or his daughter Jeannie. No luck.

One person named Jeannie Russell I connected with gave me hope. When I called her, I introduced myself and then said, "I'm looking for a Jeannie Russell, daughter of James Russell, who lost her father in a shipwreck."

Before I could say another word, she blurted out, "I'm her!"

After we talked a little further, she interrupted me. "What year did the ship sink?"

"1960," I said.

"Oh, no. My father's ship sank years before that in WWII. So, I'm not the Jeannie Russell you are searching for."

This Jeannie Russell's father was lost on a Navy ship in WWII. As we talked, she told me about the Gold Star group she belongs to. Gold Star children, whose parents were killed in war, share an emotional void. Suddenly their father or mother is no longer part of their life. Their hearts have a wound that nothing can completely heal.

"So, the Gold Star kids, like me, grow up with a hidden desire to know and talk about their fathers," Jeannie said.

"If I didn't know you were talking about WWII Gold Star kids, I would have thought you were describing me," I said.

My conversation with Jeannie made me want to connect again with Glenna Howell and talk about our fathers. I called and invited Glenna and her husband to join Ken and me at our family's cabin.

"I wouldn't miss the opportunity to talk about our dads." Glenna said eagerly.

CHAPTER 32:

Millionaire's View & Snatch

With three interviews under my belt, I was finally ready to meet Betty Lou Mackie.

I followed the directions she had given me, travelling through the countryside, over a cattle grate and along a gravel road up to the mountaintop. Betty Lou had a millionaire's view.

She greeted me with a smile and a twinkle in her eyes. I recognized her from the newspaper photo in Grandmother's scrapbook. Her features and hairstyle still reflected the youthful appearance pictured in the newspaper, as she sat with my mother at the Coast Guard Headquarters waiting for word of the *Marie*.

Betty Lou welcomed me inside and showed me her home. The watercolors she had painted were similar in style to some of my own: extreme detail of the selected image surrounded by a void of white space. She obviously had a passion for music, also. I ran my hand across the cover of her grand piano. I noticed several family photos and even a case where a miniature model of the Space Shuttle was proudly displayed. Betty Lou Mackie was comfortable in her familiar surroundings. She invited me to take a seat at the table where she served me a cup of coffee and cinnamon rolls.

I brought her a portable nautical chart of the Santa Barbara

Channel. I also brought her a joke gift: a bottle of "ocean air," which she had requested when we set up the meeting.

She laughed when she opened it. "I've asked others for as much, but you are the first to come through."

When I arranged the oral history interview with Betty Lou, I followed all the proper steps: advance notice, list of questions for review, Smithsonian pamphlet. But when I had asked Betty Lou if I could record our conversation, she graciously declined and instead handed me my list of questions, along with her typewritten responses.

For the more sensitive questions: What happened when Hal didn't return? Tell me about the night waiting with my mother at the Coast Guard Headquarters? She offered fair responses. The information was not new to me, because our exchange of e-mails had uncovered similar details. While I appreciated having answers to these questions, I was disappointed. I had hoped to preserve her story in her own spoken words.

"Where is this all going?" Betty Lou asked.

Again, I didn't have a perfect answer. "There is the fiftieth anniversary," I said.

Finally, I decided to give up on the idea of filming Betty Lou and simply enjoy being with her. I broached the subject of filming once more, later in the day. Again, she declined. However, this time she allowed me to snap a photograph of her.

Our day together passed quickly as we retraced the path of discovery we had been following online together.

Even though she didn't share many personal details, Betty Lou had a laser focus on the *Marie*. She knew its final resting place, its engine functionality, its structural integrity, its sea worthiness, and more. I knew the information she shared would be invaluable.

Betty Lou Mackie was a gracious lady and I appreciated her encouragement and helpfulness both online and during our meeting. Over the course of our budding online relationship, I became interested in the topic of space, largely because of Betty Lou's interest in it. Among other things, Betty Lou sent me an e-mail with amazing images from space. And my grandchildren and I watched the International Space Station as it passed over Little Rock in March 2009 because she suggested it. At that time, my interest was out of politeness.

I was not yet aware that my eyes were focused underwater when they should have been looking toward the heavens.

****

As it turned out, when I was in Mariposa I divided my time between Betty Lou and a girlfriend of mine from school. When I learned that my girlfriend would be in Mariposa for a family occasion I scheduled a rendezvous. I spent a day with my girlfriend, her family, and her friends. One of her friends sat next to me at dinner and I learned he was a retired Air Force pilot. When I asked him if he knew about the C-119, to my delight, he replied, "I've flown them!"

"Tell me, can a C-119 retrieve a package from midair over an ocean?" I asked.

"Sure, with a special hook the C-119 can snatch all kinds of things," he confirmed.

I had become accustomed to little coincidences like this, and I was delighted to gain some insights. I also wondered what the C-119 snatched from the Santa Barbara Channel the Friday after my father and the *Marie* went missing.

CHAPTER 33:

Engagement

Later, Glenna Howell-Griffin and her husband Jeff Griffin joined Ken and me for a weekend at the cabin. To prepare her for the experience, I said, "Think of it as a step above camping. You have an indoor toilet, phone, microwave, and TV, but you get to sleep under a star-filled sky." I also mentioned that we would have a chance to enjoy eating, hiking, and sharing memories.

When Glenna and Jeff arrived at the cabin, the guys sensed they should disappear and leave us girls with a chance to connect. I was delighted when our conversation went immediately to our fathers. Recognizing the opportunity, I asked, "Do you mind if I record our conversation?"

"Sure," she said.

I already had the video camera in place on its tripod. I pressed the record button and went back to Glenna's side, ready to capture and preserve the Howell family memories.

"What do you remember?"

"I remember as a child, when we lived in Goleta. Lobsters were everywhere on the ground."

I opened my laptop and pulled up the photos that I believed were Glenna's dad, holding monster-sized lobsters. I had a dozen images of dad and his friends hunting, diving, and with a bounty of abalone and lobster. I showed her the pictures.

"That's my dad!" Glenna squealed, pointing to one of the men in the picture.

"I thought so. It is so cool to find a picture of your dad with all the lobsters." I said.

"Our dads were childhood friends," she said. "That makes us like family."

Feeling like daddy's little girls, we became giggly as we looked through the folder of images on my computer. It felt a little strange.

I don't giggle. I haven't since I was two. But it comes so easy with Glenna.

I'd collected over three hundred photos of my dad, but I had sorted some into a folder that included the images of interest to both Glenna and me. And she had brought some photos of her own.

When we came to the end of the images, we flung our arms around each other in a hug. We both smiled as we sank further into the couch.

"Tell me again. What do you remember of the *Marie* event?" I asked.

It was good for us both to talk about the shipwreck and our fathers, and I was delighted that I'd set up my recording equipment. We got the need to talk out of our system. Then we spent the rest of the weekend creating new memories: grilling, walking, star gazing and laughing.

When, I asked Glenna how the *Marie* affected her, she had little to say. But, I got my answer when we went on a simple hike, a walking path along a lake with some gentle ups and downs. After we had gone one mile, we stopped for a rest. When Glenna and Jeff opened up their pack, I noticed they had everything one might need for a wilderness mountain climbing emergency.

"Where's the kitchen sink?" I asked, smiling.

"You can never be too prepared," she said confidently. "Snakes, leg breaks, dehydration, shipwrecks, etc."

I understood completely. I, too, had a propensity for risk management. Glenna wanted to be ready for whatever life might place on her path.

And so did I.

****

After Glenna and Jeff departed, my brother Jim joined us for a brief visit. Since I was on a roll, I set up the recorder once more and asked Jim to share his memories.

I'd already made a list of the stories that I had heard Jim tell. Since he remembered much more than I could, I wanted to encourage him to recall as many details as possible. I set my equipment up on the deck because it was a perfect day: warm light, but cool under the shade of tall trees. Our nation's flag waved in the distance behind Jim's shoulder as I began the interview.

"Tell me what you remember of Dad."

Jim recounted the story of when Dad took him to the beach, left him on the rocks, and went diving.

"What do you remember about dad's scuba diving?" I asked.

"I remember he made everyone's wet suits. He made me and Rick wet suit bathing suits. They were really uncomfortable, similar to a Speedo type swim-suit, but just a little bigger. Not like the sexy Speedo. And the old style wet suit material was smooth on both sides, not the cloth covered that we are used to nowadays. And it was rather snug. I must have been four or five years old running around and rolling in the sand. It was the most uncomfortable thing. It would actually rub a rash in you when you got sand in your delicate area."

I remembered seeing my brothers Jim and Rick wearing those trunks jumping around on the grass in a water hose spray. I saw it in a film clip in our old family films. I was pleased knowing I could align yet another image with a recorded memory.

"How did you find out about the loss of Dad?" I asked.

"No memory at all," Jim said.

"What about when they told you that your dad wasn't coming

home?" Ken asked. He had sat down with us and listened.

"No memory. When I try to remember, it's blank. I think I blocked it out." Jim answered with a childlike shrug of his shoulders.

"Didn't you ever question why he was lost?" I asked.

"There were those court documents in a box in our family's garage," he said.

I thought back to 1986 when Jim and I looked over a box of court documents before they were trashed. I had been renting two rooms from Mom in our family's home. After I'd been there only a few months, Mother had to sell the family home in Goleta and return to her place of birth, three hundred miles north to the San Francisco Bay area. I was frustrated that I would have to find a new place to live. I was a single parent, and not making the income I needed to thrive in the Santa Barbara or Goleta area.

Making the wound deeper, Mother took what was of interest to her and left me to clear out 24 years' worth of material that had accumulated in the family's garage and attic. I invited my brothers in for a weekend to help me clear the attic and move boxes to my condo. Instead, they came into town, played at the beach, went to the golf course, ate my food, rummaged through the family stuff, and moved one box each to my condo. Then they left town.

With no time, no funds, and no storage space, I was forced to trash everything, including the box of the *Marie* court case records. I loved and respected my brothers, and at that time I was peeved at their ambivalence to my predicament. But we were all immature. In time they would redeem my admiration at a commemoration in California and another in Arkansas.

When I ran out of questions for Jim, I pressed the stop button. I hoped he understood the treasure trove of memories that he held. I was pleased that we had preserved them.

****

After the cabin visitors and family departed, Ken and I drove down the mountain to replenish supplies and conduct cabin business. We were ready to transfer the cabin ownership from Mom's irrevocable trust to its beneficiaries. Originally, I proceeded like a turtle with Trust activities, patiently doing the easy and clear tasks. Ken had encouraged me to "pick the low-hanging fruit."

I knew that once the transfer document was signed and filed in the county recorder's office, it would be part of the cabin's permanent chain of records. The document had to be accurate, because my signature would be on it. Then, like a line of dominos falling, today's filing would trigger other changes, including property taxes, insurance, responsibilities and rights transferring from the trustees (Ken & me) to the new owners (My brothers and me). Later, Ken and I would have to send out transfer documents to the beneficiaries who had to sign and accept both the right and responsibility for the cabin.

Taking this next step was the right thing to do, but I didn't know what the future held for the cabin and its family. My heart sank. Although the necessary steps to resolve the Trust's cabin-related issues were clear, it was less clear how to resolve the cabin families' childhood assumptions and expectations that impact relationships.

I had been trying to "build a better boat," – a sound legal agreement to govern the cabin family operation – before transferring ownership. Then I realized it was too late.

My family was already on the boat.

CHAPTER 34:

Coffee Talk

During my next adventure in the Los Angeles area national archives, I spent the night with my brother Don and his family. The next day he and I were going in search of the court case files. I knew they existed, but I had so far been unsuccessful in finding them.

That morning, Don's wife said, "Come with me to 'Coffee Talk' time."

Coffee Talk was a regular gathering of the neighborhood women. Their motto was 'Come as you are,' and they were serious. The approved dress code included sleepwear and gardening gear.

I had danced with girlfriends in Hawaii and shared refreshments afterwards, but for some reason, the thought of having to participate in idle girl talk scared me. I was raised with boys, worked with men, lived with a man, and wanted to know my father. I had deflected Lily's invitations on other occasions, but today I felt guilty because I was taking her husband away with me.

"Okay, one cup of coffee."

I nudged my brother on my way out. "Come rescue me if I'm not back in an hour."

I followed Lily out the door, down the street, and through her neighbor's front door. I was greeted with smiles and a hot cup of coffee.

Surprisingly, when the doorbell rang an hour later and Don walked in to rescue me, I didn't want to leave.

"One more cup," I begged.

I wanted to stay with these women who welcomed me and my shipwreck into their circle. I had told the 'Coffee Talk' circle the whole story, everything from Grandmother's scrapbook to the family myth about the Russians kidnapping an eminent scientist, the CIA, the dreams, and my father. Their response was refreshing. When I shared my thoughts about the shipwreck with Ken, his eyes glazed over. Even my brothers encouraged me to 'cut to the chase.' These ladies understood the emotional and mental hoops my heart and mind were jumping through.

I gained energy from these ladies who shared an hour with me. And like adding fuel to a fire, their attentiveness flared up my passions. I wanted to tell them more of my story.

When I was investigating, I had to be objective as I reviewed and documented my sources and findings. But in this circle of friends I let my hair down and I felt real and complete.

I smiled as I bounced out the door toward Don because there was a mission to complete. But I was also aware that deep in my heart I harbored a child's desire for a happy ending, where my daddy would appear and rescue me.

Just like all the white knights do for their beauties.

****

My decision to bring Don into the process of research was born out of necessity and opportunity. Necessity because I needed extra arms. Archivist Mr. Wormser told me the only way to locate Federal Court files without a case file number was to review the civil dockets within the targeted timeframe.

It was also an opportunity to connect with my brother, because Don was in between jobs. I welcomed the chance to bring him with me because the shared experience would give Don a window into my world. After we signed in, the staff instructed Don in the policies and procedures, and soon he was approved to conduct research.

After we made our requests, we sat at separate tables in the glassed-in reviewing room and waited for the source documents to arrive. Soon, an assistant entered pushing a cart full of boxes.

"We have more where this came from," the assistant said. Before he allowed us to begin, the assistant reviewed the rules for researchers: one box, one folder, no ink pens, no erasers, no licked fingers, and so on. Then the assistant took a seat at his table and kept careful watch on us.

Don and I went to the cart and each pulled a box and returned to our respective tables and began reviewing dockets. We searched through reams of documents, looking for a docket bearing the name Raytheon along with the names Beardsley, Terres, Howell, McCaffrey, Mackie, Russell, or Lovette.

Our bodies grew stiff and cold in the air-conditioned room as we raced against the clock. Just before noon, Don said, "I got something."

His head tilted downward as he read the sheet before him. I rubbed my eyes and took a breather to give Don time to review the document. Finally, Don said, "It looks like the docket is for a related case, but not the main one."

He handed me the sheet, and I confirmed his assessment. We had to keep looking. Just in case, however, I did submit a pull-slip to have these records retrieved.

An hour later it was my turn to say, "I've got something."

I placed a docket flat on the table so we could both see it.

We agreed. "This is it."

It was noon, and we had been hard at it for several hours. I grabbed a pull-slip, entered the appropriate details, and handed it to the attendant. Mr. Wormser would have to complete and approve the form before they could pull the records.

"Let's take a lunch break," I said. It would give the staff time to retrieve our sources and us a well-deserved rest before we continued. We found a seat in the warm sunshine in the third-floor balcony cafeteria where we could thaw out a bit. After lunch, we returned to the cold, archive reviewing room.

Two boxes of United States District Court records were waiting for us. We each grabbed a box and began reviewing the court case files for Hooker Howell vs. Raytheon. [85]

Don and I approached our respective boxes of source documents differently. In connection with his job, Don had offered testimony in more than one court case and had handled court records. He was keenly aware of the documents to zero in on: contentions, findings of facts, opinions, conclusions, rulings, and stipulations to rulings. He quickly placed tabs around those documents.

I on the other hand approached the documents like a hound-dog, chasing squirrels and following them wherever they led me. Don was focused; my efforts were scattered. Don was quick; I took my time. Nevertheless, I grew to appreciate the path Don forged through the court records. In the end, both approaches complemented each other.

We left the archives with a stack of copies of the documents that I would examine back in my office.

CHAPTER 35:

The Court Case

After returning to Arkansas, I spread the court records out in my inner office. We had found two dockets, two civil cases that I would later learn were combined into one. Judge E. Avery Crary presided over the case. [86]

Armed with a pencil and a stack of multicolored tabs, I sat in a comfortable chair at a brightly lit table and began reading. I marked the details that I planned to return to later.

I grew up believing the shipwreck was the fault of the boat, the boat owner, or the Russians. As I reviewed the court records, I saw the truth wasn't as obvious as I had allowed myself to believe.

The documents made it clear that the court handled a potentially explosive situation wisely and with respect. Documents from the discovery process fleshed out a list of the contentions and the issues of fact to be addressed:[87]

- ☐ Was the *Marie* lost at sea, as alleged?
- ☐ If so, where and when did such loss occur?
- ☐ What was the cause of the loss of the *Marie*?
- ☐ Who was entitled to recover damages?
- ☐ Did the sinking or loss of the *Marie* occur in the Pacific Ocean more or less than a marine league from the shore of the State of California?

☐ Was the occurrence an inevitable or unavoidable accident?

☐ Who owned the vessel *Marie* at the time of her loss or sinking?

☐ Was the vessel *Marie* inadequately equipped and maintained and without proper survey and inspection in such a manner that she became, and was she unseaworthy at the time of her loss?

☐ Was there negligence in the maintenance and/or operation of the vessel?

☐ If the Raytheon Company is found to be such an owner or charterer as to be entitled to limit liability did Raytheon have knowledge of any fault or negligence in connection with the loss of the *Marie*?

☐ Along with a list of issues that sought to identify if there was an assumption of risk by Howell or Lovette.[88]

I continued to read and tried to understand the key details.

The plaintiffs sought due compensation for the loss of their loved ones from one or more of the defendants, including Mr. Dowse, McCaffrey Brothers Sporting Goods Store, and Raytheon Corporation.

As for the defendants, Richard Weston Dowse, the owner of the *Marie*, contended that Raytheon chartered the boat and didn't return it. Raytheon contended that an undetermined accident occurred, and the terms of the contract were clear that they and McCaffrey Brothers Sporting Goods were to cover their respective losses.

Richard Weston Dowse, owner of the *Marie*, was the first witness. He testified that he had been copartner with Hugh James McCaffrey in McCaffrey Brother's Sporting Goods Store since January 1957.

Mr. Dowse told the court that a Mr. Murray, the previous owner of the *Marie*, used it to gather abalone from divers around the Santa Barbara Channel Islands. Rather than each diver making an individual trip to bring abalone to market, one boat would pick up the abalone from all the smaller boats.

"An unfortunate accident happened with Mr. Murray's boat," said Mr. Dowse. "He had come in one night late with a load of abalones, approximately ten tons. There were a couple of...old outlets along the side of the boat which had not been properly plugged, and the water – the boat being loaded, and so forth, in the harbor – the water lapped up and got in and the boat sunk in the harbor there. They had to dive down and take the abalone off and they raised it the next day, but in the process Mr. Murray had a heart attack and decided to sell the boat."[89]

At that time, the *Marie*, a WWII landing craft, had already been converted to a sport and utility boat.

After purchasing the *Marie*, Mr. Dowse made improvements. He extended the cabin, refurbished its bottom and hull, added a 12-foot lifeboat, and tuned up its engine (which he later overhauled). In his testimony, Mr. Dowse clarified that the *Marie* was not fitted with a galley, sleeping accommodations, or a radio transmitter.

According to Mr. Dowse, he and Mr. McCaffrey used the *Marie* for sporting trips, "...at least once a week or once every two weeks, depending on weather and season," As joint partners in the McCaffrey Sporting Goods Store, they used the *Marie* for the "creation of good will in the business."[90]

Mr. Dowse testified that Mr. Russell, "...an employee of Raytheon, who was also a good friend...of Jim McCaffrey and Dale Howell..." wanted to charter the *Marie*. Mr. Russell "... had this equipment, which he would like to test, and that he would like to use Jim McCaffrey and Dale Howell and the boat *Marie* in testing it."[91]

Mr. Dowse continued, "At first I told him I didn't see how I could let them use the *Marie*, because I didn't have a license to charter as such, and then we decided that he could use it, but we would not make any charge for the use of the *Marie*."

Mr. Dowse recounted how they believed that by not charging for the use of the *Marie*, they would probably not be subject to licensing requirements and restrictions. With this as their understanding, an agreement was made.

By the end of the trial, Mr. Dowse would learn that the court held a different perspective.

****

Next, Mr. George MacFarland took the witness stand. As the last one to see the *Marie*, MacFarland described for the court what he saw as the *Marie* was being loaded and boarded. As it departed from the harbor on June 7, 1960, "the *Marie* was low in the water." He could not see her water-line mark.[92]

"Did you notice in the loading of the material you mentioned whether there were any boxes indicating or marked *explosives*?" asked Mr. McLeod, attorney for the plaintiffs.

"No, sir," replied MacFarland.

As I continued reading the witness testimonies, I wondered why the lawyers asked each witness about explosives. Much later, I'd wonder how the boxes of electronics would be identified today. Ordnance? Weapon System?

The next witness was Miles Cobert Burke, Raytheon's purchasing agent. Mr. Burke completed the arrangements for the contract between Raytheon and the McCaffrey Brothers Sporting Goods Store. The Raytheon Company issued a purchase order on company letterhead. He explained that Mr. Russell was a design engineer for mechanical, experimental or manufacturing items in infrared. He also said that Mr. Russell oversaw this project and had funds allocated to him for expenditures.

Mr. Burke explained that before completing the arrangements, he called two other competitors for bids, as it was standard policy. "I told [Russell] that in my opinion there was quite a bit of difference and I couldn't understand it or why there should be. And it was shrugged off by Mr. Russell…. He was satisfied with the equipment, so the discussion was dropped." Mr. Burke said he contacted Mr. McCaffrey and completed the purchase order.[93]

The purchase order, a contract agreement, was entered into

evidence as Exhibit-one. The contract specified that McCaffrey Brothers were to furnish:

> Necessary services, material and equipment to transport, by ship, Raytheon employees to waters adjacent to Santa Barbara County Line. Seller to supply the following
> (1) one ship
> (2) one ship operator
> (3) two skin divers (one of which may be the ship operator)
> (4) sufficient air and equipment to adequately outfit four people for skin diving operation.
> Seller to be notified at least 12 hours in advance of requirement.

"To your knowledge, Mr. Burke, did any of this equipment, which was either purchased or supplied by Raytheon itself for the *Marie*, or to go on the *Marie*, include anything in the nature of explosives, to your knowledge?" asked Mr. McLeod.

"So far as I know Raytheon at Santa Barbara has never purchased any explosives," Mr. Burke replied.

Later, the topic of explosives came up again. "Do you have any business carried on there that has anything to do with explosives or rocket fuel or anything of that sort at all?" asked Mr. McLeod.

"Nothing whatsoever," said Mr. Burke.

When Burke was asked to describe what he knew of the Raytheon equipment tests conducted underwater, his answers aligned with the basic details that I understood to be true. This was comforting because it confirmed the accuracy of what the retired Raytheon engineers told me. I had feared that the information that they had shared might be classified and that I could get them in trouble if I told their story. The court case and records were in the public domain, which gave me confidence and peace. But little was said about the project or its program test in the courtroom. And a project name or number was not identified on the records.

Burke continued, "This was an experiment to be conducted on the floor of the ocean, which he told me was about 30 feet down in the water." He went on to explain, "The program itself is classified by the US Government." He said that he was not that familiar with the actual experiment itself, but he confirmed that, "It was a secret program, or using secret equipment, and the experiment itself was classified secret."[94]

When McLeod asked Burke to describe the business that Raytheon carried on in Santa Barbara, he responded, "Mainly a research and development organization, with a limited production capacity." He also confirmed that Raytheon Santa Barbara was doing research and development in electronic communications, and that the experiments dealt with communication underwater.

Mr. Burke's description agreed with the Raytheon Company's lawyers' description: "Raytheon was engaged in a program of development of certain electronic equipment. As part of that program, Raytheon found it desirable to subject the equipment to certain tests which involved using divers to place the equipment on the ocean floor in calm clear water of specified depths and to make certain tests and measurements on the equipment while so placed."[95] The Raytheon lawyers' description also clarified that they hired the vessel the *Marie* as transportation to and from the desired locations.

Mr. McLeod said, "Mr. Burke, in connection with these various classified projects or jobs, whatever the proper terminology is, was it the policy of your company to permit outsiders to be present, without authority, to be around a classified project?"

"No, it is not a policy," Mr. Burke answered.

"Would then, to your knowledge, by the policy of the company, anybody be permitted to come along on the *Marie* on this project merely as a pleasure proposition?" asked Mr. McLeod.

"They shouldn't. I have no idea if anyone did." Mr. Burke responded.

"They should not?" echoed Mr. McLeod.

"They should not," said Mr. Burke.

Burke was dismissed.

Stanley D. Crane, another Raytheon employee, was sworn in and took a seat. He began his testimony by informing the court that from 1944 to 1961 the Raytheon Corporation had employed him, both in the City of Chicago and in Santa Barbara, California. "From 1956 to 1959 I was manager of their counter measures department in that locality." He had since moved to another government contractor, the Aerospace Corporation. Mr. Crane, explained, "I was manager of [Raytheon's] engineering operations in Santa Barbara, particularly from the years 1959 through 1961."

McLeod asked, "The years 1959 and 1960, did you have a member of the personnel named James Russell under your supervision?"

"I had a gentleman named James Russell under my supervision, but not directly so. He was directly under the supervision of Dr. Maxwell D. Krasno, who was under my supervision," Mr. Crane replied.

"What was Dr. Krasno's capacity under your supervision?"

"He was the department head or the department manager for the infrared department."

"Then was Mr. Russell directly under his, that is, Dr. Krasno's supervision?"

"That is correct," Mr. Crane confirmed.

That statement jolted me back into the present. I had heard the name Max Krasno before. It was the name that the retired Raytheon engineers had mentioned fondly as the ringleader of the Raytheon rooftop *imagineers*. However, until I read the court transcripts, I didn't understand that it was Dr. Max Krasno's men and project who were lost on the *Marie*.

I shuffled through the court papers, and confirmed that Dr. Krasno wasn't on the list of witnesses. He had, however, submitted a written deposition that had been returned in the '70's along with all the other Exhibits. Exhibits were often returned "to conserve space" the archivist had explained to me. I wondered what Dr. Krasno's deposition or testimony would reveal. I made a note to search online to see what I could learn about Dr. Maxwell Krasno.

I returned my focus to the trial records, to see what else Stanley Crane had to say.

"Can you tell us approximately when this project began or when you first knew of it, whichever you can tell us?" asked Mr. McLeod.

"To the best of my recollection, discussions concerning this project and the nature of the research involved extended back to the early portions of 1960. At that time, we were preparing a research budget for the company's self-sponsored research, and the subject of this particular program was mentioned and discussed in detail," answered Mr. Crane. [96]

"Were you familiar with the inventory of the Raytheon Company that was necessary to load on the *Marie* to carry out the experimentation?"

"In general, yes," replied Mr. Crane.

"Can you give us any estimate of the approximate total weight of all of the equipment and material of the Raytheon Corporation that was necessary to load onto the *Marie* for the purpose we discussed?"

"I am afraid I can't give you that exact amount now. At the time of the Coast Guard inquiry, following the loss of the *Marie*, I think I did know it in some detail. But I am afraid I couldn't give you a good answer right now."

McLeod prodded further. "Well, it need not be exact. Can you give us an approximation? The number of pounds?"

"It would be under perhaps five or six hundred pounds," Mr. Crane said.

I placed the court testimonies aside, and pulled out a report that I assumed was generated because of the Coast Guard inquiry. I flipped the pages, and read on page three, "The equipment on board weighted approximately 1200 pounds, free board was about two foot."

I thought, either Mr. Crane had a poor memory or deliberately suggested a low estimate. Or, the Coast Guard record accidentally added an extra 1 or 0 on either end of the number to a correct weight of either 120 or 200.

The Coast Guard's eight-page report was, for the most part

accurate. However, as I scrutinized each detail, I found a few that were questionable. First, at the time of the report Paul Lovette was believed to be hired crew, a diver, and strong swimmer. It was later determined that he was likely a novice and on the vessel for personal reasons. Second, Lovette's body was recovered at a position of 34° 12' North, 119° 35' West, and a typo in the Coast Guard report had left off one of the ones in 119. Third, recovered items were listed as four bodies, two plywood hatch covers, several life preservers, and "…to date no other equipment has been recovered." But, I had identified that a bucket and a life preserver with a sweatshirt tied to it had also been recovered.[97] Finally, the Coast Guard report also stated, "The three other persons (Beardsley, Terres, McCaffrey) aboard perished – their bodies or effects have not been recovered." I concurred with some of the statement. However, until I could find a report of what "data" the Navy and Air Force recovered on June 10, 1960, I wouldn't know how accurate the statement was, because at the very least, I believed the electronic equipment was recovered.[98]

I put aside the Coast Guard report and returned my attention to Stan Crane's testimony.

Mr. Crane continued to describe the report submitted after the *Marie*'s first test was conducted. According to his testimony it was a "… written report, which was submitted to me by Dr. Krasno as a routine research report for the month." It would have been, he continued, "from Mr. Russell, Dr. Beardsley and others who accompanied them."

The May report confirmed that, "The experimentation was somewhat disappointing. They had not achieved all the results they would have liked, but it encouraged them to try several more voyages."

They achieved some *but not* all *the results.* I knew it was a reference to the scuba diving trip and the men made the weekend before.

He also told how the report was a summary document, and "… only indicated the nature of the results, the location at which they had been secured and the intention to continue."

"You stated that either Mr. Russell or possibly Mr. Beardsley would give instruction, (to the scuba divers) right?" asked McLeod.

"Yes, it could have been so."

The judge interjected, "Mr. Beardsley was aboard?"

"Yes, Dr. Beardsley was aboard the vessel," said Mr. Crane turning to the judge.

"May we establish who Dr. Beardsley was, please?" asked McLeod.

Mr. Crane responded, "Dr. Beardsley was an employee of Raytheon, who was quite an eminent scientist...." He added, "Dr. Beardsley was a consultant on the staff of Dr. Krasno."

It appeared to me that the court was befuddled for a moment. Perhaps the judge, who had taken on the responsibility for the two combined dockets, may have still been getting up to speed. Or it may have been that since Dr. Beardsley's spouse didn't join in on the lawsuit, the judge had a momentary disconnect with Dr. Beardsley's presence on the *Marie*. In fact, it would be a while before I had a reasonable guess as to why Nell Beardsley kept her distance from joining the other spouses and the lawsuit.

The examination continued:

McLeod: All right. Approximately when, please, in 1960 was Mr. Russell placed in charge of this particular project?

Crane: I am afraid I can't give you an exact date. I don't recall.

McLeod: Could you estimate it was sometime early in 1960 was Mr. Russell placed in charge of this particular project?

Crane: In the natural course of events, the research budget would probably be approved in the first quarter, so that the designation of Mr. Russell must have been some time after that.

McLeod: Thank you. Now, as such, with Mr. Russell in charge of that project, did he, as such, have direct supervision of the experimentations involved in the project?

Crane: He was directly in charge of the implementation of this experimentation, to coin a word. Actually, his colleague, Dr. Beardsley, Dr. Niel Beardsley, was one of the chief proponents of the method and experimentation to be used. It was Mr. Russell's responsibility to carry these methods out. He was the project manager, not its conceiver.

McLeod: I take it you were familiar in your position at this time with the methods used and what was done in these experimentations?

Crane: Only in the general sense. Not in detail.

McLeod: All right. Was this at the time, as you understood it, a classified project?

Crane: Yes, it was.

McLeod: That is, classified at least to some extent by the U.S. Government?

Crane: It was a military security classification.

McLeod: All right. And, of course, I do not want you to violate any of those provisions, but can you tell us this, Mr. Crane, did not the actual carrying out of these experiments on the vessel *Marie* involve going to various locations in the ocean?

Crane: Yes, it would be necessary for the *Marie* to transport equipment and personnel to designated spots.

McLeod: All right. Now, can you tell us when it would get to a particular location – I think it has already been testified to here that this equipment, whatever it may have been, was lowered to the ocean bottom, the ocean floor.

Crane: That is correct.

McLeod: Now then, in further conducting experiments from there, it would be necessary, would it not, for the skin diver not only to go down – well, first, it would be necessary for the skin divers to go down, would it not, to the ocean bottom?

Crane: Yes, they would have to place the equipment in the proper position relative to each other.

McLeod: How would that be determined on the vessel itself?

Crane: To the best of my knowledge this would be by vocal communication, using either sound power or wire telephones.

McLeod: Then the skin divers would be, would they not, under constant direction by whoever was directing up above on the vessel itself?

Crane: At the time of placing the equipment this would be true.

McLeod: Would not this process be continued as they moved on to various locations?

Crane: I should clarify that. The moving on to various locations would probably not occur within the course of any one trip.

McLeod: Was the vessel to be used as anything more than a conveyance between the time it left Santa Barbara and the time where it reached the project or project site?

Crane: I would say in general this is correct.

McLeod: Mr. Crane, as being in charge, apparently in full charge of this particular department, would you permit, as a person in charge of this, anyone to attach themselves or go on a trip like this simply as a pleasure trip for themselves?[99]

Crane: It would certainly be out of order to so do.

Over the eight days of the trial, a long line of witnesses followed, but Mr. Crane was not asked to return to the stand.

As I continued to review the testimonies and records, I noticed how the legal counsel was very conscious of the classified nature of the project.

****

The court devoted a lot of attention to determining Dale Howell and Timothy Lovette's involvement with the *Marie* expedition, because it wasn't clear who worked for whom and because it was these men's former-spouses who initiated the lawsuit.

Raytheon contended that, "... Loren Dale Howell, was one of the skin divers furnished to Raytheon by McCaffrey Brothers under the contract. The other, Paul Timothy Lovette, who was either the second skin diver furnished by McCaffrey Brothers, or, as Dowse has testified... was permitted to go along on the trip for the ride without pay. In any event, he was not employed by Raytheon."[100]

Mr. Dowse had told the court that Paul Timothy Lovette was not employed or paid by McCaffrey Brothers Sporting Goods. Apparently, Mr. Howell had asked just before the fatal trip if Lovette could come along. According to Dowse, Lovette's presence was by "...authorization of Mr. Jim Russell."[101]

Later, the court stated that "…Lovette had no part in the project of Raytheon, nor in the operation of the *Marie*, and was on board solely for his own pleasure at the request of decedent Howell."[102] This ultimately filtered into the court's Judgment: "Plaintiffs sought relief under the provisions of the Jones Act, 46 U.S.C. 688, by jury trial, but the jury determined that Howell and Lovette were not seamen." [103]   And in the Preliminary Jury Verdict, Howell was found by the jury to be "a maritime worker, not a member of the crew," while the jury also found Lovette to be neither a seaman nor a member of the crew but, "a guest or visitor."[104]

CHAPTER 36:

Judgment

Over the course of the eight-day trial, a parade of witnesses took the stand before the plaintiffs' and defendants' attorneys offered closing arguments. Afterwards, the court began the process of determining jurisdictions.

Before the final judgment was given, the court offered what appeared to be an extensive written summary of the evidence, testimonies, and relevant laws. The summary described that the toxic paint layer on the *Marie*'s wooden hull was a first line of defense against the harsh elements of the sea. And that the *Marie*'s hull was damaged by the maintenance that was provided by "sloughing off" sea growth by a diver's gloved and tooled hand as he inspected the hull's surface. In addition, it was pointed out that the *Marie*'s hull paint had likely lost its toxicity (facilitates detachment of sea life growth) because it was wooden, and that a wooden hulled boat needs to be pulled from the water and painted every year. A "working boat" requires it more often, every nine months. Mr. Dowse confirmed that the *Marie* hadn't been pulled from the water or painted in two years.

The following judgment was issued:

Considering all the evidence ... the court concludes that the *Marie* was unseaworthy on June 7, 1960, and that Mr. Dowse knew or should have known of that fact, that the condition was the result of the negligence of the owner, that the defendants are liable under the Death on the High Seas Act, and that petitioners' liability is not limited by the provisions of 86 U.S.C. 181, et seq.

JUDGMENT of DISMISSAL

In accordance with the foregoing Findings of Fact and the Conclusions of Law, IT IS ORDERED, ADJUDGED AND DECREED:
(1) That the Complaint of Plaintiffs, ... dismissed defendant RAYTHEON COMPANY.
(2) That the Cross-complaint of RICHARD W. DOWSE, against RAYTHEON COMPANY be ... dismissed.
(3) That defendant RAYTHEON COMPANY have judgment against Plaintiffs ... for its costs of suit herein.

These conclusions were followed up with the court STIPULATION FOR JUDGMENT, signed September 17, 1963,[105] awarding a total sum of $295,000.00 to be divided between the plaintiffs and claimants.[106]

It was a dollar figure half the amount reported in the newspaper article that had lead me to pursue the archives for the case file in the first place. I assumed that either Grandmother's scrapbook was missing a report with the update, or a reporter had jumped the gun and failed to follow-up with the final judgment.

My attention was keen on what the court also identified as the remaining two chief issues of fact:
1. What caused the *Marie* to disappear?
2. What was her status at the time as of charter?[107]
****

I reviewed the case records with mixed emotions. Initially, I was numb. Then I became annoyed as I read my age listed as being three years old at the time of my father's loss.

I was two years old!

I was also humbled, because the two-year-old in me had to grow up. I realized that my childhood beliefs, such as, "it was the boat's fault," were simplistic. The truth was a much more complex reality.

In truth, nobody really knew what happened or why.

I had believed the McCaffrey family owned the boat, and my heart sank as I learned the truth. I was frustrated when I realized that Grandmother's scrapbook included only the preliminary judgment. The article was one of the final news pieces Grandmother placed in the scrapbook, reporting a dollar award almost twice the amount awarded in the end.[108] My heart ached to think that although my mother received some financial compensation to care for four children, my grandmother received nothing to lighten the burden of losing her son.

I also had mixed feelings when I realized that Mrs. Constance McCaffrey was seven months pregnant with their fourth child when her husband was lost at sea. On top of that, she had to deal with a lawsuit against her husband's estate.

After digesting the case files, my confidence soared. I thought I knew just about all there was to know about the *Marie* shipwreck and the events surrounding it. I believed I had discovered everything that the National Archives had to offer, not to mention family records and personal testimonies. However, even as my confidence soared, uncertainty nagged. Like a sonar ping, it seemed to be saying, "Something's missing. Keep up the search. There's more to discover."

If I'd had an intimate awareness of electronics, I might have recognized that, although the court clarified what was *not* on board the *Marie* (explosives), it failed to identify what *was* on board. However, one thing was certain: Raytheon was exonerated.[109]

I was pleased with this conclusion because it offered me a green light to approach the Raytheon Company once again. I saw no reason why Raytheon shouldn't welcome being part of an event in honor of those lost on the *Marie*.

CHAPTER 37:

Venue For An Anniversary

I believed Raytheon's exoneration represented the final piece of the *Marie* puzzle. Now I could commit my time and resources to spearheading a June 2010 activity for the tragedy. And it was going to take a lot of time and resources, because I now believed the event should honor more than my father.

When I first learned that my family had never held a funeral or memorial for my father because they believed that he was still alive somewhere, I made plans to honor him with a small, family gathering. At the 50-year anniversary of the shipwreck, I wanted to remember my father's life by gathering with my three brothers, singing a few hymns, and tossing a wreath into the ocean. But God had other plans.

As I listened to my heart, I knew we needed to expand any activity to include the families of all the men who were lost, along with the company that had lost an entire project team—Raytheon. With Ken's encouragement, I outlined a basic project charter and anticipated budget. My new goal was to create a memory at the fast approaching fiftieth anniversary. However, I believed everything depended on Raytheon's involvement. I needed to keep the plans flexible until I heard from them.

I felt that Raytheon's clearance of wrongdoing was my green light to approach the company again. However, because my other attempts had failed, I planned to approach Raytheon differently. I wanted to pique their interest, and I had done my due diligence this time.

Therefore, I went to Raytheon Santa Barbara headquarters on Hollister in Goleta, armed with a simple letter requesting a brief face-to-face meeting with the general manager. I wanted to invite them to participate in a June 2010 anniversary of the *Marie* shipwreck.

I designed and created a presentation folder with images and information that summarized the story from Raytheon's perspective. The folder included news items from 1960, quotes from Raytheon's newsletter, reports about scholarships Raytheon representatives awarded to UCSB engineering students in the names of the engineers lost (Beardsley, Mackie, Russell, Terres). I also included the headline *Raytheon is Exonerated*, along with a link to a website I had created.

I didn't want to overwhelm them with information, but to spark an interest and schedule a face-to-face meeting while we were in town. I tried to anticipate their initial concerns, and I used every bit of influence I had. I even asked Ken to sign the letter as Colonel Kenneth H. Newton (US Army, ret.). I knew his signature would add credibility.

The sun was bright and the air crisp when we arrived at Raytheon Santa Barbara headquarters. Ken waited in the car while I went inside to drop off the letter and presentation. Package delivered, I returned to the car, and we drove to the Santa Barbara Harbor.

My next step was to initiate a relationship with the Santa Barbara Maritime Museum (SBMM). I hoped the museum would agree to be the event's sponsor. Contributions to the anniversary event could go to the museum, a nonprofit, tax-exempt organization. As I saw it, it was a win-win.

The Santa Barbara Maritime Museum was a perfect place for the event. Its building was not only at the harbor, it was the site where the Coast Guard orchestrated the 1960 local search and rescue efforts for the *Marie*. Mom and the other spouses gathered there to wait for news. Recovery teams deposited wreckage and debris from the *Marie* there.

The museum was ideal for another reason. Many of its exhibits highlighted the fact that over the years the Santa Barbara Channel had claimed hundreds of ships. In that respect, the *Marie* tragedy was not unique. The Channel is a dangerous place.

Ken and I had an appointment to meet with Greg Gorga, Executive Director of the SBMM. As Mr. Gorga ushered Ken and me back into his conference room, I felt as if we were entering a ship captain's cabin. Rich wood paneling, seafaring décor, and artifacts lent an elegant atmosphere to the room. After some pleasantries, I handed him a presentation folder, customized with information slanted toward the museum's unique interests.

I told him about the *Marie* shipwreck, the plans for the first gathering at the 50-year anniversary, and my hope to find a nonprofit sponsor.

I brought two books to bolster my case. First, I showed him a book I purchased in the museum's bookstore: *Shipwrecks, Smugglers and Maritime Mysteries* by Eugene D. Wheeler and Robert E. Kallman.

I flipped the book open, and my fingers pointed and read, giving due drama as if the words floated on the waves. "One of the strangest boating accidents of the 1960's was the disappearance of the *Marie*...."[110]

"That's what a member of your board of directors said about the *Marie* shipwreck," I said.

Next, I pulled out a hardcover, coffee-table-sized book. "Here's the response of the Santa Barbara community," I said. I showed him the cover: *Santa Barbara News-Press' HEADLINERS: A History of Santa Barbara from the Pages of its Newspapers 1855-1982.*[111] Next, I turned to a page with a compilation noteworthy stories, including the *Marie* shipwreck.

"The *Marie* shipwreck was one of Santa Barbara's mysteries in 1960, and I believe it is worthy of devoting resources to a 50th anniversary remembrance," I said.

I explained where I was in the preparation process, and that I hoped to get an official commitment from Raytheon that week. I also clarified that I intended to hold an anniversary event somewhere no matter what the museum or Raytheon decided.

I asked, "Given what I have shared with you, would you and Santa Barbara Maritime Museum consider sponsoring the event and being the beneficiary of any charitable contributions?"

The museum's participation would be huge. If SBMM tossed in their hat to the effort, then when I approached Raytheon I would be doing so from a stronger position. The event would then be about serving the community, not merely about honoring seven men. I had noticed a gleam in Mr. Gorga's eyes when he opened the presentation folder. He smiled and said that he was open to the idea of hosting the anniversary gathering.

He continued and suggested, "The museum could put together an Exhibit on the *Marie*."

I love that idea!

An exhibit at the SBMM would give the *Marie* commemoration respectability and exposure. Additionally, such an exhibit might justify someone investing time and money to produce a documentary, something I hoped Raytheon would be willing to do.

"I will have to run this all through the SBMM system," Mr. Gorga said, mentioning a board of directors and the curator. Later, in a private tour of the museum, he showed us a central location, visible from almost everywhere in the museum, that would be available for both an exhibit and a gathering. It even included an 80-inch plasma screen monitor, where a maritime documentary entertained and educated.

The space fueled my desire to see the exhibit become a reality.

I'm going to make this happen.

Mr. Gorga pointed upward, toward a model airplane suspended above us. "The museum has a connection with another government contractor," he said. He recounted the story of Lockheed Corporation's beginnings in Santa Barbara before it grew into a leader in the Aerospace Industry. I wanted to tell Mr. Gorga that four Lockheed men may have a roll in the *Marie* story. Ken was delighted with the *Surf's Up* exhibit, a display of Santa Barbara's legendary surfers, surf memorabilia, and surf industry. He had taken up surfing when we were stationed in Hawaii.

Mr. Gorga said, "Our curator, Jennifer Wiesnewski finished this recently." He then added, "We just lost her to the Clinton Library in Arkansas."

It was a casual comment, but it immediately struck a chord in me. I knew that a woman named Jennifer with a unique last name lived and worked near me. I also knew she had experience with displays at the SBMM. I made a mental note to follow up with her.

As our tour continued, I mentioned two SBMM board members whom I was attempting to gain their support of the commemoration: Robert Schwemmer, with the National Oceanic and Atmospheric Administration (NOAA), and Fred Benko, with the Condor Express Whale Watching Tours.

"Robert Schwemmer's efforts produced the wreck diving display," said Mr. Gorga as he waved a hand in the direction of the model of the torpedoed Montebello Oil Tanker.

"I'm hoping that the anniversary activities can work with the Condor Express to include a wreath laying ceremony at sea," I said.

"Fred and Hiroko Benko will likely extend SBMM's discount," he replied. He went on to tell me that Bob Schwemmer with NOAA would be dropping by later that day and that he would mention my visit.

"Budgets are tight and I have little else beside the use of our name to offer you," he confessed. He made it clear that, for the most part, I was on my own. Also, I would still be expected to pay the reservation fees for use of the museum for the event, but I would get a non-profit rate assuming the effort was sponsored by the SBMM.

Given these boundaries, I still believed an alliance with the Santa Barbara Maritime Museum was desirable.

We departed with a handshake and a smile. Later that day I received an e-mail with electronic files of the SBMM logo in color and black and white. I updated the *Marie* presentation to include the logos. The Santa Barbara Maritime Museum was now the "presenter" of the *Marie* anniversary activities which would, if nothing else, add credibility and community spirit to the entire effort.

By day's end, Bob Schwemmer with NOAA made contact. We

scheduled to meet over lunch on a sidewalk café at the marina and next to the museum.

Next, I got a call from Raytheon. "Can we set up a meeting with our Public Relations and Human Resource Managers?" an assistant asked.

"Yes," I replied. If she only knew how delighted I was to hear those words. We arranged a meeting for a few days later.

Everything was lining up in our favor.

****

Ken and I arrived early for our lunch meeting with NOAA's Bob Schwemmer. We chose a table under an umbrella to shield us from the August sun.

Mr. Schwemmer walked up to us confidently, carrying a legal-size folder. I wasn't sure what he looked like because the online pictures I'd seen always showed him in a scuba diving suit with mask and snorkel.

After some casual conversation, he handed me a folder. "The *Marie*'s records," he said nonchalantly.

Ken asked Mr. Schwemmer about his work with the Santa Barbara Maritime Museum's board of directors and the Montebello shipwreck display, giving me time to review the folder's contents.

The folder contained more than twenty pages of documents, dating between the 1940s and '60s. I dismissed the top document, titled, *Rescue Coordination Center*. It contained inaccurate information that I had seen before. In fact, I had called NOAA some time ago to correct the errors.

My heart skipped a beat when I turned the page and I read the header on another document: *Eleventh Coast Guard District Search and Rescue Diary*. Under the title in all caps was, CASE CONTINUES. Was this the missing SAR report?

I wanted to ignore everything else and focus my attention on that single document, but I turned the page. I skimmed the rest of the folder's contents and noted that these included, *US Coast Guard, Oath of Master to Loss of Document for Bureau of Customs, Report of Violation, Designation of Home Port of Vessel with the Treasury Department's Bureau of Customs*, and so on. Each page bore the footer, "Reproduced from the holdings of the National Archives Pacific Southwest Region."

I had a stack of documents with the same branding.

I glanced again at the Coast Guard's RCC report, considering the original source of misinformation that apparently continued to feed NOAA's records, news reports, and publications. I imagined that whoever completed the form on June 9, 1960, never realized how many people would access it.

For the most part, the details reported in the report were accurate. But family members notice the little things. One man's last name was misspelled. Two other men's first names, including my father's, were incorrect. The document listed Dad as James. Dad's name was Diego, which in English is either Jim or Jimmy. Never James. Even Dr. Niel Freeborn Beardsley's first name was misspelled, with the letters "i" and "e" transposed.

In addition, the document described the location of the shipwreck as being in the "vicinity of 34-12N 119-35W." That was where Paul Timothy Lovette's body was recovered. Nobody knew the location of the shipwreck. Finally, the form listed the date of the tragedy as June 9, 1960 which was the date when Paul Timothy Lovette's body was recovered, not the date of the shipwreck.

To some, these might seem minor mistakes. But to family these were huge errors that were compounded every time someone repeated them. The form I was reviewing had never been fact-checked or updated. Thus, those who accessed this record unknowingly repeated the errors. I thought of times when I had butchered the spelling or pronunciation of someone's name, and I felt humbled.

Mr. Schwemmer told us about the Montebello oil tanker that was featured at the museum. "It was sunk by a Japanese submarine torpedo attack in World War II." He had devoted years spearheading a taskforce to ensure the tanker's oil didn't pose a threat to the environment.

The submarine attack reminded Ken of a Japanese submarine attack off California's coastline in WWII, against the Ellwood Oil Field on the north side of Santa Barbara.[112] In his military history class at the

University of California, Ken assigned his students the task of finding information about the first submarine attack on the continental west coast of United States. "It always surprised students that Japanese submarines attacked the USA just a few miles up the road," Ken said.

"There were many other submarine attacks on the Pacific Coast,"[113] Mr. Schwemmer added. I listened as the two men continued a friendly discussion over history discussing the hundreds of submarine attacks launched against the continental US on the Pacific, Atlantic and Gulf coasts.

I wondered, *Should the Marie be on a list of enemy attacks?*

During a lull in the conversation, I asked him, "How and where did you get these records?" I nodded toward the legal file.

"I called the National Archives and they sent a copy," he said with a smile.

There was always more to learn about finding information in the Archives.

"Thanks for the file. I'm trying to find everything I can about the *Marie* – good, bad, and questionable." I felt bewildered, because I had searched the same archives, but hadn't located this file of records on the *Marie*. The folder tab was labeled #253652. Inside, each document bore the ID #253652. I had been led to believe that all I needed was the name of the *Marie*. I hadn't searched Los Angeles boating records because I understood that the *Marie* was moored in Santa Barbara.

The waitress delivered our lunch, and as we enjoyed our sandwiches Ken asked, "Bob, what are your NOAA's Sanctuary boundaries?"

This was an important question and I was glad Ken asked it. At the moment, I didn't fully understand the importance of ocean boundaries. However, in time I'd grow in my awareness of the invisible boundaries that distinguished United States' waters from international waters and the *Laws of the Sea* that governed everything from military underwater installations to pirates.

"Our boundaries run from the shore out six miles," he replied. He explained that his responsibility included both the Pacific coastline and the Santa Barbara Channel Island.

As Mr. Schwemmer elaborated on the Sanctuary, my mind drifted to what was of importance to me in NOAA's Sanctuary: Finding the sunken *Marie*.

My thoughts went to grandmother's scrapbook and the news report about the abalone divers who found a sunken boat in 1969. The divers believed the boat was the *Marie*. My understanding of that find was that, if the abalone divers had found *Marie*, then the boat was probably resting in the NOAA Sanctuary and wasn't lost in the middle of the channel. From what I could tell, the discovery was never validated. Therefore, it remained a mystery.

Apparently, NOAA's records didn't identify any sunken boats at the site of the abalone divers find, said to be 2.5 miles from the shore side of Santa Cruz Island and 1.5 miles east of the Big Cave (Painted Cave), in less than 50 feet of water. One of my objectives in connecting with Bob Schwemmer was to encourage him and his colleagues to locate whatever vessel was down there.

"It's a shame you don't know what is located off Santa Cruz Island, no matter if it is the *Marie* or not," I said.

Mr. Schwemmer returned my grin and encouraged me to pursue a grant and bring in a small submersible submarine. "Funding and time is tight with NOAA."

I reminded him that if the abalone divers find was accurate, the sunken vessel in question was in less than 50 feet of water. "A very reachable depth even for Ken and me," I said. I also pointed out that since the 1969 divers didn't confirm the find, whoever located the *Marie* could claim finding rights. "If I had more time in the area, I would go diving there myself," I added.

I became a certified scuba diver in my senior year of high school. I had had only one open ocean dive before I met Ken and later moved to Hawaii. That dive was out at Santa Cruz Island on a sailing and diving weekend with my younger brother Don and Peter Edwards, a friend of my brother Jim's, who could also captain a sailboat. Peter had permission to use my brother's sailboat while Jim was out of the country. I would discover later that Peter held a clue to locating one of the *Marie* widows and the Russell family.

"Tell me more about the online list of shipwrecks that I originally complained about," I asked, reminding Mr. Schwemmer of my initial contact with him. At the time, I was peeved that the list of 35 shipwrecks sunk in the SB Channel didn't include the *Marie*. I had sent him copies of sources that validated that the *Marie* was indeed a shipwreck and should be included on his list. Bob had replied graciously. And I began to learn about the purpose of that list.

"The spreadsheet online is a listing set up for kids and teachers," Bob said, explaining that it was a tool that teachers used in classrooms. "It gives them real information to use and spark an interest in developing skills in setting up and using a database that the students can use in searching, sorting, and assessing," he said. "It's been well received."

I felt ashamed because I'd complained, failing to realize that over 700 shipwrecks qualified for the list, but they offered the kids a small selection so as not to overwhelm them with data.

As our lunch meeting ended, I felt that my main objective was accomplished. The *Marie* milestone was now on Mr. Schwemmer's and NOAA's radar. He had offered me a window into NOAA's world of tracking submerged objects and I was grateful that he was now aware of the upcoming *Marie* anniversary.

CHAPTER 38:

Rebuffed

With the Santa Barbara Maritime Museum on board and the event on NOAA's calendar, my thoughts turned again to my upcoming meeting with Raytheon. I had no idea how Raytheon would choose to participate. Would they want to take over the effort? Would they want to influence the activity to ensure it was both professional and respectful? I postponed making concrete plans until I understood their needs.

When I first approached Raytheon's corporate headquarters in Boston, the results hadn't been positive. Since then, I had done my homework. I hoped this time that Raytheon would respond favorably.

I paused at the top of the steps of Raytheon's Building-One and looked back across Hollister toward the Santa Barbara Airport and the Goleta Beach beyond. It was familiar territory. I had passed by the front of this building countless times as a child. I had always known it as the place where my father had worked. The retired engineers had offered me insights into what went on behind its doors and upon its rooftop. Now it was time for me to enter what had once been my father's world. I turned and continued through the door Ken held open for me.

Raytheon's Mangers of Public Relations and Human Resources led us back to a small, professional-looking office. Ken and I sat facing them across a small conference table. I gave them an updated presentation folder with the Santa Barbara Maritime Museum logo strategically placed. I explained that since we'd arrived in town, the museum had signed on to the anniversary activity. I was pleased when the HR manager's finger quickly pointed to the pictures I had included of Dr. Bob Watkins.

"That's Dr. Watkins," he said to the other manager as if Dr. Watkins was a legend in his own time. I had taken the photos at the morning gathering at Dr. Bob's home and at the Raytheon Retiree's picnic.

"I learned more from your website than I got from an investigator hired to put together some information," said the HR manager.

During our interview, I learned that the presentation we had originally left with the Raytheon Santa Barbara General Manager had been given to the PR manager, and since she knew nothing of the *Marie* shipwreck she had distributed a company-wide e-mail in search of someone who did.

The HR manager had responded.

As they browsed the *Marie* website, and had noticed that the link to Raytheon wasn't correct. "It should link to Space and Airborne Systems," they informed me.

I made a note of this.

They asked me to clarify the details of the invitation I had extended to Raytheon to participate in the anniversary activities.

"Can you elaborate what you mean by participate?" PR manager asked.

I explained that I hoped we would work together toward defining Raytheon's role. I could only imagine the various ways that Raytheon might want to handle such an event: control, influence, or just say a few words of condolences, perhaps?

"Is it agreeable for you to go forward with the PR manager as your contact," the HR manager asked.

"Yes. Of course."

I tried to sound professional, but inwardly I was ecstatic.

I now had a name, a face, contact information and a verbal agreement from someone willing to explore the next steps.

I was on Raytheon's radar.

With our objectives reached, it was the right time to graciously bring this first-touch meeting to a close. I heard Ken's advice echoing in my head.

Leave them wanting more.

"Thank you for meeting us on such a short notice," I said looking from one manager to the other.

PR manager stood and said, "I will have to go, because I have another meeting."

I stood and followed her into the hallway. Ken turned to the HR manager, "When did you first hear of the *Marie* Shipwreck?" he asked.

"I had been at Raytheon 30 years and had heard nothing of the shipwreck. And a few years back, I got a somewhat belligerent call that concerned me enough to have our security look into the matter," he said escorting us down the hallway.

I had made a call around that time, after I learned about the Lost at Sea Memorial's dedication. My behavior had been respectful. I wondered who else had called.

As Ken and I departed, I was confident that I had a foot in the door, and that we would all work toward a successful anniversary activity.

As a follow up to our meeting, I sent an e-mail a few days later with a more complete response to the manager's question about how Raytheon might participate in activities. I also included how I believed Raytheon could be helpful in the ongoing *Marie* research, by revealing the program and project names and numbers. These were important puzzle pieces I had yet to locate.

I received a response.

"It was also a pleasure to meet with you and your husband and learning more about the *Marie* commemoration. I look forward to keeping the communication lines open. I will be in touch in the next 2-3 weeks." [114]

I took note of the e-mail signature: Manager of Communications, Tactical Airborne Systems, Raytheon Space and Airborne Systems. I corrected the Raytheon link on the *Marie* event website.

I was pleased. Finally, Raytheon and I were connected and communicating.

****

Three weeks passed with no further response. I waited a few weeks more, reasoning that these things always take longer than anticipated. When September was drawing to a close, with still no response, I knew it was time for me to take another step toward Raytheon. A polite memory jog seemed appropriate.

On September 22, 2009, I e-mailed my Raytheon contact.

Just wanted to make sure you hadn't forgotten about our dialogue. Needless to say, I've been working non-stop on planning and coordinating different facets of the *Marie* commemoration. It seems like that's all that I do, but thank goodness my husband pulls me out for some golf and tennis....

Best wishes,

Teresa

When I didn't get a response to my second e-mail, I began to get concerned. I shared my frustration with Ken. "No word of acknowledgement," I said. "Not even a note confirming that they're busy."

Ken took a pen and paper and wrote "Raytheon" in the center. He circled it and then began drawing arrows out from it and identified the people or entities I had approached or could approach to offer a possible course of action: PR, HR, Raytheon Santa Barbara's General Manager, Santa Barbra newspaper, Santa Barbara's elected officials, Navy League of Santa Barbara, Corporate HQ in Boston, etc.

I recognized it as a mind-mapping technique.

As he diagrammed, Ken talked out loud. It quickly became clear that I had only directed my recent efforts to Raytheon's Santa Barbara office. I had not yet communicated with Raytheon's Corporate Headquarters in the Boston area to invite them to attend or participate in the *Marie* anniversary activities.

Handing me the mind map, Ken left my office sanctuary. I was comforted to have his empathy and his assistance. And I was grateful because he helped catapult me over the wall I faced.

As the white oaks began dropping acorns, I drafted another letter to William Swanson, President and Chairman of the Board of Raytheon in Boston. I included a presentation folder with the letter, and on October 2, 2009 I shipped out a priority package with a tracking slip. In the cover letter I mentioned that I would follow-up with a phone call in ten days, on October 12, 2009. I also sent a copy to Scott Jackson, Raytheon Santa Barbara. In the letter, I thanked him for the opportunity to meet his HR and PR representatives, on August 10, 2009. I hoped this might motivate him to respond.

Ten days later, on October 12, 2009, I placed a follow-up call to Raytheon Headquarters in Boston.

William Swanson's administrative assistant, answered.

"Hello," I began, "this is Teresa Newton-Terres and I am calling as a follow-up to a letter and presentation that I sent. It was about an invitation for Raytheon to participate in a commemoration of the *Marie* shipwreck on June 4-6, 2010 in Santa Barbara, California."

The assistant was polite and respectful as she told me that such invitations were handled by another person. "Would you like me to transfer you?" she asked.

"I can give her a call," I said after getting the contact number and thanking her for her time and help. I wanted to do my homework and learn a little bit about this manager before I called.

By the end of the day, I made a second call to Raytheon and got the Communications Manager's answering service. I left a brief message: "William Swanson's office asked me to follow-up with you. I look forward to hearing from you."

I never got a phone call, letter, or e-mail response from Raytheon in Boston, but by the end of the day on October 12, 2009, the Communications Manager from Raytheon, Santa Barbara, connected with me by e-mail.

> Hi Teresa,
> Just a quick e-mail to let you know that our business corporate office is still reviewing the *Marie* commemoration package to determine how we can participate. I will be in touch with you as soon as I hear from them.
> Thanks for your patience.

The communication was short and simple. It offered no timeframe for when I might hear back from them. But at least it was encouraging, because the e-mail stated that they were determining *how*, rather than *if*, they would participate.

A few weeks later, in Nov 2009, a brief message about a June 2010 *Marie* anniversary was included in the Santa Barbara High School Alumni newsletter because four of the lost (Howell, Mackie, McCaffrey, Terres) were SBHS alumni.

I knew Raytheon's Communications Manager was a SBHS alumni too. So, I hoped the newsletter offered an opportunity to connect again. Also, enough time had elapsed so that touching base would be acceptable. I sent her a brief e-mail.

Again, no response.

The mighty oaks were bare, with acorns rotting on the ground, when I received a response from Raytheon. While the introduction was thoughtful and respectful, I was baffled by the letter's message.

Dear Ms. Newton-Terres,

Thank you for your recent request to support the *Marie* commemoration. I reviewed your request materials thoroughly. The loss of the *Marie* and the men on board was devastating for the families and the Santa Barbara community. Our hearts continue to go out to everyone who suffered from this tragedy.

We value the time and resources you and the committee members have invested in the historical research. We also value the opportunity presented to Raytheon to support and endorse the commemoration. Unfortunately, we are unable to support your request.

Raytheon's philanthropic and local giving program focuses its support on Science, Technology, Engineering and Mathematics (STEM) education of middle and high school aged children. We actively support STEM programs in schools and community organizations with a STEM focus. Your request is outside of our philanthropic and local giving focus.

Again, thank you for the invitation and opportunity and best wishes for a successful event.[115]

I read it once. Then I re-read it. Next, I found Ken and handed it to him, shaking my head. "I'm baffled," I said. "The anniversary activity was assessed as just another charity request." I sputtered as Ken read the document. "The shipwreck is a Raytheon-family historical event and an opportunity."

"Boggling," Ken scratched his head.

I grabbed the letter and returned to my private space.

After my initial emotions settled down, I began considering my options. One option was to do nothing. On the other hand, I could assume that I had failed to communicate again, and try one more time. This time I would make a request that was so simple that Raytheon couldn't refuse: merely to come and offer condolences.

Dear…,

"Thank you for responding to my invitation for Raytheon to participate in the *Marie* commemoration. My request was and is simply, that someone represent the Raytheon Company at the *Marie* commemoration ceremony and reception Saturday, June 6, 2010 and give suitable and brief remarks (2-5 min)."

I addressed my response and sent the original. I also sent copies to the Raytheon leadership in Boston, Santa Barbara, and El Segundo. From this effort, I obtained no response. No response from Raytheon in Boston. No response from Raytheon in Santa Barbara.

As a last-ditch effort before the June activities, I sent a general invitation to the Raytheon leadership.

Again, no response.

I was forced to conclude that, although Raytheon's retired engineers had welcomed me into their family ranks, for whatever reason the Raytheon corporation chose not to be a part of the *Marie* anniversary activities.

CHAPTER 39:

Building a Tidal Wave

The chilly air seeping through the window panes signaled the arrival of winter. It felt like winter in my heart, too. I had hoped for Raytheon's help in learning about the shipwreck—and my father—but that was not to be. I had believed Raytheon Corporation wanted to be part of a 50th anniversary activity.

Throughout the Christmas season, in addition to the usual busyness, my long-buried childhood desires surfaced. I had little time to allow waves of resentment and stress to swell, but they rolled in all the same.

"I want *my* father." That was the unspoken desire of my heart. When I was a child I placed this request annually on Santa's list, albeit with invisible ink.

Santa never came through.

Christmas was frustrating for me when I was growing up. Every year Mother took my three rambunctious brothers and me up to the cabin for the entire Christmas break.

"Skiers ski," was her motto. So, every Christmas we skied. It wasn't much of a Christmas. My friends got new dresses; I got new ski gear.

Although I found Mother's annual Christmas retreat frustrating,

I nevertheless had good memories of those times. The cabin's simple pleasures, the warm fires, hot meals, board games, even Mother's single bag of decorations, all lent themselves to the reason we celebrate Christmas, by remembering and honoring a birth. Ironically, now I also preferred to escape the Christmas season by retreating to the high snow-covered Sierra Nevada Mountains.

I made it through Christmas and New Year's, but my thoughts continually circled back to the looming deadline. If there was to be an anniversary activity, I had only five months to organize and promote it. Unfortunately, I didn't have the funds, time, manpower or creativity to bring it about on my own. I had made plans based on the assumption that Raytheon would participate. I had delayed other decisions in hopes of having their influence and guidance. Now, those other opportunities that I had counted on were collapsing, one after another.

I had lined up a caterer but now their fees and contract terms were too expensive. I had arranged for a film company to create a short documentary for the museum exhibit. But I had counted on funding from Raytheon and I was now going to have to back out of it. Even the Santa Barbara Maritime Museum, which initially offered to develop an exhibit, backed away. "Times are hard and funds and staffing are already over committed," I was told.

After the Christmas decorations were put away, the *Marie* anniversary was front and center, and I faced a mountain of concerns: I didn't live in California. I didn't know how to find the other families.

I can't manage an event without Raytheon's help.

These words repeated like waves pounding a shore.

Emotions snowballed as I considered the shipwreck story, Grandmother's grief, Grandfather's search, Mother's letter written from the cabin's deck speaking of dreams, sweatshirt signals from my father, Russian trawlers, submarines, storms, and a data pick-up.

Something was picked up. Was it Dad? Was he kidnapped?

I felt as if a noose were tightening around me, and thoughts of suicide began to creep in. My "Terres' tooth" was sore from my repeated pressing on it.

One day, as Ken cleaned his rifles for an upcoming hunting trip, I found myself staring at them. I had never shot a gun. I feared their presence in my house. Yet now I found myself thinking about using one on myself.

"Please keep these locked up," I told Ken.

I don't know if he understood what was in my mind.

On a short drive to the grocery store a few days later, the child's cries of my heart were so strong. *Dad may be alive. No one is rescuing him. Go find Dad. Bring Dad home. I want Daddy.* Like a tsunami they crashed through a barrier of suppressed wants and desires, threatening my well-being.

As I drove, I imagined crashing into one of the tall oak trees that lined the path. It would be so easy. I immediately hit the brakes, pulled over to the side of the road, and sat there. I was numb. I couldn't think. I wanted to escape. I felt like I had no life to live. I sat by the side of the road and tried to pray.

"Our Father who art in heaven…"

In my heart I knew that God wanted better for me. I had lived through other tough lessons and pain caused by not listening to God's voice. So, as I sat there in the car, I heard a still small voice like gentle waves on the beach.

Live to see the glory of God.

I began to think about my daughter. I had caused enough issues in her life. I thought about the impact my suicide would have on those I left behind. My grandchildren. Sitting in the car that afternoon, I saw barren leaves blowing in the freezing wind.

I stayed there until I felt I could trust myself to move on.

Back home, I hid in my inner office, my cave. The two paper star chandeliers that I'd hung above either side of my desk to bring me joy, bathed me in dim light.

A shadow passed by. Then I heard Ken say, "Action cures anxiety."

I looked up and saw him standing in the doorway.

Did he read my thoughts?

I offered him a weak smile. Ken's "Fig Newton" wisdom always had merit, but I didn't want to put it into motion.

"You can always do a pot-luck on the beach," he said.

I didn't want to do anything, anymore. I was weary of it all.

Besides, if Raytheon wasn't going to acknowledge the shipwreck's anniversary, why should I? Why put the effort and expense into such a thing? Why should I even do a beach gathering for my brothers? Why should I do anything?

Looking up, I gave Ken another feeble smile. As he disappeared, I noticed to the right of the doorway the wall-hanging. "I can do all things through Christ who strengthens me." My eyes moved further to the right to a framed Old Spanish Days Fiesta poster. It held an iconic image dating back to 1923 of a troupe of dancers and musicians, dramatically posed. I bought it because I liked it. I had no idea it was part of my own family history until Uncle Albert, on a recent visit to our home, pointed to one figure in the dance troupe.

"You know who that is?" Uncle Al asked.

"Who?"

"It's my father. Your grandfather."

My eyes strained through the dim and lingered on the image of my young grandfather. The framed poster was propped on the left edge of my desk, a door turned sideways straddling two sawhorses. I took in a deep breath and blew out slowly, as if to blow away my mental fog.

To the right of the poster was a picture of my grandparents dancing together at Fiesta. My gaze continued to the right and found two images of my daughter. My heart warmed as I remembered the days she wore the red satin costume in her youth and the polka-dot dress as she performed with a troupe for the Embassy of Spain in Washington D.C. in her teens. And to the right of these was an image from this past Fiesta, where Ken, Uncle Al and Aunt Lynda, and I had dawned costumes for an evening. I smiled at the memory of my Southern Gentleman as a well-dressed Spaniard. On the other side of my desk was the collage of news and images from the shipwreck. I reached out and caressed the lines on my grandfather's face.

I took in another deep breath.

Then, I stood up and turned the switch and the room flooded with light revealing walls covered with poster-paper—my shipwreck timeline. The timeline was useful, but it was also covering images of my family.

I stepped over a pile of papers and uncovered inspiring artwork and images of my family—celebrating and dancing. Three photos showed my grandfather as a dashing young man with his dance troupe.

Their lives were not void of hardships, but they were ... dancing.

I looked back at the shipwreck's collage. Grandfather was at the helm searching the sea for his son.

Who's at your helm? Then? Today? Do you trust God?

Looking around the room, I found a container behind another stack of papers. I blew off the dust and put it on my desk. Inside was a treasure: a pair of black leather shoes and a set of castanets. I put on one shoe and then the other.

Then, I shuffled aside the collection of documents and books that blanketed my floor. I hit the play button to a musical piece. As the intro resonated, I raised my hands high, twisting and twirling my wrists to extend my fingers, circling like a fan. And my muscles strained to remember, *my feel-good power move.*

My grandparents and I danced classical Spanish dances with defined steps. My daughter, however, learned flamenco. A form of dance inspired by gypsies which flourishes with personal improvisation. I first took flamenco with my teenage daughter.

Spontaneous movement in performances wasn't part of my youth, but in the protection of my cave, it was freeing. As the musical phrase began, my blood surged, and the depression that had engulfed me like a fog lifted.

One leather heel hit the floor. Then the next. And the next.

I did one musical phrase with my hands and heels. Then, I returned to my treasure box. Holding the silk encasing, I removed my castanets. "A cousin in Spain made these for you," Grandmother Terres said as she placed them in my hands after returning from a trip. I looped twine around one thumb and then the other. And as the next musical phrase began, my fingers reverberated a quick ripple of beats – wood beating on wood like a drum.

Raising them high, I danced my heart out.

With the rhythms and beats, my emotional storm subsided.

*Why should I do something? To gather all the worthy stories. To compile the myths and memories. To find and face the facts. So we can…*Dance!

As the music quieted, I heard a faint voice inside me whisper, "Consider all things."

I looked to grandmother's scrapbook. And I starred. Then, I grinned as I saw in my mind's eye the Raytheon Company newsletter from July 1960. It contained an article recounting and responding to the *Marie* tragedy. And I realized that the *Marie families* would not have to go without hearing from Raytheon.

Ken was right. I needed to reassess. It was not too late to make changes. It was okay to do nothing. Or I could return to the idea for a simple family gathering focusing on my father. Or I could press forward and honor all the men who were lost.

I had a collection of stories from three families and several retired Raytheon engineers, all of whom were interested in the anniversary. A pile of information from original sources cluttered my office and told of a mystery that needed to be solved. And I had already found three of the seven families.

As I danced, my goal became clear: Organize and host a 50[th]anniversary for family, friends, and a community. I had no time to lose because I was going to face a mountain of work, and it all had to be done in five months.

"God willing," I said, "I will juggle all the balls."

****

My first concern was funding. I was now planning to host an event located two thousand miles away. The Santa Barbara Maritime Museum had offered space for a *Marie Remembered* exhibit, and even though they had pulled back from producing it, the door was still open to have it there.

"The space is available to you," Mr. Gorga had said, "if you have a museum-quality film." The more I thought about creating an exhibit, the more I became like a young lady shopping for a wedding dress. I wanted it. However, as a project management professional, I knew that, as a bride-to-be can undermine a wedding with unrealistic desires, my desire for a memorable exhibit was potentially dangerous. If I wasn't careful, I could torpedo the whole event by trying to do too much.

I wanted the exhibit because it would tell the story of the *Marie*. I didn't want to be the one to tell the families what happened to their husbands and fathers. I had collected information, interviews, pictures, and documents. I believed someone more qualified than I could assemble it all into an exhibit.

I just needed the money to pay them.

I brainstormed a short list of ways to generate funds and one idea kept presenting itself: A book. I assumed that a publisher would pay for the story and assign a ghostwriter to write it. The upcoming, first-ever *Marie* anniversary event would provide a perfect marketing venue. At least, that's what I thought.

On this assumption, I drafted a proposal for a book titled, "Mystery of the *Marie*." Ken edited the proposal to ensure the context was dynamic and appealing, and I sent it out to a handful of literary agents.

I waited for the calls and contracts to come in. Instead, I received form-letter rejections.

Feeling the sting of the rejections, I took a few days to consider the need, my desire, and my priorities. I could always self-publish a book, but if I tried to produce it by June, all my resources would be devoted to writing it and funding it. But the purpose of the anniversary activity was not a book, but a gathering for the families of seven men lost.

I needed to consult Ken, but he was notoriously difficult to nail down when it came to scheduling time to discuss my "shipwreck thing" as he called it. Today, I brought the shipwreck event up while I sat next to him, watching basketball on TV.

"The story seems destined to be told, but a book is not going to fund this event," I admitted. "I believe God wants more than a pot-luck. Our personal bank account will have to bankroll the brunt of the expenses." I told him.

"God isn't in it," Ken said. He pointed the remote control at the television and switched to a different game.

I had poured out my heart and soul, and in four words he shot me down.

I stormed from the room and went back into my inner office. I closed my eyes and sat still for a few moments.

I turned on my computer and opened a file. It was my first attempt to write the *Mystery of the Marie* myself. Throughout the document, I added a selection of phrases: "God said … God moved me to … God's glory." Then I hit the print button.

I remembered some Bible study insights that Ken had recently shared with me: husbands interpret a wife's requests as either nagging or seduction. And they preferred seduction. So, I went and put on a short skirt, high heels, fluffed my hair, and slicked my lips. Then, I went to meet my other half.

Ken was still watching the game.

At the next commercial, I snuggled close, pouted, and handed him the printed pages. "See, God is throughout this project," I said. As he turned toward me, he smiled. The look in his eyes said that he would give me whatever was within reason to succeed.

It was a turning point.

I understood better how to approach Ken, and he saw how God was all over the approaching event.

BUILDING MOMENTUM

The next step was to create interest in the upcoming *Marie* anniversary, was going to require the best of my talents. As part of my project-management work, I had facilitated similar activities across the nation, and I was a trained graphic designer. Thus, events and event planning weren't unknown to me. Although the *Marie* event was unique and only a few months away, I knew what I needed to do. The initial step was to nail down my objectives. First, I needed to motivate people to gather together and to be willing to pay a fee to do so. I needed a logo to distinguish the *Marie* anniversary communications. At first, I tried the image of a compass and a ship's wheel, but I kept returning to the collage I created for the Prodigal Son Art Festival. That single image told the story of the *Marie*.

My art piece would be the event's logo.

Immediately, I began placing my new logo on all *Marie* event communications – website, cards, letterhead, invitations, and newsletters.

By February 2010 I sent out a *Save the Date* newsletter and postcard to a network of interested people, personal friends, and family.

Although I had a general framework in mind, there was much to do before I could begin announcing an event for June 4-6, 2010 weekend, let alone opening registration.

Paramount was my objective to connect with four key families: Beardsley, Lovette, McCaffrey, and Russell. Friends and family had been influential in helping me locate the Howell and Mackie families, and I hoped to find similar help in finding the others. Meanwhile, I began casting a wide net to locate the families by researching online.

I reviewed Dr. Beardsley's obituary, but it offered little insight into where to find his family. His wife, Nell Beardsley, was said to have survived him; however, I had no luck searching on her name. Perhaps Nell was a nickname.

I found a list of publications online, dating as far back as 1915, but these appeared to be targeted at math and physics teachers and were of little interest to me. In fact, I found them confusing. I found other publications of his published prior to 1946. "These are so outdated," I said to myself. The topics were technical in nature. Did Beardsley solve a problem? Or was it that he proved a hypothesis incorrect? I was baffled, and flippantly deemed them irrelevant.

I searched online ancestry records but, again, found little useful information and no trace of where to find his family. I found census records from 1900, 1930 and records from his military service in WW-I, but nothing related to his service in WW-II, military or civilian.

As I searched, I remembered the name Dr. Maxwell Krasno. The court case transcripts reported that Dr. Krasno had brought Dr. Beardsley in as a consultant. The retired Raytheon engineers had also mentioned Dr. Krasno.

I googled Maxwell Krasno and instantly got some hits. I found links to patents for a signaling device and system but, believing Krasno's patents were of little importance, I moved on. I found one file, titled *Some Early Lead Salt Detector Developments.* [116] I recalled Bob Wilke's words, "We thought we could detect the side of the submarine."

Anticipating a treasure trove, I opened the file. One phrase jumped out at me. "The contract monitor, Niel F, Beardsley, (Krasno 1961)." [117] Nothing more in the body of the document mentioned Beardsley or Krasno, but the bibliography contained an intriguing reference: *In Memoriam, Dr. Niel F. Beardsley, Proc IRIS, 6, (1961).*

Now I just had to find a publication or periodical known as *Proc IRIS.*

CURATING AN EXHIBIT

I believed that others were far more suited to curating an exhibit, but unless someone else stepped up, the task would be mine. There was so much I didn't know, and I felt terribly insecure. I had no idea where to start, but there was a lady in Arkansas who did. She had recently curated one of the Santa Barbara Maritime Museum's newest exhibits, and it seemed more than coincidental that she was placed in my path.

"Jennifer works at the Clinton Presidential Library as one of its curators," Mr. Gorga had said in passing when he heard I lived outside Little Rock, Arkansas.

I took a chance one afternoon and stopped by The Clinton Library. "I'm looking for one of your curators. Her first name is Jennifer and her last name starts with a W and ends in ski," I told the receptionist.

"No one works here by such a name," he told me. "I'm less familiar with the folks in the National Archives," he said as he handed me a card. "Try contacting them."

After I returned home, I sent out a simple e-mail to the address the receptionist gave me. Within the week, I was meeting Jennifer Wisnewski over dinner. Jennifer was an attractive young woman with crystal blue eyes and long blond hair, but it was her gentle spirit that was most attractive. The Clinton Library used her expertise with each rotating exhibition.

I explained to her what had taken me to the Santa Barbara Maritime Museum and my hopes for June 2010. I told her that I had hoped to have corporate funding for the *Marie* event, but that it had fallen through. I asked her if she would consider a free meal, coffee, and friendship in return for any creativity and professional expertise she could share. She agreed.

Now someone with the skills to develop an exhibit had joined the team.

One evening Jennifer came over to our house for dinner. After the meal, I cleared the table and then set a huge box filled with photos, artifacts, and resources in front of her. "How do you create an exhibit from materials such as this?" I asked.

She rummaged through it for a few minutes, and then raised her head and smiled. "All you have to do is tell a story."

CHAPTER 40:

Infrared Information Symposium

Jennifer was a key element in pulling an exhibit together. However, I still needed to track down the other four families. Locating Dr. Beardsley's family was proving a difficult, but intriguing, process.

Skimming the preface and introduction to *Some Early Lead Salt Detector Developments*, I noticed that this 55-page report was produced by the Air Force and created by the University of Michigan to show the historical development of detectors, specifically pre-crystal detectors.

I jumped ahead into the body of the report, and skimmed the section that referenced Dr. Beardsley as a contract monitor for a Syracuse University contract. Did that mean he worked for Syracuse University? Continuing to the Bibliography, I read again the reference: *In Memoriam Dr. Niel F. Beardsley, Proc IRIS, 6, 1961*.

What was *Proc IRIS*? I assumed it was a publication where I would find a remembrance of Dr. Niel F. Beardsley. But despite an Internet search on the meaning of the acronym, I found no publication with that name—not from 1961 or any other year.

I closed my eyes and turned my thoughts to God. After a few minutes, I decided to go upstairs for a cup of coffee. In the process, a new idea flowed into my mind.

One option was to contact the university referenced in the

detector development report. Perhaps a reference librarian could point me in the right direction. Returning to my keyboard, I located the report. Michigan University had written the report but, the section mentioning Beardsley was entitled *The Syracuse Effect* and described research at Syracuse University under **Henry Levinstein**. I called Syracuse University information and asked for the library. "May I have the reference librarian, please?"

My call was sent from the switchboard to a librarian who, in turn, forwarded me to the Science and Technology Library.

The reference librarian came on the line. "This is Mr. Keays."

"Hello, Mr. Keays," I said. "I'm looking for a resource and I believe it's in your holdings." I gave him the details.

"Can you e-mail me your request?" he asked.

I did as he asked, and Mr. Keays responded within an hour.

"I'm not finding many libraries that own Proceedings of IRIS. Syracuse does not. ... the USAF Academy seems to have one volume of this.... I can't determine whether Lockheed Martin has it or not."[118]

Within minutes, I was online, looking for contact information for the Air Force Academy Library in Colorado. No luck. Then, I looked for a Lockheed Library. Another strike.

I re-read the document *Some Early Lead Salt Detector Developments*, this time I read each word of the section entitled *The Syracuse Effort*. I needed another clue, a hint of where to find a copy of *In Memoriam*:

> The interest of the military in developing improved infrared sensitive detectors has been described. Paul Ovrebo, as has been noted, had been in charge of tests of the Kiel IV at *Wright Field*, Ohio. He, naturally, felt the need for improved detectors, and did his best to encourage groups to undertake research toward that objective.
>
> After surveying the field of infrared detectors - development, Levinstein concluded that PbS cell development was in good hands, And PbSe and PbTe offered the more promising new paths.

The latter seemed better suited for experimental investigations. *Support for this work, it must be noted, came from the military with a desire to create improved infrared detectors. The contract monitor, Niel F, Beardsley, (Krasno 1961) worked in close liaison with Levinstein to assure that that goal would be met* [emphasis added].[119]

However, the Syracuse effort was directed toward understanding the mechanisms of photoconductivity, and thereby aimed to improved cell production.

Dr. Beardsley's authority as a contract monitor apparently came via Syracuse University or the military at Wright Field, Ohio. I had tried Syracuse University, but not the military.

A quick search revealed that Wright Field was an airfield located in Ohio. It was part of the U.S. Army and U.S. Army Air Corps research center during WWI and WWII. With the creation of the U.S. Air Force in 1947, the base transitioned to what is now Wright-Patterson Air Force Base. It is also home to the National Museum of the United States Air Force and the Air Force Institute of Technology. I found an Air Force Institute library phone number. "I have a resource I'm looking for. Who can assist me?" I asked. They gave me an e-mail, and I zipped out a request. In no time at all, I got a call from one of the Air Force Institute of Technology research librarians.

"I can access the document, but it's classified, and we don't have the means to declassify for the public," the librarian informed me kindly.

"Would it help if I have a dependent's military ID or that my husband is recently retired military and has a security clearance?" I asked.

"Sorry, but we don't have the means to process and declassify it," the librarian repeated.

I took a long deep breath. *What do I do now?*

The librarian gave me the next step.

"It may serve you to try the Navy because they sponsored the publication. And if that doesn't work then try the University of Michigan because they are the producers.

"Since you seem to know a lot, can you tell me what Proc IRIS stands for?"

"You are looking for the sixth Proceedings (Proc) of the Infrared Information Symposium (IRIS)."

I decided to approach Mr. Hodges, one of the archivists at the Navy Yard. He had helped me before and I hoped he would be able to once again. Unfortunately, even he turned out to be a dead end.

"If you haven't already, try contacting the Ruth H. Hooker Research Library at the Naval Research Laboratory (NRL)," he wrote, explaining that this office is the gatekeeper for the documents belonging to the Office of Naval Research (ONR).

While I had Mr. Hodges attention about the IRIS proceedings, I decided to ask him about something I had previously failed to mention, the tropical storm alerts during the *Marie* SAR. He found a resource, a booklet with a powerful cover image.

"It's a pearl!" I exclaimed. Mr. Hodges had originally compared the process of diving into his archives as a search for pearls of information.

The booklet from the Navy Yard archives was emblazoned with an image of a lightning bolt piercing a thunder cloud, below were the snow-capped words STORM Project: Fleet Marine Force Pacific.[120]

This booklet contained references that were strikingly similar to those I found in the Command History from the Western Sea Frontier (WSF).

The STORM Project pages defined a purpose, "...to support emergency operational deployment... involving actual or potential enemy opposition under conditions short of general war...". Returning to focus on the WSF document, I read of the THIRD MAW being out loaded under either the STORM concept or under conditions of general war. With some Internet research, I understood who was sent out as being the services finest. The Third Marine Aircraft Wing (3rd MAW) - The top guns from Mirmar Naval Air Station, the Marines at El Torro.

FIG 32: Storm Project booklet cover. Reproduced from the holdings of the Navy Yard, Washington D.C.

Recently I had read of a situation where in 1966 there was a mid-air collision and nuclear weapons were lost in the waters off Palomares, Spain. Marines were sent in to surround the assets until an appropriate recovery team could be assembled. Apparently, there were some who believe the law of the sea to be 'finders keepers' and thus the treasures of a nation and its allies were protected from piracy, ignorance, or enemies.[121]

Returning to the Coast Guard Station log alerts, given what I think I know, I believed that a storm of Marines went out on Thursday, June 9, 1960 at 4:15AM. With that, the gap between the vessel's expected return and first sign of actions taken decreased on the timeline by hours.

The pearl was a key.

The booklet was tantalizing, but I forced myself to set it aside. If I continued following new trails and expanding my circle of research, I would never bring things together for the fast-approaching anniversary.

"I have to put further research on ice," I told myself as I reluctantly set aside the "lightning bolt" booklet along with a long list of other unresolved questions and actions.

If the anniversary activities didn't come together, I would have nothing. I would have failed everything.

Besides, I was on an important hot trail that would directly serve the June event. I had to find Dr. Krasno's *In Memoriam*, a document that was, for some reason, tucked away in the classified publication, *Proc IRIS.*

I called the NRL's Ruth H. Hooker Research Library.

"I'll transfer you to classified holdings," the receptionist said.

When the librarian came on the line I summarized my mission and asked if she could help me get the *Proc IRIS* declassified.

"It's a six-year process," she informed me.

"Okay. Where do I begin?" I was in this for the long haul. If it took six years, so be it.

"Send an e-mail with your request, telling why you want the requested information and how you intend to use and distribute it once you have it."

I was disappointed, but prepared for whatever it took. By day's end I sent off an e-mail with the requested details, and explained that I needed the document for an upcoming gathering to honor Dr. Beardsley and his six companions lost in a shipwreck.

I checked my e-mail the next day and found a message from the NRL's Research Reports Library. I downloaded the attachment: *In Memoriam: Dr. Niel F. Beardsley* by Dr. Maxwell Krasno.[122]

I turned my gaze upward and breathed a prayer. "Thank, you." I believed that a divine hand moving on hearts and minds orchestrated the result.

As I read the *Memoriam's* three pages, I had no idea where its details would lead me.

CHAPTER 41:

Remembrance Before Honor

As the days passed, I was like a juggler, managing multiple tasks such as finding families, planning an event, creating an exhibit, and funding the effort. I was concerned that I would drop a ball, and I was becoming more stressed every day.

For some time, a small voice in my head had told me that I needed to connect with my pastor, Bill Parkinson. I believed the time had arrived, so I set up an appointment. Over the course of the next month, he had to re-schedule twice.

I knew that I needed to seek out the Parkinsons' prayers and wisdom, so I persisted. Persistence paid off, and soon I was sitting face to face with Pastor Parkinson, discussing my needs, desires, and confusions. His counsel was invaluable.

"In the funerals and memorials that I've been a part of," he said, "you help people remember so they can honor the memory."

I wrote down, "Remembrance comes before honor." I also jotted down his comment that no one's life can be captured in its entirety. The core good of that person's life must serve as a pivotal point. Pastor Parkinson's wisdom was based on experience, and it comforted me. He understood that I wrestled with the desire to close the gap between the known and unknown in the shipwreck mystery. He closed our time together by praying for God's purpose to be revealed, and for it to serve His will. Tears moistened my eyes because someone sat alongside me praying for the work I was drawn to undertake.

As he prayed, I saw in my mind's eye: *Marie Commemoration Event — To Remember, Honor, Rejoice.*

I was encouraged and strengthened because of our time together. I also had a valuable new resource. "You may want to consider talking with Lee Burrell of Light Productions," Pastor Parkinson told me. I realized that I might not be able to afford Light Production's services. However, I knew that an initial consultation is usually free, so I had nothing to lose by calling them.

"Lee Burrell," the voice on the other end said.

"Hello, I am Teresa Newton-Terres. Pastor Parkinson at Fellowship Bible Church recommended that I give you a call." I told Lee why my pastor recommended that I touch base with Light Productions.

"What are you doing for lunch?" Lee Burrell asked. By noon we were sitting across from each other.

My story, which included engineers testing infrared communication technology under water, appeared to intrigue Lee, and I quickly learned why. Lee Burrell had a master's in electrical engineering. His thesis focused on the guidance system of an intercontinental ballistic missiles (ICBM), specifically the point when the guidance system switches from SONAR to Infrared.

"I left the Electrical Engineering field to support Campus Crusade and Family Life Ministries," Lee said of the career path that lead him to start Light Production, a full-service film and video production company.[123]

Lee offered to help create a cost-effective solution that would, in his words, "Get you through the commemoration."

It was a deal made in heaven.

Would the film be of a quality that the Santa Barbara Maritime Museum would approve? I didn't know the answer, but I trusted this opportunity and decided to take the next steps forward and let the chips fall where they may.

CONNIE MCCAFFREY

I had dragged my feet making the connection with the McCaffreys, telling myself it was because I wanted to know the full *Marie* story before I contacted them. The McCaffrey family tugged at my heart for several reasons. Just like my father, their father's body was lost at sea and never recovered. In addition, James McCaffrey's widow had the added burden of being seven months pregnant, with a store to manage, and a court case to defend.

I almost didn't want to burden the McCaffrey family by bringing the shipwreck back into their lives. But a commemoration of the *Marie* wouldn't be complete without them.

Swallowing my insecurity and pride, I called the number that was on the business card Bud Bottoms had given me. "I'm looking for a McCaffrey family member," I asked as a pleasant voice answered.

"This is Patrick McCaffrey."

I introduced myself and the purpose of my call. "I'll send you more information so that you can share it with your family."   I verified his e-mail and street address, and then I followed up the call with an e-mail and a letter. I included a newsletter and a Save-the-Date card.

It was a beginning. I was now connected with the McCaffrey family. Patrick had given me his mother, Constance's, phone number, so my next step was to call her. I wasn't sure how she would react, but I knew she was expecting my call.

"Good morning, Mrs. McCaffrey," I began. "This is Teresa Terres daughter of Jim Terres."

"Dear child, call me Connie," she said.

I had been fearful, but she welcomed me with open arms. In our brief conversation, it was clear that she was warm-hearted, loved God—and was in failing health.

Connie's brief chuckle was infectious as she recalled how Dawn Howell stopped by for a cup of coffee a few weeks after the shipwreck. "Before she left, Dawn said, 'Oh, by the way, I'm suing you.'"

Connie chuckled again, telling me that she understood the need of these young mothers to take care of their families. What I would most remember of my brief conversation with Connie had nothing to do with the *Marie*. It was the way she said, "I know there is a God because who else could create the beauty in a sunrise or sunset."

After a brief introduction, I said good bye. If I had known that would be the only opportunity I would have to talk to her, I may have tried to speak with her longer. But at that time, I didn't want to push her. Her family had said she was growing frail, and I didn't want to tire her out.

As I hung up the phone, I had such a desire to sit by the side of this gracious woman. I had been wrestling with the idea to go to California to tie up loose ends before the commemoration event activities. This conversation fueled my resolve.

THE RUSSELLS

"Have you connected with the Russell family yet?"

The e-mail from Peter Edwards, my brother Jim's friend from the Santa Barbara City College's Marine Technology program, intrigued me. Why was he asking about the Russell family?

Years ago, Peter had taken my brother Don and me on an open water scuba diving adventure, which I now realized was in the waters off Santa Cruz Island. It was my first and only dive in the Santa Barbara Channel.

Peter had checked out my MarieEvent.com website and had some interesting news.

Referring to the people listed on the website, Peter said, "My father and mother-in-law knew these people. I have a cousin Jeannie Russell whose mother married an uncle of mine. Helen Edwards was my uncle's second wife. Jeannie, moved to Colorado, I think Aspen, she was a friend, I think of John Denver and hung with that crowd."[124]

I knew that Mrs. Russell had remarried a man with the last name Edwards by the end of the court case, but I never imagined that she was now part of the Edwards family my brother Jim ran around with. Peter's brother, the actor Anthony Edwards, appeared in the movie *Top*

Gun and TV's *ER*.

I wasn't going to let an hour go by without trying to connect with Mrs. Russell. I went online and searched for information on the Edwards family. In the Colorado phone listings, I found a number for a Helen Edwards. Gathering my thoughts, I picked up the phone and dialed. She picked up on the third ring.

"Hello?"

"I'm looking for a Helen Edwards who was formerly Mrs. Russell."

"Speaking."

"I'm Teresa Newton-Terres, the daughter of Jim Terres who worked for your husband Jim Russell and was lost at sea."

"Well, how are you," Helen said without a beat.

"I have looked all over California for you and your daughter, and I recently got a lead that you were in Colorado." I kept the conversation brief because I didn't want to overwhelm Helen or her daughter, Jeannie.

Since Helen didn't use the Internet, I confirmed her mailing address. "I'll send you some information that you can share with Jeannie." I said.

I sent her a letter with a copy of the newsletter and a Save-the-Date card. I had limited time to build a relationship, invite them to the commemoration, and capture the core of their family story. I preferred to knit our hearts and minds together in a comfortable, face-to-face setting, but it was impossible for me to get to Colorado before the commemoration. Within days, Helen's daughter, Jeannie Russell, and I were exchanging e-mails and we quickly set a date for a phone call.

Starting our conversation was easy, but winding it up proved difficult because we reveled in the connection between two hearts impacted by the same tragedy.

"What are your memories of your father?" I asked.

"There is a wonderful picture that I cherish and love which is of me and him holding a fish and abalone. And I'm sure we had gone out fishing," she said. "There are only three pictures of me and him. I still fish and I'm a mountain gal. And I'm very much into the hunting and fishing idea of outdoorsmanship."

Jeannie shared with me how she felt her father wanted a boy because he was so preoccupied with hunting and fishing and she, being a girl, couldn't go. "I also remember a time when we went out on a small boat—my mom and dad and me—and he went scuba diving. And I was afraid of him going underwater, that he wouldn't come back. My mom reassured me that he would come back, and indeed he did."

"Do you have any theories of what happened?" I asked.

"No, not now," Jeannie began. "When I was in my twenties, I came back to Santa Barbara after being away for a couple years. Apparently, there was an engine found on one side of Santa Cruz Island. A friend told me about it and how they thought it could be the engine of the *Marie*. I had no idea. I thought it was an accident. That was the first I had heard anything about espionage or a secret mission or anything like that. Because of that, it gave me…" She paused briefly. "Oh my, he may have died for a purpose?"[125]

Jeannie went on to tell me about her tour on the Condor Express in Santa Barbara. It was the same boat I had been on and had scheduled for a sunrise wreath laying ceremony at the commemoration.

"I'm not sure how I'll get to the commemoration, but I will be there. And I will do whatever I can to get my mother there too," Jeannie promised.

I appreciated Jeannie's enthusiasm for the event and her offer to help. My gut told me, that given her mother's age, she would have her arms full just getting her mother there. So, I encouraged her to work toward attending the commemoration and bringing her mother because it would make a difference. Before our conversation ended, I asked, "Do you think your mother would be open to a phone call interview so that I could record her story?"

"She tells me so little," Jeannie said. "I'd be interested in learning what she would say to you."

I hoped for future opportunities to dialogue with Jeannie. We had laughed and cried over childhood experiences that resulted in some adult messes. But for the moment we were pleased to be on a life journey that had led us both to find strength and comfort in God.

With a green light from Jeannie, I sent another letter to Helen suggesting the idea of being interviewed and recorded over the phone. In the envelope, I also included a list of the questions I would ask and a copy of the Smithsonian booklet. Then, after a few days' time, I gave Helen a call to assess her feelings and, if she was agreeable, set up an interview date.

When I called. Helen said yes. We planned to talk five days later.

CHAPTER 42:

Interview By Phone

I began the interview slowly, with a few warm-up questions before progressing to the more targeted questions. I asked Helen to imagine we were both seated in a comfortable spot enjoying a cup of tea. I had, in fact, brewed a cup of tea for myself.

"Where did you meet Jim Russell?"

Helen told me about attending grade school with Jim, dating in high school, and marrying in college.

"Today, what are your thoughts about Jim?" I asked.

"He was ambitious, and a hard worker for what he wanted," Helen said. "While Jim was in college, which was of the same time I was, he lived in a boarding house. And he worked in their kitchen and served and did dishes for his room and board. But in all four years that we were in college, he ate peanut butter sandwiches and a quart of milk every day, because that is what he could afford."

"If he graduated with an Engineering Degree, what did you graduate with?"

"Social Welfare and Social Psychology."

"What are the first memories that come to mind about your marriage that you can share?"

"Well, what came into my mind, and I don't know why, was that he liked to fish. I have a picture of Jim and Jeannie, holding a fish up from a fishing trip. And she seemed to like fishing ever since that.

"Jeannie just sent me a copy," I said. "It's precious. Jeannie in her bathing suit and Jim, with a big fish, and three abalone at their feet."

"I don't even have that picture. That's another thing. We had so much abalone, we would have parties with six, eight, twelve people, we had so much abalone from what these guys would get."

"Jim was the project manager for Dr. Beardsley and this project. And a section leader for infrared. Did you have any added responsibilities beyond those of a regular spouse?"

"No. I had no added responsibilities. And if the project was top secret, I never knew anything about it. We didn't discuss it. He was discrete. I don't know how other wives and husbands handled those things, but we didn't discuss them."

"Do you remember any previous trips on the *Marie*?"

"No."

"My mother believed there were several others, but all I can verify as Raytheon-related is one on May 31st," I said.

"It may be entirely possible," said Helen. "But I just don't remember it."

"What can you remember about the last time? When did you expect them home?"

"I think that night," she said. "But then I was being optimistic. I had no idea that they had no radio communication. I thought that if they had any problems, they would let us know. I wasn't terribly concerned until the next morning."

"And the next morning? What do you remember?"

Helen thought for a moment. "I remember talking with George Edgar. He was probably the first to call. He was very close to Jim."

"What do you remember him saying?"

"Well, just that they were concerned and that they were overdue. And that no one had heard from them."

"When did you go down to the dock? Or did you wait?"

"I did go down to the dock. It seems like it was in the afternoon, before the Coast Guard went out. We went down there and there were a group of us waiting at the CG Office for news. I remember sitting there and some man who answered their radio said, 'Does the name Lovette mean anything to you?' Well, I had never heard of a Mr. Lovette on this little venture. So, I said, 'No.' I guess no one else did, either. It wasn't until later that we learned that he had even been on the boat.

"Shortly after that they said that they were going to stop for the night, and that they would be coming and needed the office, so we would have to go home."

"So, you were down there at that time?" I asked. "We have a news article with a photo of Mom knitting and Mrs. Mackie and Mrs. Edgar, but I wasn't aware that you were there too. Jim wasn't found until the 21st. He was the last one recovered. It was around Father's Day. Do you remember Father's Day that year?"

"Heaven's, no. I was down in Pasadena back at the house. The sheriffs came to tell me that they found Jim."

"Had you met Dr. Beardsley before?"

"Not that I remember."

"Do you have any theories about what happened?"

"I think the speculation at the time was that some of the diesel equipment just exploded and tore the boat apart. That makes as much sense to me as anything else. There was so much speculation. There were those that believed sabotage was involved but, I didn't believe that at all. It is a miracle that any of them were found, when you think of the vagaries of the currents."

"What else would you like to address?"

"I'd like to know who you have talked with."

"I've spoken with all the families but the Beardsleys and Lovettes."

"Is Connie McCaffrey still alive?"

"Yes. She is challenged by cancer, but her voice is strong and her spirits high."

"I feel real frustrated that no one knows anything about Lovette. There must be somebody out there that knows something about this man."

"I agree." I told her some of the insights I had gained into Lovette.

"I have absolutely no knowledge of him. Wouldn't the owner of the *Marie*, Richard Dowse, know? Have you contacted him?"

"Richard Dowse? Would you agree to having him involved?"

"I frankly would. I'm sure that it touched him very deeply. I don't feel any blame there. These kinds of things happen, and he was very much affected by it all. Wouldn't it be interesting if we know more about it?"

"Do I understand that you may be coming to the upcoming June commemoration?"

"Well, of course Jeannie is. I have some misgivings about it. I really don't want to dredge up all the old feelings.

"I know it must be difficult for you because of your memories and what you had to live through. I'm not going to push you, but I'm working hard to make it a memorable event for you."

"You certainly are and I appreciate that," she said. "It will be most memorable for the children."

"The details coming together are one thing, but it's the people that will make the difference."

"I don't see how you have found all of these people. I want to make one comment before I forget about it. Jeannie said that you thought it strange that there wasn't a memorial service for all these men. Well, we didn't do that in those days. People had their individual religious services, and that was it. That simply wasn't a part of our lives at that time."

"So, you didn't feel like you were deprived of a group gathering?"

"Heaven's, no. I'm kind of a solitary person anyway, so that wouldn't have occurred to me. We had a funeral and a nice service. And then when the body was found, we had a burial service. And the immediate friends gathered around afterwards for food and what not. That's how death was handled in those days."

"I'm glad to hear that you felt the appropriate closure." I mentioned how my family never had a memorial or a funeral because Dad was one of the three never found.

"So, you would always feel a little empty," she said.

"Right. We were so young, and we were never told that our dad was gone. He just never came home."

"You were two?"

"Yes. My brothers were one, four, and seven years old."

"You see, it was just another time. Another era. I don't think we shared that kind of thing with our children. We protected our children rather than bringing them into such a thing. And maybe that it was ignorant thing to do as far as their sensibilities, but that is how it was."

****

After the call, I began to think about some of Helen's comments. "We didn't do that back then." Her words lingered on my mind.

That statement echoed as I considered the gatherings and ceremonies that I had experienced with Ken and the military, including Memorial Day, Veterans Day, and Pearl Harbor. I considered my faith and my profession which also recognized traditions and milestones. Good habits, I understood, marked changing times at home and in work in such a way to help promote wisdom and prevent foolishness. Like a North Star, a Polaris, thousands of years and historical events flooded my mind with their myths and memories that I looked to as a light to guide my heart and mind.

Helen Russell's words were intended to be comforting and reassuring.

I considered the hundreds of pictures, the songs sung, and the film that I had of my father. I looked toward Grandmother's scrapbook where I knew there was a Raytheon Company newsletter with words suggesting a great loss.

Those that love well find a way, to forgive as forgiven, and to live well.

Had the *Marie* been just another ship with a hodgepodge of people lost at sea, then a group gathering might not have been appropriate. But these men were lost in the service of their country.

CHAPTER 43:

Before and After

What was churning in Dad's mind?

My *Marie* timeline expanded as I considered this question and the day prior to the fateful sunrise departure. I had disregarded including on my timeline the day prior to the *Marie's* harbor departure thinking of little importance. As I circled back to review the transcripts of news articles, I realized that I needed to include the day prior, Monday, June 6, 1960, to the fateful mission Tuesday, June 7, 1960.

I reviewed the news that told of Dad's activities. Raytheon officials reported, "… Diego S. (Jim) Terres, flew a Santa Barbara Flying Club plane out over the island the day before the expedition in order to check on weather and water conditions….Terres filed a flight plan with the Federal Aviation Agency showing his flight over the island on the day before the Marie's trip."[126] I heard a brief mention that Dad knew how to fly in the process of gathering oral histories for the Old Town Goleta Cultural History Project. And I was pleased to confirm his capability with this news report.

Dad made a reconnaissance flight.

I speculated that Dad's reconnaissance flight may have included a buzz above the *Marie*. There was another article. It reported that Bryant, Howell and Lovette, "took the *Marie* out on Monday." The article continued, "Bryant told officers that Lovette had to have Russell's permission to go along on the trip. Lovette was not a skin-diver…" and, "They put 100 gallons of diesel fuel into the tanks when they returned so the *Marie* would be ready for the following day, Bryant said." The news also reported, that Bryant was "…a university student and skin-diver that had been scheduled to work for Raytheon on the trip but had been unable to go."

The court case discoveries and testimonies reveal that, later Monday evening, Lovette connected with Mr. Dowse and then Mr. Russell to gain approval to join the *Marie* the next day.

The following day was a sunrise departure on the *Marie* with the men who never returned alive.

By Thursday evening, bright lights were reported out at sea.

I read the details in the news reports and those in the original source documents. And the differences intrigued me. For example, what were the mysterious "flares" that people reported?

The Coast Guard Station log, noted receiving "five" calls from civilians reporting "flares out at sea." Investigating by landline, the CGD11 RCC informed them that a Coast Guard helicopter had been dropping flares in search of a man fallen overboard.[127] Then, in the Santa Barbara newspaper reports I read, "Two planes continued circling overhead through the night, dropping brilliant phosphorus flares to light up the scene. And scores of motorists along Pacific Coast Highway called police and sheriff's stations in alarm over the bright lights."[128]

According to another report, "The search, begun about noon yesterday, continued through the evening by the light of flares dropped by search aircraft while most of the wives of the missing men gathered in the local Coast Guard office."[129] This reinforced my understanding that one record told only the facts (five civilians, CG Helicopter) while the other sought to tell an interesting story (scores of motorists).

I wanted to build a fact-based timeline, but it wasn't as easy as I wished.

There was Dad's blue sweatshirt that surfaced. The blue sweatshirt is reported in the newspaper but it wasn't listed on an official record. And the meaning behind it is held only within our family. But, at the least, I can understand that the blue sweatshirt suggests Dad wanted to communicate something to someone.

The newspaper reported, "Adding another bit of mystery to the case, Vic Tanny (gym) officials in Santa Barbara said that Lovette and Howell had been carrying a "considerable amount of money" from collections for the company."[130] But, when I found no other collaboration or mention of this detail, I disregarded.

I also learned that Howell and Lovette's apartment was broken into the week after the shipwrecked *Marie*. This detail I have yet to confirm with fact based records, but it isn't a surprise given the news reports revealed places of residence. Thus, residences were vulnerable. And given the nature of the testing conducted on the *Marie*, I can only speculate as to what all may have been gained or removed.

CHAPTER 44:

Paul Timothy Lovette

I gazed out the window, not noticing the early signs of spring beginning to show on the ground. I continued to review my conversation with the former Mrs. Russell.

"I feel real frustrated that no one knows anything about Lovette," she had said. "I just feel that there must be somebody out there that knows something about this man."

I had already searched for Paul Timothy Lovette and had found almost nothing. On my way to Washington D.C. some months earlier, I took a side trip as I headed out of Tennessee and into North Carolina. Although I had no address, no name, and no pictures, I did have two cities: Salisbury and Canton. Salisbury was apparently where Paul Lovette grew up; Canton was where he was buried. Since Canton, a town of only 4,000, was on the western edge of North Carolina, I took a chance that I might be able to find Western Chapel Methodist Cemetery.

"How hard can a cemetery be to find in a small town?" I said.

On a hunch, I took the exit before the road to Canton, hoping it might lead to the cemetery. Instead, I found myself driving along a tree-lined hilltop. Fall colors were blazing. I found a scenic overlook, where I turned off and stopped. From the car, peering across the tree tops, I was mesmerized by the splash of colors reflecting on the dancing leaves in the light. I didn't realize it at the time, but I was in the Black Hills of North Carolina.

Where the mountains kiss the sky was Canton's motto. I believed it was true.

I found Canton before dark and drove its length several times. I found no cemetery or Methodist church. The streets were deserted, and no stores or restaurants were open. I headed forward along another country road that my map showed would eventually lead to a major road and return me to the interstate and lodging.

By nightfall, I realized I had to consider Paul Lovette "my bridge too far." If I continued to do research on him, I might jeopardize the entire commemoration.

Was it worth continuing my search for him? Maybe; maybe not. It would certainly be nice to know what he was doing on the *Marie*, since he was a last-minute addition, and neither a diver nor an engineer. And if the *Marie's* mission was top-secret, why was he even allowed on board? I wanted answers to these questions, but so far had none.

I remembered what Mom and Grandmother taught me about how to make soup when food was scarce. You don't worry about what you don't have, and stretch what you do have.

I had a news photo of Lovette's shark-eaten body wrapped in a cloth and being transported by Coast Guardsmen from the *Cape Sable* to the Santa Barbara Pier. I had a few words about Lovette that I had compiled from newspaper and court case discoveries. I had a place holder oval as part of the commemoration art-piece, waiting for an image of Lovette to fill it. And I knew where his final resting place was, where the mountains kiss the sky.

I decided to leave it there and I prayed that, if it was meant to be, the Lovette family would find me.

CHAPTER 45:

An Insider's View of the Coast Guard

Ken saw my frustration level escalating because of all the details still to be managed and knew I needed to be on site to handle them. "You need to make a final trip to California," he said. Within two weeks I found myself on the West Coast, ready to tie up loose ends preparing for the fast-approaching event.

First stop: Sutter Fox's home.

After I arrived at Sutter and Bonnie Fox's, we shared conversation and a cool drink, before Sutter and I departed for an appointment with the Coast Guard.

"Your script is in draft form," I told Sutter, who had agreed to be the master of ceremonies for the commemoration event's evening ceremony. I also confessed my struggle. "How to recount the chain of events haunts me." I told him that beyond the public story a covert story was casting a shadow on the shipwreck's timeline.

"You can't go wrong by telling what you know," Sutter said.

I took that to mean that I should focus on what was known and leave the speculations for the future, when I had more knowledge and clarity. His advice rang true.

Sutter and I departed, heading for the Coast Guard's Command Center Sector Los Angeles and Long Beach. Although the building and technology were different, it was the same command center that coordinated the SAR for the *Marie* in 1960.

When we arrived, Petty Officer Schofield, Public Affairs Officer (PAO), informed us, "There's an active SAR, so we will need to wait before we are allowed to enter the space."

I used the time to inform Petty Officer Schofield of my purpose and intent for the day. "I need to come away with footage for a documentary I'm producing," I said.

As we waited, I set up my camera and microphones, and arranged several items in the office to show them in the best light. Then I handed Sutter and Petty Officer Schofield a reproduction of the *Marie*'s SAR map and began filming. On cue, they claimed the spotlight as Sutter used the map as a prop to explain the Coast Guard's 1960 activities in the Santa Barbara Channel to Schofield.

After he finished, I gathered up my equipment and we headed to the Command Center.

The windowless room and dimmed lights made the space feel like a library. High-definition monitors encircled the room, and a large image was projected on one wall. There was a hush in the room as a couple of Coasties moved in and out of a side room.

I wondered if they were being quiet for my benefit.

The PAO introduced us to Lieutenant JG (LTJG) Dwoskin and Operations Specialist (OS2) Hall. "They can explain anything to you," Schofield nodded toward the Coast Guardsman and gave me permission to film them as they went about their work. Sutter, dressed in khakis and a dark, suit coat, continued to explain search and rescue procedures and brought in the Coasties as it suited our needs. They projected the appropriate chart onto the wall and I filmed Sutter as he discussed the historical *Marie* SAR with LTJG Dwoskin. I filmed OS2 Hall as he worked at one of the stations.

At one point, Sutter and I gathered around what looked like a large butcher-block table in the center of an open space. "This is our chart table," Dwoskin said as he pulled out a large paper chart of the Santa Barbara Channel and Santa Cruz Island. "We are ready in case the technology fails us."

Dwoskin pulled out another chart. "This is most likely a similar chart as used in 1960," he said.

I couldn't tell off hand, but I wondered if it was similar to what I had received recently in an e-mail from Dr. Cloud.

"Show me the location that is 2.5 miles North of the Big Cave, Painted Cave, and 1.5 miles from Santa Cruz's coastal side," I asked. Dwoskin's finger moved from the Painted Cave (aka Big Cave) and along the coastline to an estimated 2.5-mile distance in one direction and then away from the coastline 1.5 miles on the shore side.

An X marked the location near where the *Marie* might have gone down.

"What?" I gasped tipping the camera to one side as my jaw dropped. Before I could get a good look, Dwoskin pulled an eraser from his pocket and eliminated the mark.

"Wait!" I said. But it was too late. The X was gone.

"What did that mark mean?"

Dwoskin shrugged. "Only that someone was looking at the same spot."

The X had marked the approximate coordinates reported by the abalone divers in a 1969 news article in Grandmother's scrapbook. They believed it was the sunken *Marie* in 55 feet of water.

I wanted to linger at the map and consider the site where someone had marked that X. Unfortunately, my time in the command center was limited, and I needed to focus on the task at hand: getting footage for a documentary. I moved on.

While coming away with useful footage was my main objective, the two-year-old in me reveled in the opportunity to experience personally the command center where the Coast Guard coordinated ships, airplanes, and helicopters for the Coast Guard, Navy, Air-Force and 3rd MAW, as they searched for the *Marie* and her men. Originally, I had little interest in the part the Coast Guard played in the *Marie* shipwreck. But over time I had grown to respect their critical position as conductor of the search and rescue operations.

****

Task accomplished, I said farewell to Bonnie and Sutter and headed north to Santa Barbara, where I had a reservation to stay with Uncle Al and Aunt Lynda. My brother Don also planned to be there, and arrived soon after I did.

Don, Albert, Lynda and I drove to the harbor and walked the length of the breakwater to the *Lost at Sea Memorial*. The sky was clear and Santa Cruz Island was visible in the distance.

"What do you think your dad would be like, if he were alive?" Al asked.

I paused and looked Albert straight in the eye. My mind raced. I was blown away by the question. Then laughed, realizing that I had never thought of my dad in such a way. In my mind, Dad was untouched by this world. Now I realized Dad was only a man. No wonder I hadn't known my father. How unfair to his memory, to my brothers, to my husband, not to mention God. I had placed my father on a pedestal where only God belongs.

I smiled as we continued walking to the end of the breakwater as I shared my revelation.

We sat at the *Lost at Sea Memorial's* whales-tail benches, not saying a word. Then, we returned together, shoulder to shoulder, to share dinner before Don returned home to Irvine, CA and I returned to the activities I need to accomplish for the commemoration.

CHAPTER 46:

Cold War Mystery?

While I was in California, I decided to approach the University of California at Santa Barbara (UCSB). I hoped the effort would prove fruitful for both my ongoing research and upcoming event needs.

Perhaps an academic institution would be interested in being a part of living history.

Also, Raytheon had awarded UCSB scholarships on behalf of their four men lost on the *Marie*.

I approached the university hoping that they might have records of the scholarships and recipients. I harbored an unspoken wish that I might someday have the chance to award the Diego S. Terres scholarship. Another hope was that maybe an ambitious student or a scholarship recipient would volunteer to help with the commemoration activities. It would be a nice résumé-building activity. However, all these hopes were secondary. My primary goal was to find someone who could place the technology tests and the shipwreck into a historical context that I could include in the 50-year anniversary media.

Although it had been twenty years since I'd been on staff there, I felt comfortable walking on campus again. I worked as an undergraduate advisor at UCSB for over ten years before meeting Ken, who was at that time a professor of military history and an officer for the ROTC program.

I approached the chancellor's office carrying copies of Santa Barbara News Press articles about the Raytheon scholarships from 1961 and 1965. At the top of the stairway, the entrance was closed, blocking the access to an entire wing. I knocked on the metal door and a woman peeked through the blinds covering the door's small window. She looked me up and down. Opening the door slightly, she said, "Your purpose?"

"I was directed to see the Deputy Chancellor."

"Come in quickly," the woman said. She ushered me inside and closed the door behind me.

Now she smiled. "How can I help you?"

I showed her the news articles I carried and I explained my purpose.

"Please be seated," she said disappearing into one of the offices. A few seconds later she said, "The Deputy Chancellor will see you in just a minute if you care to wait." She pointed to the couch. Then, she returned to her desk.

Within minutes, the Deputy Chancellor greeted me and escorted me into his office. From the top floor, his office had a clear view of one of UCSB's central plazas.

He began by apologizing for any inconvenience I had experienced upon entering the office. "The building was under siege by students earlier today because of a raise in tuition," he said.

I was reminded of the 1970's, when a mob of UCSB students burned down a bank and a Taco Bell in protest of the Vietnam War. Recently, I learned that such protests were often agitated by our enemies.[131]

I handed over the three news articles, and quietly waited for the Deputy Chancellor to review them.

"I'll be right back," he said. Shortly, he returned with a binder and spread it open on his desk. Even with the news articles, he found no reference to the scholarships in his binder. "My assistant is also reviewing our online database," he informed me. Soon, his assistant entered and informed us that the records she accessed didn't include any information about the Raytheon awards.

"Try the College of Engineering," the Deputy Chancellor recommended.

I left his office and headed toward the College of Engineering. I showed the articles to a staff member and a professor. Their records showed nothing, either. "Our records are likely incomplete from that timeframe," they told me.

As I left the College of Engineering, I found myself drawn to a flyer posted by The Cold War Student's Group. It announced a movie they were hosting: *Colossus: The Forbin Project*. The flyer said it was open to anyone who was interested.

I decided to go.

Since the Cold War group was an extension of the History Department, I assumed that one of the three professors that I had recently e-mailed might attend. I had approached these professors on the recommendation of Dr. Cloud.

I took a seat at the back of the auditorium, and soon a graduate student stepped up to the podium and welcomed everyone. He offered a brief description of the Cold War Group and then introduced the group's sponsors. The three professors I had exchanged e-mails with were indeed in attendance.

The host then began a description of the Cold War era in which the film was produced, including a short list of Cold War projects: U2, Corona, Polaris, Guided Missile and Space System. He commented that these projects led to today's super computers, and thus the imaginative scenario posed in the movie we were about to watch.

After the introduction, the auditorium lights were dimmed and the film began. As attendees focused on the movie, my mind wandered to the *Marie* ceremony agenda. The agenda should include a piece placing the shipwreck and its technology into a historical context. I scribbled a reminder on my note pad.

The 1970 movie depicted an artificially-intelligent supercomputer that was discovered to have a sinister agenda of its own.[132]

After the showing, I introduced myself to the three professors and thanked them for the entertaining thriller and blast to the past. As in my e-mails, I tried to describe the infrared technology the Raytheon engineers took underwater.

"I believe it's linked to a SOSUS (Sound Surveillance System) upgrade," I speculated sheepishly.

"SOSUS wasn't in the Pacific," the professor to my side said quickly. Then he added, "Infrared doesn't work under water."

His quick response silenced me. I wondered if he was thinking out loud, and whether he was dismissing what the men on the *Marie* had attempted?

I didn't have the academic credentials of these men or their knowledge of the Cold War. But, if I was to believe the retired Raytheon engineers, infrared worked under water. How well and how far were questions I couldn't address.

I knew that I had conducted a fair amount of research into original sources. And I knew SOSUS was alive and well in the Pacific in 1960. The professors were likeable; however, it was clear the Cold War Group offered little more than a social hub. Nor did it appear to be a suitable place to find someone to produce a written piece that would place the Raytheon-related infrared communicator into a historical context in time for the commemoration.

I felt overwhelmed. The task seemed so simple in my mind. But, it was difficult for me to understand the story of the *Marie* and what they were trying to accomplish. I had approached UCSB's history department hoping someone would step forward to help, but I left the university without a historian.

It was dark when I returned to my car and drove the three miles back to Albert and Lynda's. I said goodnight and found solace in what had become "my room."

As I slept, I dreamt I was in a wheelchair beside a swimming pool. Was it Al and Lynda's pool in the backyard? I swiftly wheeled right up to the pool's side and then over and into its blue water. Sinking with the chair, I pushed and kicked away. As I broke the surface of the water and gasped for breath, my mind was filled with one thought. "You have to get rid of your handicaps."

The next morning, I drove north, two and a half hours, to the Paso Robles area, where I was to meet a few members of the McCaffrey family. I wondered who and what I would face today.

CHAPTER 47:

Influencer & Advocate

I didn't want the McCaffrey family to arrive at the commemoration without having more of a comfort level with me. Also, I needed more insight into their father, for the film and display. I needed a face-to-face to get a feeling for the heartbeat of the family.

With Patrick McCaffrey's help, a meeting was arranged at the McCaffrey's place of business, a nearly three-hour drive north of Santa Barbara. I wouldn't meet their sister, Shawna or their mother Constance until Friday evening of the anniversary activities.

From a magazine article they showed me, I learned that Jim McCaffrey was influential in hunting, fishing, and diving. As a featured writer in a sports magazine, he told of his adventures and was an advocate for preservation of the wild. He was also a respected businessman.

I learned what his mother, Constance, then seven months pregnant, had been facing in providing and caring for what was left of her family.

"Are you still angry?" Pat asked me.

"I must have some lingering grief, because I feel driven to spearhead the commemoration," I said.

I wouldn't truly understand Pat's question until long after the commemoration weekend, when he told me about his experience at the end of the big court case.

****

After I returned to Arkansas I received an e-mail from Jean Sedar, Jim McCaffrey's niece. She wanted to add her memory of Jim McCaffrey to the *Marie* event collection:

Hugh Jim McCaffrey:
A Niece's Memory of Jim McCaffrey and the
Marie

> At six years old, when I was forming my first hero worship beyond my father, I lost my Uncle Jim McCaffrey. Through all the tears, it was difficult to understand the mystery of how the boating accident happened and I was unwilling to accept my uncle being missing permanently.
>
> To me, he was just not found yet, and I imagined the "bird woman of San Nicolas..." watching out over my uncle on a nearby island until he *would* be found. I didn't grasp that the Indian woman, who was inadvertently left there in the previous century, would be long dead.
>
> My mother, Barbara Jean McCaffrey Sedar... allowed me to believe in this emotional safety net until some months had passed, and then even our shared love of magical 'Indian ways,' local lore and hopes for a miracle couldn't uphold the fantasy.

I enjoyed reading her reference to, Juana Maria, so named by the padres who rescued and buried her in 1853. The novel, *Island of the Blue Dolphins*, was inspired by the true story of Juana Maria, stranded eighteen years on San Nicolas Island. The book told of her being found wearing a feather dress—thus, the *bird woman* name. I was reminded of the story when I had interviewed Bud Bottoms. He also told a story of Juana Maria.

"Russian trappers," Bud had said, "were extinguishing the

wildlife on San Nicolas Island." According to Bud, a man went to San Nicolas on a hunting trip and to prepare an outpost for military reconnaissance. Once there, the man found footsteps in the sand and other signs of a human presence. A search party returned and found the woman who would become known Juana Maria.

She was eventually reunited with those who remained from her tribe, who had vacated San Nicolas Island for the mainland. Juana Maria had jumped ship, because her baby had been left behind. She swam ashore only to find that wolves had already eaten her child. Years later, the Bird Woman, Juana Maria, was laid to rest at the Santa Barbara Mission gardens.

Jean Sedar's remembrance of her uncle was like a ray of light passing through a prism. It helped me to see that losing Jim McCaffrey and his infectious spirit was devastating, not only to his immediate and extended family, but to an entire community of sportsmen.

CHAPTER 48:

The Father of Infrared

After I returned home to Arkansas, I read the document I had searched so hard to find: *IN MEMORIAM: DR. NIEL F. BEARDSLEY.*

It described a man of character and integrity, who had little interest in notoriety. Dr. Beardsley lived to serve. "Dr. Beardsley was the father of infrared," said one of the retired Raytheon engineers. Back then, I considered such a label a bit of an exaggeration. I had found a historical timeline of those who had influenced infrared, and it didn't include Dr. Beardsley. However, he was recognized as a pioneer.

> The contributions a man makes to his chosen field of endeavor sometimes go far beyond the work which actually bears his signature. This is particularly true of Niel F. Beardsley, a pioneer in infrared who was still actively engaged in advancing the art when on June 7, at the age of 68, he was lost at sea together with six companions on a research expedition.
>
> It is true because he was more interested in getting a job done than in signing his name to it; because his single-minded aim was to further the progress of infrared technology: and because he sought to achieve this aim not only through his own research

but through aiding the efforts of others – pointing them, exhorting them, and even bullying them when necessary.

His standards were exacting and his approach to problems sometimes startlingly direct.

The tribute moved me. It was more than just a list of accomplishments. It described the character of a world-class man:

When Dr. Beardsley joined Dr. Ovrebo in infrared work at WADC in 1946, he had behind him a long career.... During World War II, he became expert in optical shop techniques, which he pioneered for the Manhattan project, and liked the work so much that he welcomed the change to continue it at Wright Field.

On these field trips, it was evident that Dr. Beardsley as not only fearless, but actually enjoyed the danger involved. "I carried a Civilian Observer Flight Card until I was past 65," he boasted. "Then the problem was not to pass the flight examination but to get the flight surgeon's permission to take it."

Conrad M. Philippi, who worked under him at that time, recalls with amusement the dismay of the officials who could find no health or regulatory excuse for grounding this man who refused to grow old.

"During these years, Dr. Beardsley was active in measuring infrared radiation from the sky and transmission of infrared radiation through clouds, for which later purpose he once spent an entire month on top of Mt. Washington in New Hampshire.

"He also labored long and hard measuring the infrared transmission of materials, and never ceased to urge the importance of continued search for better and better windows.

"...In line with his concern for the general welfare of infrared technology was his initiative in helping to establish the Working Group of Infrared Backgrounds.[133]

I understood these words were a tiny window into the man's life. Yet the insights were valuable, because now I was enabled to start building a timeline of Dr. Beardsley's life.

I now understood that Dr. Beardsley was a scientist who worked on the Manhattan Project, the top-secret WWII effort that developed the atomic bomb and expedited the end of the war. I had initially been skeptical of Beardsley's participation in the Manhattan Project. His involvement had been mentioned in some newspaper articles, but in such a way as to hype the shipwreck's mystery and sell newspapers.

Dr. Krasno's memorial to his friend and colleague continued:

...When Dr. Beardsley came to Santa Barbara in May 1959, he had resolved to slow down at long last."[134]

Finally, Dr. Krasno brought the piece full circle by offering insight into Beardsley's final mission:

The day before that last expedition put out to sea, a younger colleague, remembering the rigors of a previous trip, suggested that perhaps he might prefer to stay ashore. Such an idea had obviously never occurred to Dr. Beardsley. He was in charge of the research; naturally he would conduct the tests. His answer was simple, firm, and characteristic: 'I think I'd better go.'

Two photos of Dr. Beardsley complemented the *Memoriam*. One was a head shot that I had seen used in several articles. The second, I assumed, was taken at one of the IRIS receptions. This photo showed

Dr. Beardsley socializing with four people, a crowd of others in the background. The memorial and the detector development report also helped me to understand the role that the physics department at Syracuse University played in Dr. Beardsley's life and legacy. He considered the students whom he mentored to be his family:

> Typically, when asked about his career, he always cited first the part he had played in the achievements of others. He was proud of his monitoring of Air Force contracts during his years at Wright Field, and especially of the contract for detector research still in force at Syracuse University after fourteen years. He regarded the young men who carried out that research as his "family," and he followed their later activities with interest and affection.[135]

As I read this touching tribute to Dr. Niel Freeborn Beardsley, my heart pined to have a memorial for my father, for all the shipwrecked fathers. That is what moved me, despite my feelings of inadequacy, to create an exhibit that would have to be approved by the Santa Barbara Maritime Museum in just a few weeks.

CHAPTER 49:

Telling a Story

Tell a story.

Jennifer Wisnewski's counsel echoed in my mind as I visited the Clinton Library and reviewed every permanent exhibit. The Clinton Library offered inspiration. I noticed the use of text, images, artifacts, film and interactive activities. No text was too small. Nothing was too detailed. Everything was visually captivating. Each display had a clear beginning, middle, and end. And although each display told a story, it held a piece of a larger story. Through my observations, I began to understand the wisdom of Jennifer's advice: "Tell a story."

IT'S MY DAD

Darting through April showers to our mailbox, an umbrella shielded me as I returned with a padded envelope with a California return address. I opened it and found a note from Glenna Howell wrapped around a DVD. The note read, "I hope you like the DVD. I think the fishing boat trip has your dad."

I brewed a cup of tea, and settled down with my laptop. For the next ten minutes, I watched a silent set of film-clips. When film ended, I watched it again, pausing for a better view here and there.

This is too good to watch by myself.

I picked up the phone and dialed Glenna.

"Hi, Glenna. It's Teresa. What a treasure."

"Oh! Oh, you got it. Let's watch it together."

We started our DVD players at the same time, and watched the images from the past together.

The film-clip jumped to a scene of a toddler and two little girls beside a blue and white airplane. The girls were twirling their skirts. "The toddler's my brother and that's my sister and me twirling skirts." Glenna said.

She didn't know anything about the airplane except that they were at the Santa Barbara Airport. Then the film-clip cut to a front yard in Goleta where the same four children were now in play clothes. We both recognized her dad, Dale Howell.

The next film-clip was solid blue, with light filtering in from above. A diver in a full, dark wetsuit entered the frame, the surface light glowing around him. Light bounced off his silver air tanks and the air bubbles that floated toward the surface. We watched the lone diver as he descended following what appeared to be an anchor line.

As the diver approached the bottom, the blue deepened but visibility remained clear. The ocean floor beyond the diver was spotted with purple sea urchins. Whoever held the camera kept up with the diver. In the next shot, the diver held a spear gun as a catch bag dangled from his side. When I watched the film alone, I hit the pause button throughout this diving clip. I wanted to examine the wet suit, the weight belt, and the spear gun. My brother Jim had a weight belt, like Dad's.

I had taken out the photo of my dad, Dale Howell, and Bud Bottoms when they were on a boat. The wetsuit in that photo of my dad fit like a glove and had a light-colored seam on the inside leg. The diver's wet suit in the film clip was well fitted and had the same distinguishing inseam on each leg. I concluded that it was my father diving.

Glenna and I were captivated as we watched. Then Glenna broke the silence.

"It's my dad," she said.

"No, it's my dad," I corrected. "Well, we know someone's dad is diving and someone's dad is filming," I added.

It was likely both our fathers, and it didn't matter whose dad it really was. The image took two divers to capture.

The film jumped and we entered the Santa Barbara Harbor marina. One and two-mast sailboats dotted the harbor. In the distance was the Santa Barbara Naval and Coast Guard Headquarters, now the home of the Santa Barbara Maritime Museum.

In the next scene, three young children sat side by side in three chairs. A dark-haired woman placed more chairs in the line and then tried to herd the boys and girls into the chairs. One girl with short dark hair stayed seated, craning her neck and watching the other kids.

"Glenna, stop" I cried.

"What? What?"

"See the girl seated with the butchered dark hair?" I asked.

"Yes."

"It's me."

"I'm the strawberry blond curly haired girl to the right of you," said Glenna.

"No. We played together?"

"That makes sense because that's my babysitter trying to line the kids up," Glenna said of the lady corralling the children.

I was no older than two at the time. Glenna was about five or six. I had one picture of myself with that haircut. I had tossed it because I looked like a boy. Here, I recognized the hair and the yellow cotton dress that I wore. It was the dress with a pocket I wore in my single memory I have of my father. I see him in the distance playing with kids at a trampoline, and I feel peace.

"There's the fishing boat. There's your dad." Glenna cried as the film cut to a new scene.

"They are on the *Marie*," I added. I recognized it first because of its unique placement of the skiff, lifeboat, which straddles the bow. Also, because the boat resembled the one in the photos Dad took during a scuba diving adventure on the *Marie* with the diving club from California Polytechnic University.

"I thought it might be the *Marie*," Glenna said.

The scene shifted to a rocky shore. The diver in the fitted wet suit, this time without the air tank, carried a mechanized spear-gun as he lumbered across the rocks and out into the ocean. He swam a short distance, waved, and then disappeared beneath the water. Soon he returned up the rocky edge of the surf to the shore, holding his spear gun in one hand while heaving a large fish in the other. But with the sun at his back and his face in dark shadow, we couldn't identify him.

"Dad's graduating project was a mechanized spear gun," Mom had said. "He got the job with Raytheon, not for his grades but for his ability to apply the theories to real situations."

A group gathered around the diver. One was unmistakably my grandfather Terres. When the diver stood, he was taller than my grandfather.

"It's my dad," said Glenna.

"No, it's my dad," I correct again. "How about this?" I suggested. "When I watch the film, it's my dad. When you watch the film, it's your dad. And when we are both watching," I paused, "it's my dad!"

"It's my dad." Glenna countered.

In truth, we were delighted for each other, no matter whose dad we were watching.

I looked toward the closet where I stored the Terres family films and Dad's presentation slide carousels. There were over twenty-four hours of footage, but I had yet to look at them because they needed to be digitized.

"I will see you soon," we both said before hanging up. The commemoration was now only a few weeks away. Glenna Howell was successful in digitizing the old home movie, and it arrived in time to be added to the exhibit's content.

My thoughts raced to the documentary I was producing, which I knew would benefit from combining a diving clip with dad's singing captured from the old 45 record Uncle Al had given me. I was in awe of technology: the photos, films, and sound recordings. They were opening a window into my father's life. Like a cherry on an ice cream sundae, these memories would add a personal touch to the exhibit, which had to be completed and approved in less than four weeks.

CHAPTER 50:

Dr. Beardsley Search

So far, I had been unsuccessful in finding any of Dr. Beardsley's family. Because the *Memoriam* said that Dr. Beardsley considered his students to be family, I turned to Syracuse University's PhD program. Maybe someone in the Syracuse University Physics Department knew something about the elusive scientist.

On Syracuse University's website, I found that the physics department had set up an annual scholarship in honor of Dr. Beardsley, which appeared to be an ongoing and active award. I e-mailed the physics department, inviting Syracuse University to the commemoration and asking for any additional information they had about Dr. Beardsley.

About noon on Saturday, I received a brief e-mail from a Dr. Goldberg.

"Dear Teresa: I too have tried to find information about Niel Beardsley. All I know is that he was a sponsor of infrared research out of Wright-Patterson AFB in Dayton, OH. Apparently, he also cooperated in the research group headed by Prof Henry Levinstein."

Dr. Goldberg sent another e-mail on Monday. "I have one address for you, but I believe it will be sufficient." The address was for a contact who was a Syracuse University Physics PhD student. I smiled when I saw that his home address was listed as Goleta, California. My home town.

Within days of the initial contact with Syracuse University, I was in contact with three former Ph.D. students of Dr. Levinstein's, whom Dr. Beardsley would also have considered as his family. These three men added inspiring quotes for the exhibit. And through them, I began to understand Dr. Niel F. Beardsley's legacy lives on in the program he initiated at Syracuse University, the students served, and the field of infrared.

CHAPTER 51:

Curating an Exhibit

I still needed to create a small but museum-quality exhibit. Toward that end, I gathered the pieces that I had for the display and documentary. I assessed the story pieces I had and the gaps that remained, and then I began piecing together the beginning, middle, and ending.

I had a host of photos and information, but the details were out-of-balance. I had one photo of Hal Mackie, three photos of Jim Russell, three images of Dr. Beardsley, several images of Jim McCaffrey, several photos of Dale Howell, hundreds of photos of my dad, and not a single photo of Paul Lovette, except for his draped body.

I wrestled with piecing together a brief biographical sketch of each victim. Paul Lovette and Dr. Beardsley were particularly problematic, although for different reasons. I had almost no information on Lovette and much of the extensive information available about Dr. Beardsley lay buried under layers of classified documents.

Another challenge was that I had no visual of what was loaded onto the *Marie*, to include a Raytheon Communicator. I began to draw a picture of an orange crate and two boxes to represent the electronics.

Ken sat beside me. "It's an orange communicator box." Ken said as he peered over my shoulder. "They didn't load a crate of oranges."

"What do you know," I sneered. I felt he always moved away

from me when I'd try to share tidbits of the *Marie* mystery.

"Suit yourself, but they didn't load boxes of fruit."

Looking him in the eye, I could tell my kidder wasn't kidding. Could my memory be deceiving me? I set my laptop aside and looked for the source documents.

"You always have to check behind me," Ken said.

I quickly found the reference, and saw that Ken was right. I also found where I had gone astray. When I read the transcripts of the court case, I got sidetracked along with one of the lawyers who asked a witness to repeat the description of the apple crates being loaded onto the *Marie*. Apple crates? Did the lawyer's mind lose track of the details or was he deliberately misleading? Either way, I hadn't tracked the details correctly.

"I was wrong. Spank me."

Ken grinned.

That exchange proved to me that Ken was paying more attention to what I was doing than he let on. I was grateful that he had saved me from making an embarrassing mistake.

The Raytheon Communicator sender and receiver were encased in orange-colored water-tight compartments. In the display, I intended to complement the orange electronic boxes with a simple orange outline of a fish. The fish would help communicate that the electronics were tested underwater.

I also hoped to add some Cold War flavor to the exhibit. Since I had little knowledge of either the historical times or Cold War programs, I believed it was appropriate to choose a representative photo. I decided to use an image of the out-loading USS *George Washington*. A Polaris submarine, the *George Washington* was the first nuclear submarine capable of launching missiles while submerged. On June 7, 1960, this submarine was in its final preparations for loading and test launching its first missile.

Placing an image of the USS *George Washington* on the display was an educated guess. I was uncomfortable making educated guesses because I wanted the exhibit to disseminate facts and not misinformation. Nevertheless, I decided to make another speculation when I included an X marking the location where many thought the sunken *Marie* might have been discovered by abalone divers in 1969.

Using the electronic chart of the Santa Barbara Channel, that Dr. Cloud had sent from the NOAA archives, I placed on the display an image to map-out the waters of the Santa Barbara Channel and Santa Cruz Island. "This is likely the chart used in 1960," Dr. Cloud had written when he sent it to me. I added an "X" to mark the possible resting place of the *Marie*: 2.5 miles east of Painted Cave and 1.5 miles from the shore of Santa Cruz Island. I placed a close-up of the chart in the background as a visual to add color and unite the display panels. I also added a Search and Rescue line drawing that had been given to newspapers, detailing where airplanes, ships, and helicopters searched the Santa Barbara Channel.

My eyes lingered on the X and then I looked closer as I compared the SAR drawing up next to an appropriately sized chart.

The X on the chart was outside of the SAR.

"Teresa, put it on ice," I told myself as I ripped my attention away to focus on the task at hand. I was running out of time and I knew it. I had an exhibit to create and get approved, not to mention people preparing to travel from across the nation and around the globe to attend the *Marie Commemoration Event*. I couldn't lose focus now, especially since I still needed to produce a 20-minute documentary about the shipwreck.

I told Anthony "Tony" May, the film editor, that my goal was to create a documentary under twenty minutes in length that provided an overview of the story. I added that it needed to satisfy the Santa Barbara Maritime Museum standards.

Tony read the overview I had drafted, including a general timeline. He considered the still images I'd compiled along with the a story-board I drafted. Then, spreading out the pieces that would contribute to the documentary, he set me to the task of digitizing the fourteen hours of footage I had shot. As each video was digitized, he reviewed them and copied interesting clips that would build the basic storyline. He wrote out lines for a professional narrator to read and record. I reviewed and edited the snippets of text, and shaped them into the final script.

"Hop in the sound booth," Tony said one Saturday after the moon had begun to raise outside. We both knew that time was ticking away, so I was going to serve as the narrator. As I read the script, I tried to eliminate the Southern accent that I had picked up. I also tried to summon up latent oratory skills. We had diminishing time for one take before we had to turn off the lights and head home.

Tony had all the pieces. The rest would require his creativity, computer, and expertise.

Despite the challenges, a 19-minute documentary that told the basic story came together.

However, I wouldn't see the film until I and Ken arrived in Santa Barbara, days before the commemoration. No time for retakes.

Was the film going to be good enough for the Santa Barbara Maritime Museum? The question haunted me.

"We have standards to uphold," SBMM's Mr. Gorga had said.

Without an acceptable documentary, the small exhibit space would be revoked and I would be left to tell the story of the *Marie* shipwreck as best I could.

CHAPTER 52:

Black Project

When I compared Dr. Beardsley's *Memoriam* with his obituaries, I noticed that both mentioned his work at Wright Field, now Wright-Patterson Air Force Base. According to both sources, he began work there in 1946; however, neither stated when Dr. Beardsley retired from working for the Air Force before moving to Santa Barbara.

One obit simply stated, "He came to Raytheon a year ago." The *Memoriam* added, "When Dr. Beardsley came to Santa Barbara in May 1959, he had resolved to slow down "at long last." It wasn't clear whether Dr. Beardsley had first retired from civilian work for the Air Force. I remembered that the retired Engineers and court case testimonies described Dr. Beardsley as "a consultant." But whom was he consulting for? The Air Force? Raytheon? What was his chain of authority? These seemed like simple questions that anyone with personnel records could clear up.

Because it was now clear that Dr. Beardsley had devoted a considerable amount of his life at Wright-Patterson AFB, I decided to contact them. I assumed someone there could clear up the retirement issue among other questions, such as what programs he worked on.

Based on previous experience, I knew that approaching Wright-Patterson, was a matter of respecting and following protocol. If I were simply conducting research, I could choose to employ the FOIA process (Freedom of Information Act). But, I wasn't merely conducting research. I had an event I was spearheading and I had an exhibit I was creating. Thus, my objective was twofold: first, to invite appropriate people to the upcoming commemoration and, second, to gain information for an exhibit.

I contacted Mr. Hancock, of the Wright-Patterson Public Affairs Office. After he had conducted some research into my request, Mr. Hancock gave me a call, informing me that he couldn't be of service to me.

"Dr. Beardsley was here, but he was not one of ours." Mr. Hancock went on to explain another reason they couldn't help me. "It was a black project then; it's a black project still."[136]

I was dumfounded. I repeated his words, "It was a black project, meaning that you can't tell me what he was working on?"

"That is correct."

I was at a loss for words. But the Sherlock Holmes in me was intrigued.

"So, where do I go from here?" I asked.

"I don't know," Mr. Hancock said.

My mind was spinning. *If Dr. Beardsley was working on a black project, to whom did he report?*

Mr. Hancock had made another cryptic comment. "I have yet to connect with the Sensing Directorate."

Who was that? Were they Dr. Beardsley's authority?

Again, I considered the statement: "It was a black project." Did *it* refer to the project Dr. Beardsley worked on while at Wright-Patterson? Or, did *it* refer to the project that he was working on when he was lost at sea? Or were both projects the same?

My understanding was that black projects might never process through usual de-classification avenues, especially projects related to nuclear technology. Others might eventually be challenged because the public has become aware of them. Programs such as the SOSUS, U-2 spy planes, and the Corona Satellite programs were highly classified until the largest de-classification effort America has ever experienced took place during President Clinton's administration.

Later that week, I received a phone message from Mr. Hancock. "Try writing the National Archives in Saint Louis. I don't think you have a chance. But it's worth a try."

What would Dr. Beardsley's civilian records reveal? I desperately wanted to learn more; however, I felt time slipping away. My gut told me to be patient and put questions about Dr. Beardsley on ice.

I ignored my gut.

I quickly drafted and sent a letter to NARA Saint Louis. I believed it was critical to confirm whom Beardsley worked for and if he retired before heading west.

Ken cautioned me against becoming distracted. "The commemoration isn't just about Dr. Beardsley," he said.

I knew that, but I also knew that I had to learn more about this elusive man.

George Washington (SSBN-598), unknown location. USN photo courtesy of US Naval Historical Center.

CHAPTER 53:

Beyond Black

As the event date drew near, I came to think of Jennifer Wisnewski as an angel with blue eyes. She walked beside me as I struggled with creating an exhibit display and film. I was amazed how she and her colleagues routinely brought together several exhibits at the same time, while I wrestled with one.

Jennifer was my encourager. We met regularly. She suggested I try using a top-to-bottom timeline because I could then use cost-effective banners. "They're easy to create, print, and display." Jennifer said. "Big museums are all using them."

We brainstormed and agreed on four panels to surround the large plasma screen featuring the film would be perfect.

"I love the outline of the orange fish," she said. "I assume you will replace it with an image of a garibaldi?" When I explained that I didn't know what a garibaldi was, she explained that it was the bright orange fish I had seen on Glenna's DVD. I promised her that I would replace the outlined fish with a photo of a garibaldi.

Before I headed to California for the commemoration, I e-mailed Jennifer the files for the exhibit's four display panels. Later we met and she brought suggestions for edits. Once I incorporated her changes, the display panels were ready for the Santa Barbara Maritime Museum's review.

I was hopeful they would also approve.

As the documentary came together, Lee Burrell suggested, "You need to record the upcoming commemoration and then re-shoot the documentary footage in high-definition film." He also volunteered to come film the event if I covered his basic costs.

Such an offer was beyond anything I could have dreamed. We made plans to include Lee Burrell and filming into the weekend mix of activities. For what purpose, God only knew.

****

The burden of the event's expenses was too great for Ken and me to bear alone. Therefore, we set up a fee structure for attendees and agreed to shoulder the balance of expenses. We also looked for creative ways to find sponsors for commemoration activities.

Bryant & Sons jewelry store in Santa Barbara funded the event invitations and postage. Bob Bryant, the owner, said, "I was supposed to be on the *Marie*." A local quartet that included retired Raytheon engineers, volunteered to bring musical entertainment. A flag folding ceremony in honor of the veterans lost in the shipwreck was offered free by our nation. Uncle Albert along with a member of the military group volunteered to play Taps. Family and friends from Arkansas and California volunteered their services as helpers. Other family and friends made financial contributions, both small and large. It all added up. In fact, the contributions snowballed so much that the *Marie Commemoration Event* was able to make a donation to the Santa Barbara Maritime Museum.

Health and other challenges threatened to keep some of the aging spouses from attending. Mrs. Mackie said, "I don't know if I can get there." Mrs. Russell lived a couple of states away and was challenged by expenses and age-related health issues. Mrs. McCaffrey lived minutes away but her cancer had progressed. "If I can make it, I will be there," she said. If these women could attend, I knew their presence would benefit all. We offered them a free pass to all the activities. It was the right thing to do. I had to have faith and believe in each decision. It wasn't always easy. Ken and I prayed. We asked our church's small group and our other friends to pray. Together, we asked God to shoulder the burdens of those with challenges and to bring all the details together in such a way that would please Him.

Although the exhibit had not yet been approved by the Santa Barbara Maritime Museum, it was time for the dream of a commemoration for my father and all the other fathers to become a reality. Ken and I loaded the car and drove west along the historic Route 66 to California.

****

We arrived in Santa Barbara with only a week to go before the commemoration. We had distributed media kits, but thus far only one news service had published a story about the event[137]. With time fast running out, I still faced the task of publicizing the event to the general public.

I'd been working on the media kit with Laura Funkhouser, and Tony May had just sent me a link to view the documentary, which had been completed while Ken and I drove west. When I mentioned the status of the film, Laura, said "Let's have an online debut."

I didn't have to think twice. "A perfect solution for the Memorial Day Weekend," I added. "But how?" I asked. We had very little time to make the idea happen.

"Edhat.com. It's a local online news and social network. Leave it to me. I can set it all up."

I thanked her. The documentary was created to serve the commemoration. I didn't want the commemoration seen as an effort to serve as a film's debut. I wanted all the children to have a chance to view the story of their fathers' loss in a safe and private space before seeing it in a public venue. And the film debut days before the commemoration weekend marked the first trip the men and *Marie* took and returned safely.[138] Thus, the *Marie Remembered* film, became a bugle announcing, "Make way. Something great is coming."

My next meeting was the most critical of all. Greg Gorga at the Santa Barbara Maritime Museum, the venue where the commemoration would take place, had the final say about whether the museum would agree to host the *Marie* exhibit. I followed Mr. Gorga into his dark, wood-paneled office for the final verdict.

"Let's watch the film together," he said, taking the DVD that had been overnighted me. I had sent Mr. Gorga the online link when I had received it but didn't know whether he had watched it. I also sent links to visuals of the four display panels. However, I had yet to get any response.

He inserted the DVD into his computer and pressed play. I sat patiently, leaning across his desk to view the film as he leaned back in his seat. He wasn't smiling, and I couldn't read his body language.

"That's my father scuba diving, and it's his voice singing," I said. "Just under twenty minutes, as you advised."

I couldn't tell what he was thinking, and he said little. Next, he went to the link in an e-mail and clicked to pull up the first of the display panel images.

"Do you have the original display panel files?" he asked.

"Yes," I motioned toward my laptop.

"Pull them up. We need to make some edits."[139]

I knew how easy it was to make mistakes and the large format had challenged me. On top of that, when I created the panels I was exhausted and operating on sheer adrenaline. I knew I probably overlooked something. I just hoped it wasn't enough to torpedo the exhibit.

Mr. Gorga opened the first of the four panels. He examined every sentence, every word. He found more than one error.

"Vessel names should be capitalized and italicized," he said.

He went on for what seemed like eternity, telling me what edits and changes needed to be made. "We have standards that the panels have to meet," he said.

I couldn't stand it any longer. I had to know. "Is the exhibit shipwrecked?" I asked sheepishly.

Mr. Gorga took out the DVD, returned it to its paper cover, and handed it to me.

"You will make the edits to the panels before printing."

It wasn't a question.

"Done."

"And you will leave a DVD for our library, along with the teak stands, when the exhibit is removed."

"Yes."

"Then," he paused, "You can have the exhibition space; but only Saturday through Wednesday, because I have another exhibit scheduled."

"Thank you. I will remove the display by close of business Wednesday."

I left happy, but also a little disappointed. I had hoped the exhibit would be up until June 21 because these dates spanned the day the men departed and the day the last victim was found. Still, I decided not to sweat the small stuff. We had an exhibit for the *Marie Commemoration Event*.

"The exhibit's a go!" I cried out to Ken when I picked him up. We headed to Kinko's, who were already alerted and prepared to complete the large-scale printing order.

By Friday afternoon, the other participants began arriving at the motel. Jeannie and Helen Russell came in from Colorado. My brother Rick had arrived from the Middle East. My brother Jim and his family drove in from Nevada, and brother Don and his family from Southern California's Orange County. Later, Sutter and Bonnie Fox came in from Los Angeles area. Others were coming from the East Coast and even two from Hawaii.

"It will be like a military ceremony," I had informed Sherri Sims, who had flown in with her husband Larry from Arkansas the day earlier to volunteer their services. "A casual social, dignified ceremony, with a sunrise boat ride."

I had experienced the basic routine repeatedly at the National Guard's Professional Education Center: remembrance and recognition, fused with traditions. The pattern was flexible and accommodated a variety of situations. Each ceremony was coordinated around a timeline and script.

I had been working long and hard on both.

As with similar events, military or wedding, we decided to have a rehearsal to coordinate the working parts. Friday afternoon, just before the evening social, those with a part in the ceremony gathered at the Santa Barbara Maritime Museum for a run-through. Although the room wouldn't be set up until just before the ceremony the next day, I could still mark out the basic plan and distribute the final version of the program's script.

After the rehearsal, we all took a short walk down the beachside boulevard to the Veteran's Administration Building for the Friday evening social, the weekend's first event. As the families arrived, many set-up table-top displays of mementoes. Among the items the Terres family placed on display were Grandmother's scrapbook, Dad's picture album, a framed photo with Dad and Mom in their Navy uniforms, and a couple of abalone shells that came from one of Dad's diving trips.

At a far end of the room, a lone small-screen monitor sat perched on an AV platform and showed the *Marie Remembered* film. Ken had directed someone to set up the printed panel display, which tomorrow would be moved to the Santa Barbara Maritime Museum.

"Those that can't make the ceremony, can preview the exhibit beforehand," He said.

I nearly panicked when I noticed that there were only three, not four, display panels. "Ken?"

Ken reassured me. "Somehow Kinko's overlooked the fourth panel. It is being expedited and will be here in time for the ceremony."

"Life certainly is one mud puddle after another," I chuckled because Ken's wisdom fit, and there was no use in getting riled up over it. "I agree, the three panels look good," I said. "And I will hope and pray that the fourth panel arrives tomorrow. Until then, we have a social to focus on."

FIG 33: Above: I'm standing with Ken on the left and F. Sutter Fox on the right as we prepare for the 50th Commemoration, the night of the "Social."

FIG 34: My brothers and I prepare for the 50th Commemoration, the night of the "Social." Standing in order of birth - Diego (Jim), Rick, Teresa, and Don.

FIG 35: Above: Dr. F. Sutter Fox at the podium to a standing room only audience at the evening commemoration, Santa Barbara Maritime Museum.
FIG 36: Left: The Centerpiece Quartet sings an encore to Sharon Sims, (USA Colonel ret.) in front of the Marie Remembered exhibit.
FIG 37: Below-Left: Santa Barbara Maritime Museum's Marie Remembered exhibit.
FIG 38: Below-Right: Mrs. Mackie receives a flag from the Honor Guard.

FIG 39: Above-Left: My daughter, Ken, and I at sunrise service standing in front of the Painted Cave located on Santa Cruz Island. Above-Right: Uncle Albert plays TAPS for servie.
FIG 40: Below the Jeff McCaffrey family pose for a remembrance.

FIG 41: Below: All the children embrace at the conclusion of the service. (My brother, Don, on right wears Dad's peacoat.)

Part-III COMMEMORATION

Marie Commemoration Artwork by
Teresa Newton-Terres.

CHAPTER 54:

The Social

At 7 p.m., a line of guests began to form, stringing past the small library, down the stairwell and into the lobby. I stood at the top landing and welcomed people. I knew and hugged everyone. We were a family by circumstance.

Jeannie Russell and her mother, Helen, were among the first up the stairs.

"Great to see you." Jeannie had her hands full with escorting her mother and had worked hard just to make it here.

I knew that Raytheon would be well represented when I saw some retired Raytheon engineers.

Glenna and Jeff Howell and family arrived. The McCaffrey Family brought enough people to fill up several tables, and despite her health problems, Connie had shown up with her daughter Shawna.

All but one...

Of those families I had connected with, I had initiated a conversation with all the children by e-mail, phone, or face-to-face. However, Shawna McCaffrey and I had yet to speak. Like me, Shawna was a sister among three brothers. It was clear her mother wouldn't live much longer. My heart ached for her and her family.

Thus, when Connie and Shawna McCaffrey arrived, I wanted to sit down and spend time together. Our hands embraced.

I want to hug these women.

The room was full and noisy and I had difficulty hearing Shawna.

I thought she said something like, "You know the story."

Our eyes met.

How do I say what is on my heart?

I wanted to convey what was swirling in my mind.

I told the story I could tell. There is more -- a submarine, a lifeboat, a storm of Marines, a data pickup, and a burning desire to know if either of our fathers or the scientist lived beyond that day.

But all I could do was look deep into her eyes.

"Welcome! Thank you for coming and bringing your mother," I said.

I have to trust the rest of the story to God.

And with that, I had to go greet other guests.

Uncle Albert and Aunt Lynda's children and grandchildren arrived.

Bob Bryant arrived, and I gave him a big hug. An article in a Santa Barbara Independent newspaper, released after the weekend event, revealed to the community that three men (Bob Bryant, Bob Wilke, Bud Bottoms) had each planned to be on the *Marie* that fateful day.[140]

Bud Bottoms arrived. "The star," Lee Burrell called him.

Lee captured video clips of the evening. He had popped out from the private library behind me where he and Laura were ready to interview and record people's memories and experiences with the *Marie*.

Filming oral histories during the weekend was a last-minute addition to our agenda. I didn't want to waste Lee and Laura's capabilities, so I made every effort to get people into the library in front of the camera.

Our room in the Veteran's Building was sparse, but came with a million-dollar view. A wall of windows provided natural light and gave a full view of the Santa Barbara harbor. To the left, the wharf projected outward with the dolphin family sculpture at its base. On the right, you could see the marina, and in the distance, Santa Cruz Island.

Once the room was blaring with conversation, the sign-in line dwindling, and the food line almost ready, Ken took command of the microphone.

"Hello. Hello. Hello. Welcome." Ken said, gaining people's attention. Chairs scuffed the plank floor as they took their seats. "The food is almost ready, but before we get started, I'd like to welcome you to the *Marie Commemoration Event*. And I'd like to introduce you to the event project manager, the investigator, the person in the dogged pursuit of the truth who helped to organize all this. If you would, please help me welcome Teresa Newton-Terres."

Ken moved to one side as I stood behind the microphone—a dangerous place for me without a script. Without written words in front of me, I tend to ramble.

A flood of emotion welled up as I looked around the room full of people who had been impacted in one way or another by the *Marie* tragedy. They were on their feet standing and clapping. They were not honoring me; they were honoring the reason we had gathered. I might be standing in front of them, but it was a shipwreck that brought us together.

"Welcome," was all that came out. Then, I looked at Ken and smiled. *Why not ramble?*

"I am overwhelmed. Someone asked me, 'Did you ever have this in mind?' And I had to answer, no." I paused for a breath and then continued. "I started out by asking one question. What happened? I couldn't find the answer, but I have found an answer in the hearts of everyone here in this room."

During the applause, Ken took the microphone. "I see the sign that our dinner is ready. Thank you for coming. The rest of the evening is yours, enjoy each other, enjoy the mementoes, and I look forward to seeing you again at tomorrow night's ceremony and the sunrise boat-ride."

****

It was dark when we finished cleaning the space. Ken and I walked arm in arm back to the motel under a clear star-filled sky.

The evening had been bittersweet for me because my daughter

Dete had called from Washington D.C. earlier. She was crying. "I woke up in the night with a busted eardrum and went to the ER. And I couldn't fly today."

"You will be right where you are supposed to be," I told her. It doesn't matter if it's in DC or at your grandfather's memorial. Yes, I want you here. And I could sure use your arms and legs. But your health is the priority." I sent her a big hug over the phone and was glad that she wasn't facing something life threatening.

Upon reaching the motel, I noticed a few people sitting and gazing skyward in the courtyard by the fountain.

My family gathered in our suite. Ken and I had commandeered the largest room in the motel with two queen beds a small kitchenette, patio, and couch seating area, it gave extra space for people to gather. While we had crossed paths for Rick's fiftieth birthday five years earlier, the last time all four of us were together was for Mom's memorial at the cabin. We shared a nightcap, and then I put folks to work, stuffing DVD covers into place and folding ceremony programs.

CHAPTER 55:

The Commemoration

I rose early on Saturday morning and went for a quick walk along the beachfront. I needed to begin the day in peace. The beloved sounds of waves, gulls, and the barking of a seal greeted me. Ken was still asleep when I returned to our room. After bringing him a cup of coffee, I dressed and left Ken to enjoy the rest of the morning on his own.

I had a breakfast appointment with three retired engineers. They had agreed to allow me to record their stories. Lee Burrell was the videographer, and my brother Don held the sound equipment. Jeannie Russell Carter joined us, to serve as an audience.

We piled into my car and drove to Dr. Bob and Rachel Watkin's home on the north side of Goleta.

Today, the opportunity I had long hoped for arrived as Dr. Bob Watkins, Bob Wilke, and Howard "Howie" Glenn agreed to come together and record a few memories.

Time was precious. We had less than three hours before we needed to return. Lee staged the seating and gave Don the microphone on the end of a boom. We settled into chairs and began recording memories.

I loved watching and listening to these three engineers bantering and giving each other grief, albeit always with respect. They had enjoyed their work, and they had served a useful purpose.

"We didn't create the science, only worked to find uses for it and solve problems," they said of their applied physics center. It was a statement I had heard before and that seemed to linger in my thoughts.

Once we had covered enough stories and our time was running short, I tried to bring things to a close. But it proved difficult to wrap up our time together. There was always one more story.

"We filled in a lot of gaps for ourselves," the three engineers said. They enjoyed having the opportunity to talk together.

While I was interviewing the retired Raytheon engineers, Dete had caught a flight from her home in Washington D.C. She arrived at the motel just as we returned from the interviews. Ken sent Dete and my brother Jim's oldest child, Marisa, on an errand to find long stemmed white roses and a simple wreath. When no wreath was to be found, a florist went into her back room and crafted a suitable one from seven natural reeds and biodegradable twine. The roses would be part of the ceremony tonight, and then tomorrow would be placed into the wreath and tossed into the sea.

Finally, my army of family and friends arrived at the Santa Barbara Maritime Museum to prepare the space. They set up the four teak frames with their panels along with the film. They also set up two central tables. One table would remain bare until four folded flags were placed upon it. The other table we decorated with seven vases, each holding a single white rose, and seven small shell wreaths where we placed battery-operated flicker candles. A sparkling blue wire ribbon was shaped and served to symbolize waves.

The Santa Barbara Maritime Museum staff arranged the chairs, podium, and directed the catering arrangements for the appetizers and chocolate river. One hundred chairs were set in rows, with a central aisle. A podium was placed to the side of the large screen in front.

****

When the ceremony began, Ken was at the podium, helping to emcee the evening. "Please begin to take your seats. This is your two-minute warning before the start of the ceremony." I took my seat on the front row, with Ken on my right and my oldest brother, Jim, on my left.

When everyone was seated, Sutter Fox, the Master of Ceremonies, stepped to the podium. "Please welcome yourselves to the first-ever *Marie* commemoration, honoring the seven men who left Santa Barbara Harbor at sunrise, on June 7, 1960." Next, Sutter asked the audience to stand and recognize those who represent the ones we gather to remember.

"In honor of: "Dr. Niel Freeborn Beardsley."

Holding a flickering candle, Hugh James (Jim) McCaffrey, McCaffrey's youngest child, walked in from the side and placed a candle into the first wreath on the table and then took a seat.

"Loren Dale Howell."

Eric Maulhardt, Dale Howell's grandson, walked in and placed his candle onto the second wreath, and then took his seat.

"Paul Timothy Lovette."

Don Terres, walked in, placed his candle into the next wreath and took a seat. I selected my brother to represent Paul Lovette because none of his family members were present.

"Harold Herbert Mackie, Jr."

Bruno Lucadello, a friend and colleague of Hal Mackie's brought in his candle.

"Hugh James McCaffrey."

Pat McCaffrey, the oldest child, placed Jim McCaffrey's candle into place.

"James Clifford Russell."

Jeannie Russell placed her father's candle upon its shell wreath.

"Diego Santos Terres, Jr."

My brother, Diego (Jim) Santos Terres III, walked in and placed a candle upon the seventh and the last wreath of shells and took his seat.

One by one, the honorary VIPs had entered and an appropriate reverence settled in the room.

"Please remain standing for the invocation."

"Let us bow our heads in prayer." Dr. Douglas Kroll, whom I first met in the Washington D.C. Coast Guard Archives, unfolded a small notepaper, and placed it on the podium.

"Almighty and everlasting God whose hand stills the tumult of the deep, we look to you as we begin this evening. Bless our time together, that it may strengthen our relationships. We pause to remember the seven men on the vessel *Marie*, who were lost at sea, fifty years ago on this weekend. We thank you for their service and their dedication. May we always remember and always honor them.

"Oh, source of all mercies, and giver of all comfort, deal graciously we pray with those still mourning the loss of a husband, a father, a brother, a friend, a colleague. Grant to all of them assured confidence in your loving care in casting all their sorrow on you. Let them know the consolation of your love through Jesus Christ our Lord. Amen."

Next, four men came to the front; a pitch pipe gently set a tone; and their voices rang out. "On a wonderful day like today…." The Centerpiece Quartet brought harmony to the opening, evidenced by the audience's rousing applause. Later they would bring an appropriate closing.

Dr. F. Sutter Fox took the podium again. "Welcome honored guests, families, and friends of the families of the *Marie's* seven men. This is a wonderful day that we can gather and remember and honor the days Santa Barbara stood still because seven men left Santa Barbara Harbor June 7, 1960, at sunrise and never returned.

"I am Sutter Fox and I have the distinguished honor to be your Master of Ceremonies this evening." Sutter went on to recognize Dr. Kroll, Greg Gorga, and other VIPs in the audience. I knew Ken had a hand at recognizing these people and I was grateful. Ken and Sutter had made several script edits today, one of which involved omitting my remarks.

"Were going to keep you off the mic," Ken had told me. "We need to keep the ceremony at one hour." They offered that as an excuse, but I knew it was because Ken feared I'd be overcome with emotion. I was silently grateful.

Next, Sutter recognized the spouses in attendance. "We have flowers to recognize and honor surviving spouses, Mrs. Mackie, Mrs. McCaffrey, and Mrs. Russell."

Sherri handed the three bouquets of flowers to the spouses. Connie had been too ill to attend, so one of her children accepted them on her behalf.

"And would the following people stand. Albert Terres, the brother of Jim Terres. Surviving children: Glenna Howell, Pat McCaffrey, Shawna McCaffrey, Jeff McCaffrey, Jim McCaffrey, Jeannie Russell, Jim Terres, Rick Terres, Teresa Newton-Terres, Don Terres."

Once the applause subsided and everyone was seated, Sutter continued, "To begin to tell the story of the *Marie*, my good friend Colonel Fig Newton will provide you an introduction which historians will recognize as a period known as the height of the Civil War era." Sutter paused and recovered with a chuckle. "Ah, Cold War era. Colonel Fig Newton."

Smiling Sutter extended his hand to welcome Ken, as they exchanged places behind the podium.

"Civil War." Ken grinned as he adjusted the microphone stand. "Of course, by the way I speak you can likely tell which side I came from."

The audience roared as Ken unfolded his script. He was in his element as he confidently addressed the audience.

"I do thank the introduction of my good friend Sutter Fox. He and I were officemates in Hawaii. And yes, Hawaii was a difficult and hard assignment." Again, the audience chuckled. "Usually I just talk and I have notes to direct me. But, tonight I have a script and I hope you will bear with me as I read it."

"Today we honor the story of the *Marie*. What a story. In fact, it was such a story that the Santa Barbara News Press recognized it as one of the 100 top newsworthy stories of the 20th Century in its book of headliners.

"What a story to remember.

"The Days Santa Barbara Stood Still. One has to venture back in time, because the story takes place during the height of the Cold War.

"Two years before the Marie disappeared, Russia launched Sputnik, the satellite that rocked America's world. Sputnik's success subsequently triggered America's determination not to be caught off guard scientifically or technologically ever again. Sputnik spurred a sequence of events that eventually led to the Marie's final trip to sea. Scientific and defense organizations were created, national laboratories expanded, scientists engaged, and project teams formed. These actions helped ensure America was more technologically advanced than any potential enemy.

"1960 was the year Presidential authority signed into existence the Peace Corps. Presidential races were in full swing and John F. Kennedy was leading in the polls, which would conclude in a few months. The Los Angeles Dodgers were seeking to repeat as baseball world champions after beating the Chicago White Sox in the World Series the previous year. The Island of the Blue Dolphin by Scott O'Dell was published. Relationships with Fidel Castro were deteriorating. President Eisenhower's Far East goodwill-tour was snubbed by Japan. The United Nations was being torn apart by operations in the Congo. It was the year of the CIA's first U-2 flight across Russia that was shot down, its pilot imprisoned, and the CIA's CORONA satellite's first successful launch into the Pacific Missile Range off Santa Barbara California's coastline.

"It was also the year a group of engineers united to serve a scientist in spearheading technological advancements in infrared sensing—underwater."

Ken took his script and returned to his seat.

"The following film will provide further background to the story of the *Marie*," Sutter added.

As the lights dimmed, the *Marie Remembered* documentary came to life on the screen in front of us.

> *On California's coastline is the Santa Barbara Harbor, and at the end of its breakwater is a memorial dedicated to loved ones whose destiny was claimed by the sea. This is the story of seven of the men honored, coming to light now after being submerged 50 years beneath the ocean, of a top-secret mission, undiscovered wreckage, and men lost at sea....*

The documentary recounted what I knew of the story, including testimony by family and friends. It helped people remember the men, the vessel, the infrared equipment they were testing, and the extensive search and rescue effort. It even recalled the folklore and mystery of the Cold War, including sightings of Russian vessels. The film concluded by recognizing Bud Bottoms and his part in creating the Lost at Sea Memorial. The film closed with the powerful and poignant words: "Regardless of the mysteries surrounding the circumstances of the ill-fated Marie, one thing is not a mystery. These men are heroes."[141]

The film brought tingles every time I watched, and this time was no different. Created for a large screen, the film made powerful viewing with its rich sound and crisp images.

How many of those present realize that it was my dad scuba diving and singing?

The house lights came back up and Sutter Fox said, "I now have the pleasure of introducing you to Mrs. Helen Wilke."

Helen Wilke unofficially offered Raytheon's voice. Even the documentary included a visual of the company's July 1960 newsletter, preserved in Grandmother's scrapbook, while I read the heartfelt words of condolence it conveyed. I wasn't going to let Raytheon Company be noticeably absent.

Mrs. Wilke said, "Some scientists and engineers are fortunate to see how their works are successful and how they can make a difference and save or improve lives. But this is more difficult for engineers who are employed in defense work. The nature of their work is secret and confidential. Few see the results of their work once the project goes into production.

"Engineers are problem-solvers. They dare to use their imagination and skills to find answers to questions which sometimes have not yet been asked. They risk being wrong, as they go into areas where no one has ever gone or even dreamed of going, as they seek solutions.

"My late husband, Malcolm McBurney, had terminal cancer. During Operation Desert Storm, he was sitting in the living room watching television one day when a US fighter jet pilot landed his aircraft and was interviewed. The pilot praised the pods under the wings of his jet for saving his life. He said an enemy missile was homing in on his exhaust flame and the countermeasures device in the pod sent out decoy signals, which turned the missile in another direction allowing him to complete his mission and land safely.

"At this, Mac jumped up out of his chair saying, 'It worked! We did it! We did it! We made a difference!' Exhausted, he sat down with a smile on his face. Mac had worked on AN/SLQ-32 affectionately known as Slick 32.

"This was a defense engineer who was able to witness his work in action, but it doesn't happen very often.

"The men of the Marie did not live long enough to see if their theories or their dream could be of value to the defense of this nation.

"To all the men and women scientists, engineers, and their support staff past and present, and to all the men on the Marie, we give thanks. We honor your name, and we honor your work. Thank you."[142]

As the audience applauded, Helen stepped from the podium. Next, Ken took the microphone to offer some additional historical context.

"With the passage of time it is now possible to piece together context for the infrared technology that was tested by the engineers lost at sea, its importance to national defense, and its legacy in many technologies in use.

"Research indicates that in June 1960, infrared systems, core technologies used for sensing, tracking, and communication networks were serving our national security interests. The evidence suggests, that it was used in some versions of the following: missiles (Hawk, Sea Sparrow, Shillelagh, Sidewinder); Polaris submarines; reconnaissance (U-2 plane); satellites (Corona /Discoverer series); and the ocean's Sound Surveillance System (SOSUS).

"Santa Barbara truly stood still in those days in 1960. Only God and possibly a select few individuals yet to be disclosed in our government know what really happened to the *Marie*, its men and equipment.

"But, what we do know, is that they were working on something important, that they were brave, courageous men, that all had family that loved them.

"50 years ago, no one knew that we would be meeting here tonight to commemorate their lives. We are proud of them and truly honor their memories. And I'm sure that wherever their spirits are, they are saying how proud they are of you—the wives, brothers, and children of the Marie."

Sutter returned to the podium as Ken took his seat next to me.

"In honor of those we remember today, we present a documentary, to those who made a difference and were in the film." I saw Dete and Sherri distribute commemoration DVDs of the film to each of the kids and those who were in the film.

"I also want to recognize the Santa Barbara Maritime Museum for their service to the *Marie* commemoration," Sutter said. Sutter went off script again adding, "We would be remiss if we didn't have a special recognition for Teresa Newton-Terres, for her role..."

Sutter's comments were cut short by resounding applause. I sat in the front row, trying to hold on to my composure. From the corner of my eye, I saw someone standing; but, it wouldn't be until I watched the filming of the event, that I saw that everyone was on their feet looking my direction. The audience's response was a kind of confirmation for me from God, that everyone there valued the event, and it wasn't self-serving.

"There really are no words to express all the work you have done and how proud everyone is of what you have accomplished," Sutter directed his comments in my direction, smiling. "And now, Albert Terres, will make a special presentation."

I knew Uncle Albert was going to make a presentation of a dolphin family sculpture, but he had told me more than once, "The sculpture is to be shared with your brothers." It was a smaller version of the fountain at the foot of the Santa Barbara wharf.

Uncle Albert came over from the far side of the room and placed the sculpture on one corner of the podium. I knew this sculpture was valued at just under two thousand dollars. Albert and Aunt Lynda had bought it as part of a silent auction for Santa Barbara High School. Al and Lynda had added a brass plate with the engraving, "In memory of Diego S. Terres, Jr. 1931-1960," and proudly displayed it in their home.

Albert continued, "My brother came from a '*Marie*,' our mother Maria, and he left with a *Marie*."

My father also left behind a Marie, Teresa Marie.

"I'd like to present this statute by Bud Bottoms to Diego's four children, Jim, Rick, Don, and Teresa. I'd like to present it to Teresa to hold and share." He emphasized the last word, share. As he did, I extended my hands because I had long admired the piece and was delighted to be the chosen caretaker of it.

"Not yet, Teresa," he bantered.

Albert continued, "Of all places I think my brother would want to be is in the ocean. And I think he is out there swimming with the dolphins." Al's hand caressed and pattered the three dolphin's heads. "There are three of these, ironically. And I think they are out there having a great time."

Tomorrow, some would recall his words as prophetic. But tonight, Al's emotions had surfaced and we were all feeling them.

"Teresa, now." Albert motioned for me to join him.

I embraced him and gladly accepted his presentation, even if I did have to share it with my brothers. It took both hands to hold the solid bronze sculpture. I smiled toward the audience and paused a moment. I didn't say a word at the podium. I hadn't thought of the three dolphins as representing the three men—Beardsley, McCaffrey, and Terres—whose bodies were never recovered, and now were swimming with the dolphins.

The applause softened as Sutter returned to the podium, "Five of the men lost on the *Marie* were veterans. Today we honor their service with a flag folding ceremony, conducted by the California State Honor Guard. Please rise."

Flags were on the center table, pre-folded, and ready to be presented. Two soldiers in dress uniforms came down the aisle and placed themselves at attention on either side of the center table. Albert took up his trumpet and stood on the far-right side in front. Another soldier stood with a trumpet on the opposite side in the back as they positioned to play *echo Taps*. Albert would play lead; the soldier would play the echo.

One soldier spoke up. "My fellow soldiers and I, are here tonight to give final military honors to our fallen comrades. This honor consists of the playing of Taps, the unfolding and presentations of flags to surviving family members. We ask all who are able, to remain standing during the playing of Taps, and current and former service members may render proper hand salute. At the conclusion of Taps, please be seated for the presentations."

Albert began playing. The soldier echoed. A sad but sweet sound reverberated back and forth and filled the space. The last note lingered as the soldiers and former service members all saluted.

A tingle ran up my spine.

The two soldiers at the front of the room took one of the diamond-shaped folded flags and held it between their white-gloved hands. One soldier unfolded an edge that had been carefully tucked inside and stretched it out. Next, the other soldier, carefully unfolded the flag, one diagonal, and then the next. Finally, they spread their arms until the flag was fully unfurled.

They then folded the flag lengthwise, and positioned it so that one soldier held the blue background with white stars and the other soldier held the section with red and white stripes. At this point, a third soldier came down the aisle and joined the other two. Grasping a corner of red and white stripes, they formed a triangle. With great precision the soldiers folded the triangle upon itself. At the final fold, one soldier reviewed the points and folds to ensure they were crisp. Then the tallest of the soldiers received the folded flag. He turned around as if on a dime, and moved to stand in front of the oldest child of Diego S. Terres, Jr. The tall soldier knelt, and offered a few private words to my brother Jim as he presented Dad's flag. Finally, he stood and saluted.

Not one sound was heard in the auditorium. Next, flags were

presented to the Howell family, the McCaffrey family, and to Betty Lou Mackie.

Later, Betty Lou shared that she had longed to be presented a flag with such respect and honor.

Sutter returned to the podium for concluding remarks. "In June 1960 seven families lost a loved one when the *Marie* disappeared. The loss of these seven men left unanswered questions and ragged edges in the lives of those left behind. Tonight, we symbolically fold those ragged edges into something more orderly. One flag. One tribute to those four veterans among the seven men. One honor to recognize the national security interest for which the ultimate sacrifice was given.

"Tomorrow is a new day. We can rejoice and commemorate the Days Santa Barbara Stood Still, June 1960.

"Before the Centerpiece Quartet ends the formal part of the commemoration, as a reminder for those attending tomorrow's sunrise wreath laying activity, the boat boards at 6:00am and departs shortly thereafter from the sea landing.

"Thank you all for helping me and the families and friends to remember and honor the *Marie*."

Sutter took his seat for the last time as the Centerpiece Quartet came front and center. They began softly and built up to a crescendo as they sang, *The Lord's Prayer*. Following this, they offered a powerful rendition of "God Bless America." They sang the chorus through once, then motioned to the audience to stand and sing along. It was a fitting end with a standing ovation.

The applause continued as the quartet returned to the sideline. As the audience began to filter out into the reception area, I wondered if anyone recognized the tall tenor as Bob Wilke, the Raytheon engineer in the film.

I wish I could convey to the audience how this man and his wife, Helen, have helped to bring this event together and helped me understand and tell the story of the Marie.

I looked around the museum and saw Sherri taking pictures with the Centerpiece Quartet while others were viewing the exhibit's four panel display. Still others were visiting the Santa Barbara Maritime Museum's other exhibits. Fifty years ago, this was the location where my mother and the other spouses gathered, where Mother knitted a sweater to keep her hands and mind busy as she waited for news. Who could have imagined that we would be gathering here tonight?

****

We returned to the motel, where my brothers joined Ken, Dete, and I in our room for a nightcap. I had recorded Jim's memories of Dad. I had spent time with Don who was too young at the time of Dad's loss to offer any memories. But, I hadn't a clue as to Rick's story. He had spent the last twenty years working overseas for the oil industry. He'd lived in Australia, Sumatra, Kuwait, Oman, and now Jordan. But tonight's activities had brought back many memories for Rick.

"I asked Mom what happened to Dad," Rick began. "I asked her several times, when's Dad coming home. Each time, Mom said, 'We are waiting for a letter in the mail.' Or, 'We are waiting for a letter from the Coast Guard.'" Rick continued to ask what happened to Dad, but with Mom's responses, he grew to distrust the Postal Service because they never brought a letter telling us what happened.

I went to bed with the thought that I lacked a script for the next day's ceremony. I had pages of ramblings but lacked well-crafted words for the sunrise wreath laying. But I was clear about two things: I would take my Bible and a bookmark. Otherwise, I was going to have to think about it tomorrow.

CHAPTER 56:

The Sunrise

Sunday morning, after waking early, Ken, Dete, and I went over to the dock to welcome everyone aboard the Condor Express. We walked down a long wooden gangplank that led to a level with a second gangplank leading directly to the Condor.

Morning fog blanketed the coastline as everyone arrived for the 6:00 am departure. Even though it was June, we dressed warmly for the occasion. Even in the summer, traveling across the Santa Barbara Channel can be chilly.

The Condor Express could cover the distance to the Channel Islands in less than an hour. We planned to make the journey across to the waters at the foot of Santa Cruz Island. We chose this destination because it was the location where some believed the *Marie* wreckage rested beneath the water. We planned to toss a wreath at that location and then tour the area and enjoy what we could before returning to the SEA Landing. By departing the harbor at six, we would arrive at our destination by seven, the same hour that our loved ones were last seen fifty years earlier. As we left the harbor, we heard a foghorn sounding. Sea lions lounged on the sandspit at the end of the breakwater, down from the Lost at Sea Memorial. Visibility was like the weather conditions that day in 1960: mostly sunny, with morning fog.

When we cleared the harbor, the captain throttled up the engines and the Condor began to cruise across the ocean waves. Those on deck felt the ocean spray upon our skin. I went below to check out the large cabin. Coffee and breakfast treats were set out at the galley bar.

People had already claimed several of the booths. At one booth, I saw Glenna's red hair peeking from under her coat. As I recalled, she had said she didn't have her father's sea legs. She wasn't alone. Others sat hunched over at their booths. My heart went out to these folks, but I knew this was a once in a lifetime experience. I hoped they would still be able to enjoy it.

As for me, I didn't have much of a plan for the day. I just wanted to experience this opportunity together, to travel to the waters at the foot of Santa Cruz Island and, hopefully, come full circle.

At a midway point, the boat slowed and everyone above deck enjoyed the antics of a pod of dolphins.

With Santa Cruz Island in view, the Condor slowed its engines because more dolphins arrived and soon encircled us. They rippled the surface, arching in the waves, breaching and falling backwards. It was magical.

"Dolphins as far as the eye can see," I heard someone say.

In the midst of the dolphins, a whale spout erupted. Then a second and a third. Everyone was on deck, mesmerized by the surrounding seas that had come to life.

"I think we are being told to have the ceremony here," Ken said after we regained our thoughts.

Recognizing he was right, I darted up to the bridge. "Stop the engines," I said. "We've found our ceremony spot."

"We are about half a mile from the designated coordinates," The captain informed me.

"Fantastic," I said. The coordinates were only an estimate.

By the time I returned to the deck, the dolphins were thinning and the whales still floated a short distance from the ship, arching in the waves. Ken had already sent Dete and Marisa to bring up the roses, wreath, and leis. I had already retrieved my Bible with its leather bookmark.

"Gather everyone to the back," I heard people saying. Glenna and the others without sea legs had already joined those on deck to see the multitude of dolphins and three whales.

I asked Dete and Marisa to pass out one lei to each person, helping to place it around their necks. Once all had gathered and were wearing their leis, we began. I still had little idea what words would come out of my mouth. But with Ken standing by my side, I was confident my feelings were true and everything would come together.

"These leis are keepsakes," I said. "A symbol of love and hope that we have come full circle."

I looked down at the white roses filling the motel's plastic ice-bucket, as I held out my Bible and opened it to the place with the leather bookmark.

"For much of my life," I said, "I believed my father hadn't listened to God when he got on the *Marie*. But in recent years, I've come to realize, who am I to judge him? That decision was between him and his God. As for me, I've spent my life *trying* to listen to God's still small voice. I didn't always get it right, but *today* I listened and I got it right.

"I hold in my hand a bookmark," I said, holding up the soft tanned skin as it blew in the gentle breeze. "This bookmark is made of deer skin. Mom told me that dad killed a deer with his friends and his friends taught him how to tan the hide. The hide was larger, but when our family home was sold, I had room for only a few things. So, I cut a bookmark from the center of the hide and placed it in my Bible. This bookmark has marked a Scripture passage that I've turned to upon going to bed and waking since I was very young. I've turned to it for wisdom, comfort, and courage. If you are a praying person, please join me."

I moved closer to Ken, because the weight and reality of all those prayers over the years and being in this place, my eyes began overflowing.

I looked sheepishly up at Ken. He understood and took the lead.

"Our Father who art in heaven, Hallowed be thy name. Thy kingdom come. Thy will be done, on earth as it is in heaven. Give us this day our daily bread. And forgive us ... as we forgive .... And lead us not into temptation, but deliver us from evil. For thine is the kingdom, and the power, and the glory, forever. Amen."

When Ken finished reading, I summoned my strength and composure and continued, "We have a plain wreath and we have roses for the core family members to take and weave into the wreath."

I motioned for family to help. Dete and Marisa and others began helping. Marisa held the wreath as Dete and I distributed white roses and encouraged people to come forward and place into the weave.

One by one, people came and attached a single rose to the wreath.

After all the roses were in place, Ken whispered, "Let me take it from here."

I was grateful he did, because I didn't know what to do next.

"Hold the wreath a moment." Ken asked Marisa who stood at the stern holding the wreath proudly to show off its simple intertwined beauty.

"What we would like you to do," Ken said loudly, "is to take thirty seconds and reflect upon those seven men—brothers, fathers, friends. Then, I'd like the children to come up and toss the wreath into the water together. Then we will have Albert play taps."

After thirty seconds of silence, Ken continued, "Lord, we come together today to remember seven men – Dr. Beardsley, Jim McCaffrey, Jim Terres, Jim Russell, Dale Howell, Paul Lovette, and Hal Mackie. We come together to finish this commemoration, and you know what a journey it has been. What an adventure for us.

"It took fifty years since that time, when those men's spirits departed their mortal bodies and now fifty years later we have a chance to come together to celebrate their memory, what they left behind in their spouses, their families, their children. We pray that their spirits know that we still love them and are thinking of them. And our hope is that they are looking down from heaven and smiling proudly, because it is a great day and a worthy occasion. In your son's name we pray, Amen.

"If the children will now come up and take the wreath together and toss it into the ocean." The children stepped forward and Ken said, "Okay, Teresa, you make the call."

"One. Two. Three!" I called out.

The wreath landed upon the rolling waves, with the flowers facing skyward.

"Love you, Dad," I heard one of the McCaffrey boys say.

For the second time this weekend, Albert raised his trumpet and began playing Taps. As he did, those of us at the center stern, moved to the side making a space for those holding flowers to come and toss their flowers upon the sea.   At the last note of Taps, I stood still arms entangled with Dete and Ken, in silence. My thoughts were wrapped up in the moment. I didn't think. I didn't pray. I just wanted to be. Silent. Humble. Grateful. I watched as the wreath floated upon the surface of the sea, and as the additional flowers decorated the waters.

The hum of the Condor's motor had never ceased, but I hadn't noticed it until now. The boat motored ever so slowly away from the wreath, leaving a trail of flowers in its wake.

FIG 42: Above: The children of the Marie unite to toss a wreath at sunrise. Dads peacoat is worn by my brother Don who stands at the center with Glenna Howell, on right, who's hand is the last before the wreath.

We all shared hugs of friendship and fellowship. Then, everyone pulled out their cameras and we all marked the memory in photos.

A few minutes later, I returned to the bridge and told the captain, "We can continue forward and use the time available to enjoy ourselves as if we were tourists." It was the signal to go visit the biggest sea entrance cave in the world and see whatever sea life was near.

Shortly, the Condor was poking its nose into Santa Cruz Island's Painted Cave. I'd been there before, but I marveled again at the island's steep cliffs that, with its pounding surf and jagged rocks, looked imposing and dangerous. From my vantage point, it appeared as if the entire coastline was made up of treacherous rocks. However, I had been to one cove scuba diving as a youth and knew there were safe harbors on the island.

After steering clear of the cave, the Condor turned and headed toward the heart of the Channel. The boat slowed again when we saw the three whales that had accompanied us earlier. On the first visit, the whales had kept their distance, swimming with the dolphins. This time, however, the three whales swam near to us. They moved steadily closer, arching, turning. It looked as if they were waving their dorsal fins and slapping their tails upon the sea. Then, they swam under the boat and surfaced on the opposite side. They turned again dove under the boat. The whales made three passes from one side of the boat to the other. Then, they rolled in the water and sent spouts of water shooting skyward. Everyone stayed on deck as the whales lingered—even those who didn't have sea legs.

"Looks like these humpbacks have taken a liking to us," the captain said over the loud speaker. He explained that the boat's bottom was completely safe for them.

Ken and Albert stood next to each other.

"I wouldn't be surprised if one started talking to you," Ken said with a grin. "Albert, it's been 50 years, what took you so long!"

"Jimmy? Jimmy is that you?" Albert shot back.

I smiled and headed toward the back. As I went, I overheard others playfully talking to the whales.

"Dad is that you?"

At that point, none of us would have been surprised if one of the whales opened its mouth and answered.

"It's time we leave these guys," the captain announced over the PA system. The whales wouldn't leave us and we didn't want to leave them, but we had to return to Santa Barbara. Then, the captain turned the Condor around and we headed back to the harbor.

Brisk wet winds outside and fresh hot coffee inside drew people into the cabin for the return trip. Since the cabin had a large screen and a DVD player, for this part of the trip, I had brought my copy of the Howell Family DVD that Glenna and I had watched together. I thought the other kids would enjoy seeing it, too.

"I have a short Howell family film. You will recognize a couple clips that were used in the *Marie Remembered* documentary, but most important you will see *all* of our fathers, Howell, Russell, and Terres being men and making memories."

Glenna was still seasick, but she poked her head from beneath her coat and came to the front where we had all gathered near the screen.

"That's my mom and my sisters and brother," Glenna interjected.

The first diver appeared diving with his spear gun, "That's my dad," Glenna added.

"It's my dad," I corrected.

"My dad," Glenna returned.

I smiled and let everyone else in on the joke. "We don't know whose dad it is. So, we agreed that when we watch the film individually, we can claim it is our dad. And when we are watching together..." I paused. "It's my dad."

"My dad," Glenna said.

"My dad," Jeff McCaffrey chimed in.

"My dad," added Jeannie Russell.

"My dad," said another of the McCaffrey boys.

In our hearts, we didn't care whose dad it was or wasn't. What we did know was that our dads loved their families and took them on an assortment of adventures together hunting, fishing, and diving.

"That's your dad?" I looked at the McCaffrey brothers who confirmed it was their dad coming from across a field with his catch in one hand, gun in the other, and his dog leaping joyfully at his heels. I saw Pat McCaffrey turn and leave the area, but I wouldn't understand why for some time after the commemoration when I learned he lost his dad and had to give up his dog all in the same week.

As everyone debarked back at the dock, I sought out Jeannie Russell to say goodbye. She would be returning to Colorado with her mother who had slept in instead of joining us on the boat.

"Life-changing weekend," Jeannie said as we embraced.

"For all us kids," I said. I squeezed harder this newfound sister of circumstance. I appreciated her heart that was willing to serve and her uplifting words of encouragement and thanksgiving.

While this was the official close of the *Marie Commemoration Event*, I would see many of these people at the open house brunch that Albert and Lynda Terres were graciously hosting at their home. During the brunch, I had another opportunity to capture more memories and stories of the *Marie*, courtesy of Lee Burrell and his camera.

****

By Monday, we all had gone our separate ways. Ken and I moved to Al and Lynda's and stayed there for a brief visit. After two nights at Albert's and Lynda's we packed up to leave.

"Albert, you said I could take a treasure with me each time I came for a visit and left." I said as I drew close and rubbed his arm affectionately.

"Well, yes." Albert looked at me and then at the dolphin family sculpture.

"Great." I reached for the opal embedded sea-turtle pendant he wore around his neck.

"Oh no." Albert grasped the pendant.

The opal sea turtle was Al's recently-purchased treasure and our agreement covered only historical family treasures.

I chuckled. "It's not often I get away with kidding the kidder."

I picked up the dolphin family sculpture. I stroked the three heads.

"Thanks for everything," I said as I turned and headed toward the car. For years, I desired every Terres family possession that Uncle Albert had. Now I just wanted to come visit them.

As we drove out of Santa Barbara on our return trip to Arkansas, I held Grandmother's Scrapbook. I had brought it for the display at the event social. I opened it and saw once more the image of Grandfather Terres and Albert at the helm, searching the sea. I flipped through the pages and my eyes skimmed the images and headlines. I saw officials and a throng of people investigating wreckage, Paul Lovette's body being transferred from sea to land, a map of the search and rescue, images and biographies of the seven men, and their funeral and memorial announcements.

"All but One."[143] I read the headline of one column that caught my eye. "I think I can consider this activity completed."

"You consider this little gathering good enough for *your* dad?" Ken teased.

I shook my head, rolled my eyes, and closed the scrapbook. Then I unbuckled my seatbelt, turned around, and placed the scrapbook in the back seat.

I was content. I sat quietly for much of the almost two thousand-mile trip, replaying in my mind the commemoration of the men, the event, and the technology surrounding the *Marie* shipwreck. I knew the purpose of the commemoration was not to solve or resolve the mystery but to remember the event and honor the men, their families and those with an interest after fifty years.

I looked skyward, grateful. I knew that God, operating through an army of family and friends, had made the event possible.

I looked over at Ken. I respected him for being himself and rescuing me when I needed rescuing. "You are my hero," I said.

As Ken and I drove east, he believed that this event was the end of the shipwreck thing in his life.

My gut told me that this was merely the end of the beginning.

Epilogue

When Ken and I arrived home, our house felt musty from the humidity that had built up with the air conditioner turned off. While I turned on the air conditioning, Ken began carrying in our luggage and the box of mail that we had picked up from the Post Office.

Our home was in order, except for my creativity room which contained remnants of my project work. A large, framed piece of artwork leaned against one corner. The image was first displayed in the Prodigal Son Art Festival, and more recently at the Santa Barbara Maritime Museum serving as the commemoration logo. It was composed of a collage of news clippings, Santa Cruz Island in the background, a beam of light shining in from heaven in the foreground, and three killer whales at the center.

I had used these three whales because I liked their graceful lines, their contrasting dark and light shapes. I intended for them to reflect a connection between the *black and white* past and the colorful present. The whales were to also offer a heartbeat at the images core. Even the whales' common-name, *killer whale*, added a hint of the sea's danger. But as I recalled the wreath laying boat ride and the whales that joined our excursion I said, "I'll have to change these to humpback whales."

"Hey, you got an interesting envelope," Ken called from the kitchen. He came into my office and handed me a thick legal sized envelope then left.

It's from the National Archives in Saint Louis![144]   I opened it and pulled out a stack of documents. The cover page was just a copy of the letter I had mailed to NARA. I'd been trying to determine if Dr. Beardsley was a government or Raytheon employee when he was lost at sea.

As I flipped through the collection, I noticed that some of the forms were handwritten. Then my heart skipped a beat when the realization hit.

"Dr. Beardsley's hand filled these out," I said after I caught my breath.

For a moment, I closed my eyes, and marveled. I flipped through the other documents, resumes, job descriptions, appreciation memos, medical slips, and health assessments. I couldn't believe the wealth of the information I held in my hands.

In my letter of request to NARA, I had simply asked for a document that would clarify for me whether Dr. Beardsley died as a civilian contractor to the military. I knew NARA couldn't simply answer questions or give out information. I assumed they would send me a copy of his final paperwork, such as a form clarifying his status as retired, relocated, or lost casualty. In my letter, I had also explained who I was and the purpose behind my request, that I was spearheading a commemoration of the *Marie* tragedy.

Instead of copying the final paperwork, however, the NARA archivist had sent me Dr. Niel Freeborn Beardsley's complete file.

The envelope had arrived while we were driving from Arkansas to California, just days before the event. Someone had tried to get this information to me before the commemoration. I didn't know who I had to thank, but I felt honored to be living in a country that trusted me with these records.

And since Wright-Patterson AFB had informed me, "he wasn't one of theirs" when he worked at their site, the question loomed: Who was Dr. Beardsley working for when he was lost at sea?

Ken, who thought the "shipwreck thing" was behind him, poked his head back in my office. "So, what's in the envelope?" he asked.

I just looked at him and smiled.

Acknowledgements

A silver thread woven in the tapestry of this book is that little progress is possible without relationships – nothing could be truer about this book project. The book wouldn't have been completed without the relationships of those who supported the effort from family, friends, colleagues and a few strangers. This story about a mystery wouldn't have been possible without a family-by-circumstance who came together and by way of respectful and relationships wove together their threads. In a way, we all wrote this book.

First, I'm grateful to Aunt Norma who valued a dusty scrapbook.

To those who dedicate their lives in service of others in the US National Guard, US Army, US Navy, US Air Force and the US Coast Guard along with NOAA and the array of national archives with their army of archivist and assistance, this book benefited because you created paperwork, preserved paperwork, and helped me find the paperwork.

Thanks to Greg Gorga and the Santa Barbara Maritime Museum because you showed me the value in remembering shipwrecks, those touched by them, and the lessons we learn from them.

To my collaborator, James Pense and his wife, Laurel who took a chance on me I'm humbly grateful. Your dogged pursuit for clarity invigorated the story. Your professionalism and friendship made the long journey enjoyable.

To Andrew McClain, your fact-finding and editorial assistance added integrity.

To my mentor, Laura Funkhouser, you showed me the value in collecting oral histories and set me on a course to navigate on a path of endless discovery.

To Uncle Albert and Aunt Lynda, you helped me capture and preserve our past while living our present with song, laughter, and a few rounds of tennis – and provided a place to call home.

To Bob and Helen Wilke, you opened up your heart and your family and you entrusted a piece of your awesome story.

To Dr. Bob and Rachel Watkins, the book didn't begin with the notes taken during a surprise breakfast, but that morning built a bridge between me and Raytheon's retired engineers that made all the difference to me and this book.

To my sisters of a shipwreck Glenna and Jeannie, you trusted me with your hearts. Talking about "our dads" and watching "our dads" scuba dive, is a treasure to hold in these pages.

To Diana Vandervoort, you saved a volunteer role for me in Santa Barbara Old Spanish Days and cheered on my efforts capturing creating this book which gave my spirit rest and rejuvenation.

To retired Captain Sutter Fox and your bride Bonnie, you were a gracious and knowledgeable guide whom I'm forever grateful to for your "family support" because it served these pages integrity in the telling of more than things related to the US Coast Guard.

Thanks also to retired Colonel Kathy Chambers whose reading of an early manuscript provided insight and inspiration.

Thanks to retired Colonel Sharon (Sherri) Sims who served this book-project as my friend who's iron sharpened my iron because your early reading of the manuscript and especially in keeping me in step with a fit life.

Thanks brother Diego, you are a powerful critic, editor, and idea-generator as the story mystery and manuscript evolved. Your attention to details in the book combined with your first-hand knowledge of technical topics and the Santa Barbara Channel offered priceless service.

To my brother Rick, you rendered brilliant service by opening up your home by the lighthouse because it was a visual reminder of the purpose of light shining in darkness as I completed this book.

To my brother Don, the list is long where you served this effort by talking of research and especially in caring for other family-related issues which allowed me to focus and complete this project. Your lovely bride, Lily, and children Matthew and Bella gave up their beds during my research trips into the national archives in the Los Angeles area.

My circles of prayer warriors with Fellowship Bible Church small-group, my life-ready ladies, and those in the MWGA - You help in the navigation of my life's waters with grace, abundance and joy which gave me a cocoon from which I could birth this book.

To Michael Hyatt & Co, I could have lost my way during some dark days where you served this effort as a lighthouse so I could navigate to a safe harbor.

To my Colonel Ken (Fig) Newton family, I'd have only a shipwreck if it wasn't for my children and grandchildren— you add colorful threads in the tapestry to the legacy of Colonel and Mimi T.

To my dearest Dete, your acts of service and your playful spirit is a source of motivation to me when I was tempted to give up. Your determination that I snorkel Key Largo's Christ of the Abyss, served as a carrot to motivate my completion of this book project.

To my dearest Ken, who served God, me, our household, our family and our community which in turn served to inspire me to go the distance. God brought us together for this purpose. From here to eternity— I'm eternally grateful. To God be all glory.

APPENDIX

FIG 43: Above: The Marie is envisioned using a white line super-imposed on top of an image of a landing craft.

FIG 44: Left: Original image of the Marie reproduced from the holdings at the College Park, MD, National Archives.

FIG 45: Left: The Marie with snoozing Cal Poly San Luis Obispo's scuba diving club after an adventure to find the legendary monster lobsters.

Scan to view the film and timeline.

Dr. Niel F. Beardsley, 68, Raytheon staff scientist, was considered a pioneer in the art and science of infrared. Dr. Beardsley had been influential in the "seeing in the dark" technology. During World War II, he pioneered optical shop techniques for the Manhattan project, and liked it so much that he continued the work in 1946 at the Air Technical Intelligence Center (ATIC) at Wright-Patterson Air Force Base, Ohio.

Among his work at Wright-Patterson, he monitored the ATIC contracts and was especially proud of the contract at Syracuse University, N.Y. for detector research because it was still in force after fourteen years. Dr. Beardsley regarded the people who carried out the research as his "family."

Loren Dale Howell, 32, expert scuba diver who would help to place the electronic equipment underwater. Dale was a Santa Barbara Skin Diving Association president and a veteran who served in the Army at Point Barrow, Alaska, with the Seventh Armed Cavalry Division in Korea, and at the Army's Arctic Fighting and survival school in Japan. He was a Santa Barbara High School graduate, class of 1946. Dale's father, the late Loren (Butch) Howell, was the 1958 man of the year in Goleta. Dale left behind a wife and four children.

Harold Herbert Mackie, Jr, 32, Raytheon electronics engineer, served in the Navy as aviation electronics technician from 1946 to 1948. He was a native of Santa Barbara and graduated from Santa Barbara High School in 1944 and UCSB in 1953, with a BS in physics. He was active in the community, including the American Radio Relay League and the SB Chamber of Commerce as Sound Products co-owner. While both serving as Alhecama Theatre volunteers, Hal and the former Betty Lou Curtis met and later married.

Paul Timothy Lovette, (Not depicted), 37, had been in Santa Barbara four months from the Los Angeles area and was a native of Salisbury, N.C. He had been working as as a salesman for Vic Tanny's gym. He left behind a wife and two children.

* CONTINUED on page 384:

Hugh James McCaffrey, 30, was the captain of the *Marie* and project scuba diver. McCaffrey, with Richard W. Dowse, co-owned the McCaffrey Sporting Goods store that his father and uncle founded in 1899. He graduated from Santa Barbara High School in 1949 and attended UCSB. He served in the Army and was a Korean War Veteran. As an avid sportsman, his adventures and articles in publications like Skin Diver Magazine inspired many outdoorsmen. He left behind a wife who was expecting their fourth child. Jim was one of the three victims never recovered.

James Clifford Russell, 32, Raytheon engineering section manager and the project manager. A native of New York whose parents relocated to Los Angeles when he was a youth, he became a Merchant Marine before graduating from UC Berkeley with a degree in mechanical engineering. He was an avid fisherman and scuba diver. He left behind a wife and daughter.

Diego Santos Terres, Jr., 29, Raytheon mechanical engineer, served in the Navy during the Korean War as a jet engine mechanic aboard the aircraft carrier USS Yorktown. He graduated from Santa Barbara High School in 1948 and the California Polytechnical University at San Luis Obispo in 1959, with a BS in mechanical engineering. He was an accomplished scuba diver and pilot. Jim's father, Diego S. Terres, Sr., immigrated to Santa Barbara from Spain as a young boy and later developed several commercial properties in Old Town Goleta. Jim left behind a wife and four children. Jim was one of the three victims never recovered.

Scan to view the film and timeline.

RAYTHEON COMMUNICATOR

RAYTHEON SANTA BARBARA OPERATIONS

SANTA BARBARA, CALIFORNIA   JULY, 1960

IN MEMORY

Dr. Niel F. Beardsley
Raytheon Staff Scientist

Loren Dale Howell
Crew Member

Paul T. Lovette
Crew Member

Harold H. Mackie
Raytheon Electronics
Engineer

James H. McCaffrey
Crew Member

James C. Russell
Raytheon Engineering
Section Manager

Diego S. (Jim) Terres, Jr.
Raytheon Mechanical
Engineer

Man in his search for knowledge always has had to confront nature, in the air, on land, or at sea. Since the beginning of time this has been so. Only among the brave, the pioneers, will you find men who willingly meet nature in the quest for knowledge alone. The men aboard the Marie were dedicated to this purpose.

We have suffered a great loss. To all of us, these men were exceptional and outstanding co-workers. To many of us, they were our closest friends and to the Raytheon Company four were valuable, trustworthy, technical employees.

Where our loss is great, how overwhelming must be the grief of the wives, children, and relatives of these men. How great a burden must be their sorrow. To these families who have lost their loved ones, we offer our deepest heartfelt sympathy.

Gordon Humphrey

AN OPEN LETTER OF APPRECIATION

During the past several weeks we have had cause to witness the organizational efficiency of the United States Coast Guard, the remarkable coordination they have developed in sea and air work, and particularly the high degree of thoughtful and understanding service provided by Coast Guard officers and enlisted men. We all can be extremely grateful that we have such an organization to call upon when their help is needed.

To Captain Zittel, Chief of Operations, we extend a special vote of thanks. His overall direction and ability was reflected in the efficiency of all search operations.

To Lt. C. V. Cowing, we express deep appreciation for his continuous effort in diagraming and communicating the overall pattern of the sea and air search. The senior rated men who was responsible for the actual patrol boat operation of 95334 and 83320 was QM1 Jimmy Spears. To him

and his hard working crew we extend a deep and heartfelt thank you.

To QM1, John Westbury, we owe a debt of gratitude. His quiet thoughtful and understanding manner, his close grasp of all details, and his efficient management of the Santa Barbara Coast Guard Station during a trying time was indeed outstanding.

We also thank YM1 Ray Wilkinson and Jack Moore who were on duty at the Santa Barbara Coast Guard Station. These men displayed unusual tact and judgement by being extremely helpful to those who asked their help.

We are also grateful for the services, so efficiently performed by the Santa Barbara County Sheriff's Office. To Sheriff Ross, Sergeant Russel Eskilson, Deputy Fritz Patterson, Detective Clayton J. Cornish, Mrs. Mary Hernandez and the many others who were so understandingly helpful.

"We Could Not Have Suffered a Greater Loss" — Mr. Adams

Expressing deep concern for the men and families of the men lost on the "Marie," Mr. Charles Adams, Chairman of the Raytheon Company Board of Directors, said upon his arrival in Santa Barbara, "We could not have suffered a greater loss than we have through this sudden tragedy. The sad news affects us all and while I am here I would like to meet the families of these men to express, on behalf of the entire Raytheon Company, our deepest sympathy."

Dr. Beardsley and his wife Nell bought a home at 3932 Foothill Rd. more than a year ago when he joined the staff at Raytheon here. A native of Wadsworth, Ohio, he studied at Hiram College, Ohio, took his master's at Northwestern and his doctor's degree in physics in the University of Chicago.

Harold Herbert Mackie, Jr., is a native of Santa Barbara, and graduated from UCSB in 1953, majoring in physics. He joined Raytheon four years ago. He met his wife, the former Betty Lou Curtis of Santa Barbara, in 1954 when they were working on an Alhecama Theater production and they were married here in 1955. The couple live at 26 La Cudena.

James Clifford Russell, 32, engineering section manager, has been with Raytheon Co. for four years. He attended the University of California at Berkeley, graduating in 1951 with BS in mechanical engineering. He and his wife Helen and his daughter Jean, 9, live at 3616 San Jose Lane.

Diego S. (Jim) Terres, Jr., 29, mechanical engineer, has been with Raytheon Co. for nearly a year. He is a graduate of California Polytechnic College in 1959 in mechanical engineering. He and his wife Marian and four children live at 68 Alpine St., El Encanto Heights. The children are James, 7; Ricky, 4; Terry, 3; and Donald, 1.

Scan to view the film and timeline.

FIG 52: Above: In the Raytheon Company, Santa Barbara Operations, Newsletter, July 1960, lease read the General Manager's words above that begin, "Man in his search for knowledge…" because I believe they hold truth.

Notes

(Endnotes)

1 Shipwrecks, Smugglers and Maritime Mysteries, by Eugene D. Wheeler, Robert E. Kallman, 1984, page 96.

2 For a listing of the newspaper articles, see the Bibliography.

3 The Old Town Goleta Cultural Project launched in 1998, spearheaded by Laura Funkhouser along with professional historian Fermina Murray, who received a grant from The Fund for Santa Barbara. The project collected oral histories from dozens of past and present residents, business and property owners, and community members to include the Terres family. https://www.noozhawk.com/article/072010_laura_funkhouser_the_right_new_look_for_old_town_goleta For another perspective of Old Town Goleta, California, and historian's Laura Funkhouser and Fermina Murray's efforts see (One of my Grandfather Terres' buildings he built is labled as #7): http://goletahistory.com/old-town/

4 https://www.facebook.com/pg/National-Guard-Professional-Education-Center-379287698788981/about/?ref=page_internal

5 The National Guard State Partnership Program. http://www.nationalguard.mil/Leadership/Joint-Staff/J-5/International-Affairs-Division/State-Partnership-Program/

6 Nuttall later raised in rank to retire as Major General James Nuttall, https://en.wikipedia.org/wiki/James_W._Nuttall

7 Cutter Docks to End Vain Search for Missing Men: Five Presumed Dead, Santa Barbara News-Press, Sunday Edition, June 12, 1960. In this article an image includes Raytheon Co. Santa Barbara General Manager, the equipment division general manager at

MYSTERY OF THE MARIE

Waltham, MA, and the manager of the western region.

8 www.Raytheon.com

Apparently, the "shot heard around the world" is a phrase originally memorialized by Ralph Waldo Emerson in his 1837 poem Concord Hymn. I'm aware of three opinions as to what is being referred to in the skirmishes in MA as the "shot": (1) A symbolic first shot from a Patriot's rifle. (2) An order sent out by King George III to confiscate the colonists' guns, https://www.westernjournalism.com/the-shot-heard-around-the-world/ (3) And recently I heard the shot described as the order shouted by a Patriate, "Shoot by God, shoot"said a recent tour guide. https://en.wikipedia.org/wiki/Shot_heard_round_the_world

10 "Mystery of scientist's '53 death grips son," by Scott Shane of the Baltimore Sun, re-published in the Arkansas Democrat Gazette, Sunday, September 12, 2004.

11 Isaiah 41:1-13

12 Dad and his roadster are featured in "Images of America, Hot Rodding in Santa Barbara County," by Tony Baker, Arcadia Publishing, 2014, page 62 and 66.

13 I drew this image of Dr. Bob's napkin. Then, I tossed the napkin away. I regret tossing it now because it was a Dr. Bob original.

14 Interview reconstructed from authors notes from the surprise breakfast, 2005. Also, supported in part by Oral History interview June 2010.

15 www.Raytheon.com

16 The surprise breakfast dialogue is reconstructed from author's notes which I scribbled during the activity, August 2005. I was also assisted by stories repeated during the Oral History interviews at the same site between three of the engineers, June 2010. And a search of the New York Times, offered confirmation of the Soviet submarine topic:

> -"Soviet Submarines Held A Major Peril," Special to the New York Times, December 15, 1960
> -"Pacific Fleet Sees Many Red Warships," Special to the New York Times, October 21, 1954
> -"House Realigns Defense Budget: Votes 39.3 Billion for Arms, Stressing Missile Work – Pentagon Takes Cuts," " by Hanson W. Baldwin, The New York Times, April 17, 1959

17 Reconstructed from interviews between Bob and Helen Wilke and the author, August 2005 - June 2010

18 Dad's mystery song turned out to be, "By the Way", Warner Brother's Music Corp., Jo Stafford sings the hit tune here in 1948: https://www.youtube.com/watch?v=TBqQWnOF5Kg Interestingly, here a selection of pictures show me how

much my mother in her youth looked similar to Ms. Stafford. Perhaps, my father believed the same? https://sonichits.com/video/Jo_Stafford/By_The_Way

19 "Coast Guard Ends Search – Final Cutter Trip Due In Hunt for Five MISSING MEN Believed Dead", Ocean Hunt Off, Santa Barbara News-Press, Saturday, June 11, 1960, by James Schermerhorn, News-Press Staff Writer

20 "Saved by Dolphins", by Michael Fessier Jr., Los Angeles Times West Magazine (A Sunday magazine), July 2, 2006.

21 "Saved by Dolphins", by Michael Fessier Jr., Los Angeles Times West Magazine (A Sunday magazine), July 2, 2006; interviews by Don Terres 2006; phone and face to face interviews with James "Bud" Bottoms by author in 2006, 2009, 2010.

22 "Your Dad saved his life" said Bud Bottoms to my brother Don and later to me. Along with this statement, Bud goes on to say that McCaffrey, Howell, Terres and he went rafting on a local river and he (Bud) on one rapid was pinned by brush and debris along with the current. And Dad came rushing down the river and spoting Bud, Dad swooped in and dislodged the dam setting Bud free. Later, Dad shared his Spanish Bota bag filled with wine as they rested on the banks of the river. The days adventure is recounted in words and images in the news article: "Four Skindivers Conquer River," Santa Barbara News-Press, Tuesday Evening, April 8, 1958.

23 "All But One", 'Marie' Victim Died Of Shock, Exposure, Santa Barbara News-Press, Friday Evening, June 17, 1960.

24 Men's Fraternity. Curriculum helping **men** to explore authentic manhood and the critical issues they face in our ever-changing culture (at home and at work). www.mensfraternity.com/

25 Mustard Tree Art Productions, The Prodigal: An Exploration of Luke 15, 2008 http://www.mustardtreearts.com/ .

26 Six Lost in Channel Science Test; Body of 7th Man Found, Santa Barbara News-Press, June 10, 190, Page A-1.

27 Sande, Ken, The Peacemaker: A Biblical Guide to Resolving Personal Conflict, Baker Books, Michigan, 2004

28 Lewis, C.S., The Chronicles of Narnia: The Horse and His Boy, HarperCollinsPublisher, USA, 1954

29 See Appendix: Timeline Version 1

30 The incident between a USA sub and Japanese fishing vessel included the USS Greeneville and the Japanese-fishery high-school training ship, Ehime Maru. Ken's officemate and our friend was USCG Captain F. Sutter Fox, Liaisons to the USPACOM. The collision occurred on 9 February 2001, about 9 nautical miles (17 km) off the south coast of Oahu, Hawaii, United States.

31 A little known fact, is that the infamous John Walker served on the USS Razorback with a top secret cryptographic clearance. Years later, Walker would become "The U.S. Navy's Biggest Betrayal." Two sources proved useful – a book by Pete Earley, *Family of Spies: Inside the John Walker Spy Ring*, Bantam, 1988; Linked by way of the U.S. Navy: "The John Walker Spy Ring and The U.S. Navy's Biggest Betrayal", by John Prados, September 2, 2014
https://news.usni.org/2014/09/02/john-walker-spy-ring-u-s-navys-biggest-betrayal

32 http://www.USSGrowler.com, http://www.wa3key.com/growler.html

33 *Foreign Relations of the United States, 1958–1960*, United Nations and General International Matters, Volume II, Editors: Suzanne E. Coffman, Charles S. Sampson, Government Printing Office, Washington, D.C., 1991 https://history.state.gov/historicaldocuments/frus1958-60v02 (Included are documents on "Laws of the Sea")

34 *Foreign Relations of the United States, 1958–1960*, Editors: Suzanne E. Coffman, Edward C. Keefer, and Harriet Dashiell Schwar, Government Printing Office, Washington, D.C., 1992 https://history.state.gov/historicaldocuments/frus1958-60v04

35 Ibid

36 The U-2: http://www.coldwar.org/articles/60s/u2_incident.asp

37 'Maire' Fund Proposed, by Markham Field MacLin, Santa Barbara NewsPress, Friday Evening, June 17, 1960. Within this letter to the editor, Mr. MacLin suggested a fund be started because he and his wife were classmates at Santa Barbara High School with three of the crew members. I don't know if his words inspired the funds that would be awarded later to UCSB students; but, his words about the U-2 were a gift, linking me to the context of the times.

38 Shadow Divers: The True Adventure of Two Americans Who Risked Everything to Solve One of the Last Mysteries of World War II, Robert Kurson, Ballantine Books, 2005.

39 The Museum of Science and Industry (MSI), "*U-505 Submarine*", 5700 S Lake Shore Dr, Chicago, Illinois

40 The Museum of Science and Industry (MSI), Exhibit - Honor, Courage, Commitment: United States Navy, 5700 S Lake Shore Dr, Chicago, Illinois.

41 The letter to "Los Bailadores Dance Group" was on letterhead stationary "California Interscholastic Federation and C.I.F. Protection Fund" and signed by Dorothy and Bill Russell, dated June 13, 1960. The Russell's and the Terres' are families that date back to the families involved in Old Spanish Days initiation.

42 Committee Meeting Minutes record this fact. Shown and told to me by Diana (Russell) Vandervoort, Noches de Ronda Chair.

43 The documents filed by then Marian H. Terres a "Creditor's Claim" and a "Complaint for Damages" listed defendants as individuals and co-partners of a McCaffrey Brother's Sporting Goods and its co-partner's Richard W. Dowse and Hugh James McCaffrey's estate.

44 The research I conducted at NARA Los Angeles at Laguna Niguel was, in fact, conducted starting 22-26 June, 2007. I place it here because it fits into the flow of the timeline. . Also, I did conduct an additional visit in August 2007 after the Santa Barbara Fiesta too along with a couple other brief visits to the site.

45 Shadow Divers: The True Adventure of Two Americans Who Risked Everything to Solve One of the Last Mysteries of World War II, Robert Kurson, Ballantine Books, 2005, page 186.

46 History of USS Norton Sound (AVM-1), Ships History, Navy Yard, Washington D.C., page 3.

47 Pacific Missile Range, The Comptroller Annual Report, The Effective Use of Money, Material, Manpower, Year Ending 30, 1960, Page 42. The four ships listed on this page being PVT Joe E. Mann, USNS Haiti Victory, USNS Dalton Victory, and USS King County.

48 History of USS Norton Sound (AVM-1), Ships History, Navy Yard, Washington D.C., page 5.

49 ALL HANDS: The Bureau of Naval Personnel Career Publication, Feb 1965, Number 577, Polaris A-3 Deploys in the Atlantic & Pacific, pg 20.

50 ALL HANDS: The Bureau of Naval Personnel Career Publication, Feb 1965, Number 577, Polaris A-3 Deploys in the Atlantic & Pacific, pg 20.

51 *Command History of the Naval Air Force, U.S. Pacific Fleet* , 1960

52 Reconstructed from e-mails sent between July and August, 2007 between Sutter Fox and author

53 Ibid

54 Ibid

55 The Albatross UF-1G1294, Sutter corrected me in an e-mail Aug 14, 2007, between Sutter Fox and Teresa Newton-Terres.

56 "6 Lost in Channel Science Test; Body of 7th Man Found," Santa Barbara Newspress, June 10, 1960, A-1.

57 Finding of Body at Sea Spurs Hunt for 7 Missing on Secret Mission, Los Angeles Times, June 10, 1960.

58 Search coordinates for the Marie were listed on the *Cape Sable*'s deck log as 34^0 11.5'N x 119^0 30.5W, and entered between 000-0400 (4AM), Friday, 10-June-1960.

59 Reconstructed from e-mails in August, 2007 with the author.

60 Ibid.

61 The e-mail I edited out the words "two" and "five of" from the original text so that it was clear and accurate because the Marie took out crew, Raytheon staff, and a guest. Here's John Stites full sentence " We had learned the M/V *Marie* along with **two** crewmen had been hired by Raytheon Corp. to take **five of** their people out to a point off Santa Cruz Island for the purpose of testing a classified underwater piece of equipment, possibly some sort of Sonar." (John Stites, e-mail with author 24-Aug-2007)

62 Six Lost in Channel Science Test; Body of 7th Man Found, Santa Barbara News-Press, June 10, 190, Page A-1.

63 Reconstructed from e-mail conversations with author.

64 Ibid.

65 The *Ehime Maru* and USS *Greeneville* collision occurred off Oahu, Hawaii, on 9 February 2001. It was between between the United States Navy (USN) *Los Angeles*-class submarine USS *Greeneville* (SSN-772) and the Japanese-fishery high-school training ship *Ehime Maru*. For more information, review these sources: http://www. cpf.navy.mil/subsite/ehimemaru/legal/Executive_Summary3.pdf AND https://www.ntsb.gov/news/press-releases/Pages/USS_GreenevilleEhime_Maru_Collision_Update.aspx

66 Reconstructed from e-mails in September 2007 with the author.

67 Reconstructed from e-mails in September 2007 with the author.

68 Six Lost in Channel Science Test; Body of 7th Man Found, Santa Barbara News-Press, June 10, 190, Page A-1.

69 Telling of a May 2007 dream.

70 Dale Howell served in the Army at Point Barrow, Alaska, with the Seventh Armed Cavalry Division in Korean, and at the Army's Arctic Fighting and survival school in Japan.

71 E-mail February 7, 2007 from Eric Maulhardt to author.

72 Glenna Howell, reconstructed conversations from interview notes from July 2008 and Glenna Howell oral history film and transcript from, August 2009.

73 The Coast Guard report found in the Glenna Howell family archives has a simple

heading "UNITED STATES COAST GUARD." It is a memo format. However, it is addressed as a "Reply to Officer in Charge, Marine Inspection." And what's also unique, the "reply" is placed on top of the "memo" formatting that is, in fact, "From: Senior Investigating Officer, Long Beach" and the "to" identified a Coast Guard authority by title and not by name, "Commandant (MVI) and the "Subj:" was identified as "M/B MARIE, O/N 253 652; disappearance of resulting in loss of life." To my mind this was the Search and Rescue (SAR) I sought. However, when I showed it to the Washington D.C. Historian, the report was said to offer more information than what a SAR would offer. Thus, I was and am somewhat baffled. Thus, I'm left to wonder, "What would the SAR include?" And, "Why would this report be in a private family archive and not in a National Archive?"

74 "All But One", 'Marie' Victim Died Of Shock, Exposure, Santa Barbara News-Press, Friday Evening, June 17, 1960.

75 Joshua 1: 6-9, New American Standard Bible. This experience occurred Feb 1, 2008. And, for the ease of retelling these events, I believed it best suited for this time and place in the writing and retelling of events.

76 The U.S. Route 50 stretching across Nevada is known as the "The Loneliest Road in America" which Wikipedia said was first called it by Life Magazine in 1986. https://en.wikipedia.org/wiki/U.S._Route_50_in_Nevada

77 In showing the Coast Guard report ("M/B MARIE, O/N 253 652; disappearance of resulting in loss of life," *United States Coast Guard, Memo from Senior Investigating Officer to Commandant (MVI), July 27, 1960*, to the US Coast Guard Historian, Washington D.C., the officer believed the report to offer me more details than what an official SAR included.

78 Santa Barbara News-Press, 6 Lost in Channel Science Test; Body of 7th Man Found, Friday, June 10, 1960, page A-1.

79 Santa Barbara News-Press, "BELIEVED TO BE 'MARIA'[sic] –Wreckage of Boat Found Off Island", by Charles Ireland, November 6, 1969, page A-6.

80 "MARIE Story Told At CG Hearing", Santa Barbara News-Press, Wednesday Evening, June 15, 1960

81 "Wreckage of Boat Found Off Island: Believed to Be 'MARIA''", Santa Barbara News-Press, Thursday Evening, November 6, 1969

84 Western Sea Frontier, Treasure Island, San Francisco, California, Command History, 1960, Reproduced from the holdings of the Ships History, Naval History and Heritage Command, Navy Yard, Washington D.C., page 3.

85 Civil Docket, United States District Court For The Southern District of California Central Division, In the Matter of the Petition of Richard W. Dowse, et al., Dawn Howell Hooker, etc., et al., Plaintiffs, vs. Raytheon Company, etc., et al, Defendants, In Admiralty No. 495-61-EC (Civil No. 235-61-EAC).

86 Civil Docket, United States District Court, 235-61-EC, Hooker vs. Raytheon Company (Complaint for damages for wrongful death, under Jones Act, Death on the High Seas Act, and Common Law Action for Wrongful Death). (This docket was located after the Civil Docket for the United States District Court, 495-61-EC).

87 JOINT PRE-TRIAL CONFERENCE ORDER, No. 235-61-S, Filed July, 27 1962, listed the following:

The following issues of fact, and no others, remain to litigated upon the trial:

A. Was the *Marie* lost at sea, as alleged?

B. If so, where and when did such loss occur?

C. What was the cause of the loss of the *Marie*?

D. Who are the survivors or beneficiaries of Loren Dale Howell, deceased, and Paul Timothy Lovette, deceased? Who are entitled to recover damages, if any, under the applicable statute?

E. What are the damages, if any, sustained by the survivors or beneficiaries of Loren Dale Howell, deceased, and Paul Timothy Lovette, deceased, as a result of their respective deaths?

F. What burial expenses, if any, are the said survivors or beneficiaries of Loren Dale Howell, deceased, and Paul Timothy Lovette, deceased, entailed to?

G. As to each defendant, was Loren Dale Howell a seaman or member of the crew of the vessel *Marie* employed by that defendant under the Jones Act, or was he a passenger or visitor aboard the *Marie* under the Death on the High Seas Act, or under the California Wrongful Death statutes?

H. If said Loren Dale Howell was such seaman or member of the crew under the Jones Act, what are the amount of damages, if any, for the conscious pain and suffering sustained by said Loren Dale Howell until the time of his death?

I. As to each defendant, was Paul Timothy Lovette a seaman or member of the crew of the said vessel *Marie* employed by that defendant under the Jones Act, or was he a passenger or visitor aboard the *Marie* under the Death on the High Seas Act, or under the California wrongful death statutes?

J. If said Paul Timothy Lovette was such seaman or member of the crew under the Jones Act, what are the amont of damages, if any, for the conscious pain and suffering sustained by the said Paul Timothy Lovette until the time of his death?

K. Did the sinking or loss of the *Marie* occur in the Pacific Ocean more or less than a marine league from the shore of the State of California? In either case, did the loss occur in the territorial waters of the State of California?

A.   Was the occurrence an inevitable or unavoidable accident?

B.   Was there assumption of risk on the part of Loren Dale Howell and/or Paul Timothy Lovette?

C.   Were said Loren Dale Howell and/or Paul Timothy Lovette contributory negligent?

D.   Who owned the vessel *Marie* at the time of her loss or sinking? Was the Raytheon Company the owner, or operator and/or chatterer of the *Marie*?

E.   Were either Richard Dowse or Hugh James McCaffrey, or both, documented as Master or Masters of the *Marie* at the time of her loss or sinking?

F.   Was Hugh James McCaffrey negligent in the maintenance and/or operation of the vessel *Marie*? Was McCaffrey Brothers Sporting Goods negligence in the maintenance and/or operation of the vessel *Marie*? Was Richard Dowse negligent in the maintenance and/or operation of the vessel *Marie*? Did the Raytheon Company operate or maintain the *Marie* and, if so, was it negligent?

G.   Was Richard Dowse negligent in his selection of a master of the vessel *Marie* at the time of its loss? Was McCaffrey Brothers Sporting Goods negligent in its selection of a master for the vessel *Marie* at the time of its loss? Did the Raytheon Company select the master of the vessel *Marie* and, if so, was it negligent in such selection? (Raytheon contends this is not a proper issue under the pleadings.)

H.   Was the vessel *Marie* inadequately equipped and maintained and without proper survey and inspection in such a manner that she became, and was allowed to remain, unseaworthy at the time of her loss?

I.   If the Raytheon Company is found to be such an owner or charterer as to be entitled to limit liability, did Raytheon have privity to or knowledge of any fault or negligence in connection with the loss of the *Marie*?

VII:

The exhibits to be offered at the trial, insofar as presently known, together with a statement of all admissions by, and all issue between, the parties with respect thereto, are as follows:

A.   Ship's documents of M/V *Marie*. Foundation is waived.

B.   Partnership Agreement between Richard W. Dowse and Hugh James McCaffrey, dated January 2, 1957. Foundation is waived.

C.   Document designedated Purchase Order No. 41-1-GF-1873, and other documents relating to said transaction. Foundation is waived.

D.   United States Hydrographic Office Chart No. 5202 for Santa Barbara Channel and environs. Foundation is waived.

E.   United States Weather Bureau reports for the period June 7-10, 1960, inclusive, for the area of Santa Barbara Channel. Foundation is waived.

F.   Death Certificates and autopsy reports on Loren Dale Howell and Paul Timothy Lovette. Foundation is waived.

VIII:

The following <u>issues of law</u>, and no others, <u>remain to be litigated</u> upon the trial:

A. Which defendants, if any, were such chatterers of the *Marie* at the time of her loss, if such accident occurred, as might be considered owners within the meaning of 46 United States Code, Section 182, et seq., or any other applicable law?

B. Is there a presumption of unseworthiness arising from the loss of the *Marie* under these circumstances, and, if so, against whom?

C. If the loss is determined to have occurred within the territorial waters of California, would this Court have admiralty jurisdiction? Will the Death on the High Seas Act apply?

D. Were Loren Dale Howell and Paul Timothy Lovette, or either of them, contributory negligent or did they, or either of them, assume any risk?

E. Did the loss of the *Marie* occur under such circumstances as to give rise to a presumption of negligence under the doctrine of res ipsa Loquitur, against anyone and, if so, against whom?

F. If Raytheon Company is found to be such an owner or chatterer as to be eligible to limit liability, are they entitled to limitations?

G. What duty, if any, did each of the defendants owe to each of the plaintiffs?

IX:

CROSS-CLAIMS AND ISSUES THEREUNDER

1. Defendant Raytheon has filed a Cross-Claim against defendant Richard Dowse individually and doing business under the fictitious name of "McCaffrey Brothers Sporting Goods" and McCaffrey Brothers Sporting Goods alleging a right to be indemnified by Cross-defendants for any recovery by plaintiffs against Raytheon by reason of the relationship of Raytheon and cross-defendants. A second count in the Cross-Claim alleges a similar right to indemnity by reason of the terms of a written contract between Raytheon and Cross-Defendants The cross-defendants have answered this cross-claim denying the material allegations therefore and asserting the defenses of unavoidable accident, sole negligence of Raytheon, and limitation of liability.

2. Defendant Richard Dowse has filed a Cross-Complaint against defendant Raytheon for $5,000.00 damages for the loss of the vessel *Marie*. Raytheon has answered this cross-complaint denying the material allegations and asserting the defenses of the terms of the written agreement between the parties, and an agency relationship between McCaffrey Brothers Sporting Goods and Dowse.

3. The only additional fact admitted by the cross-pleadings is that Dowse was the owner of the *Marie*.

4. The additional issues of fact under the cross-pleadings are:

A. Was McCaffrey Brothers Sporting Goods the agent of

Dowse in supplying the services, material and equipment under Raytheon's purchase order?

B. Was there any act or omission on the part of McCaffrey Brothers Sporting Goods or its agents, employees or subcontractors which caused any loss to Raytheon in the principal action

C. Was there any agreement between Raytheon and Dowse for the return of the *Marie*?

D. If there was such an agreement, was the failure to return the vessel the result of any fault of Raytheon?

E. Did Raytheon have exclusive control, possession and command of the *Marie* at any time on the last voyage?

F. If Raytheon had exclusive control, possession and command of the *Marie* on her last voyage, did her loss occur with the privity of knowledge of Raytheon within the meaning of the Limitation of Liability, Act 46 U.S.C. Section 183 through 186?

G. The amount of damages, if any, sustained by Dowse.

5. The additional issues of law under the cross-pleadings are:

A. Is Raytheon entitled to be indemnified by Dowse and / or McCaffrey Brothers Sporting Goods for any loss which may be suffered by Raytheon in the principal action by reason of the relationship of the parties under the written purchase order?

B. Is Raytheon entitled to be indemnified as in "A" above by reason of the specific provisions of the written purchase order?

C. Does Raytheon have any liability to Dowse for the loss of the *Marie*?

D. If Raytheon does have any such liability, is Raytheon entitled to limitation of said liability under the Limitation of Liability Act, 46 U.S.C. Sections 183 through 196?

88 JOINT PRE-TRIAL CONFERENCE ORDER, No. 235-61-S, Filed July, 27 1962

89 Civil Case No. 235-61-EC Transcript Testimony of Richard Dowse, page 15-19.

90 Civil Case No. 235-61-EC Transcript Testimony of Richard Dowse, page 61.

91 Civil Case No. 235-61-EC Transcript Testimony of Richard Dowse, page 79.

92 MEMORANDUM OPINION FOR USE IN PREPARATION OF, FINDINGS OF FACT, CONCLUSIONS OF LAW and JUDGMENT, Filed July, 8 1963, IN ADMIRALTY NO. - NO. 235-61-EC and 495-61-EC, page 13.

93 Purchase Order No. 41-1-GF-1873, dated March 31, 1960.

94 Civil Case No. 235-61-EC Transcript Testimony of Mr. Miles Cobert Burk, page 19.

95 DEFENDANT RAYTHEON COMPANY'S PRE-TRIAL MEMORANDUM OF CONTENTIONS, page 2, No. 235-61-S, filed July 27, 1962.

96 Civil Case No. 235-61-EC Transcript Testimony of Mr. Stanley D. Crane, page 66.

97 While mom had first mentioned that dad had taken a bucket out to get items for our family fish tank because it was in need and a cousin had alerted me to dad's sweatshirt. But, it was after searching my transcripts from the newspaper articles that confirmed these details for me. Read of the bucket and blue sweatshirt find in this article: Coast Guard Ends Search – Final Cutter Trip Due In Hunt for Five Men, By James Schermerhorn, News-Press Staff Writer, Santa Barbara News-Press, June 11, 1960.

98 Findings of Teresa Newton-Terres research aligning: Coast Guard and Navy Ship Log, Coast Guard Light House Log, etc.

99 Civil Case No. 235-61-EC Transcript Testimony of Mr. Stanley D. Crane, page 71.

100 Defendant Raytheon Company's Pre-Trial Memorandum of Contentions, page 2-3, No. 235-61-S, filed July 27, 1962.

101 Civil Case No. 235-61-EC Transcript Testimony of Mr. Richard Dowse, page 43.

102 MEMORANDUM OPINION FOR USE IN PREPARATION OF, FINDINGS OF FACT, CONCLUSIONS OF LAW and JUDGMENT, IN ADMIRALTY NO. - NO. 235-61-EC and 495-61-EC, Filed July, 8 1963, page 20.

103 MEMORANDUM OPINION FOR USE IN PREPARATION OF, FINDINGS OF FACT, CONCLUSIONS OF LAW and JUDGMENT, Filed July, 8 1963, IN ADMIRALTY NO. - NO. 235-61-EC and 495-61-EC, Page 10.

104 UNITED STATES DISTRICT COURT FOR THE SOUTHERN DISTRICT OF CALIFORNIA CENTRAL DIVISION, Civil Action No. 235-61-EC, PRELIMINARY JURY VERDICT, Filed June 4, 1963, page 2.

105 STIPULATION FOR JUDGMENT, Filed September 17, 1963, IN ADMIRALTY, NO. 235-61-EC and 495-61-EC.

106 STIPULATION FOR JUDGMENT, Filed September 17, 1963, IN ADMIRALTY, NO. 235-61-EC and 495-61-EC.
- Dawn Howell Hooke, as administratrix of the Estate of Loren Dale Howell, decease $43,329.48
- Marjorie L. Garrett, as administratrix of the Estate of Paul Timothy Lovette, deceased $7,500.00
- Marian H. Terres, as administratrix of the Estate of Diego Santos Terres, Jr., deceased $78,661.17
- Helen T. Russell, as administratrix of the Estate of James Clifford

Russell, deceased $80,423.11

- Betty Lou Mackie, as administratrix of the Estate of Harold Herbert Mackie, deceased $45,851.31

107 IN ADMIRALTY NO. NO. 235-61-EC and 495-61-EC, MEMORANDUM OPIN-ION FOR USE IN PREPARATION OF, FINDINGS OF FACT, CONCLUSIONS OF LAW and JUDGMENT, page 3, Filed July, 8 1963

To offer more insight let me add:

To identify court jurisdiction, since the *Marie* was neither located nor recovered, the court made the following stipulation based on the facts it had available at the time: The vessel *Marie* sank at approximately 34 degrees 12 ' N 119 degrees 35 ' West longitude or to the eastward thereof. After identifying a mid-Santa Barbara Channel point, the courts continued, "It is stipulated for the purpose of jurisdictional determination" the *Marie* was more than three miles from either mainland or the channel island.

I recognized the coordinates. They were the same coordinates where Paul T. Lovette's body was recovered. I remembered that there were those who believed his body had been dragged by sharks. And I wondered if it mattered if the *Marie* sunk within California State Territorial waters because the 1969 finding by two abalone divers was said to be within the three nautical miles of Santa Cruz Island.

To address the question, "When did the *Marie* sink", the court's judgment was, "It appears from the testimony of Mrs. Moffit, formerly Mrs. Mackie, that the boat disappeared some time during daylight hours on June 7, 1960, being the day it left Santa Barbara for the area of experiments, to wit, clear water of about thirty foot depth probably off the shore of Santa Cruz Island." The court might have preferred a more scientific and concrete timeframe, but this testimony apparently was suitable. Thus the date of the *Marie*'s sinking was identified as June 7, 1960.

In reviewing the conclusions and opinions, I believe, Judge E. Avery Crary did an excellent job of outlining the line of reasoning and law that led up to the decisions and judgments. With respect to the cause of the disappearance of the *Marie*, that the "requisite legal cause may be found from evidence of negligence and/or unseaworthiness on the one hand and disappearance of the vessel on the other." (The court referenced: W.R. Grace & Co., vs. Charleston Lighterage & Transfer Co., 193 F. 2d 539 at 542-543.) Although the case referenced was different, the example case turned on the failure to properly maintain and inspect the vessel, and the court determined (by analysis of law and by reasoning) that the sinking was due to its unseaworthiness in that case and, very likely, the *Marie* case as well.

My eye and mind return to Judge Crary's statement, "**requisite legal cause**…" which leads my mind to consider the question, "What is the chance that there is a discrepancy between the "legal cause" and the "actual cause"? But, to answer this, more information is needed.

Regarding the need for an operating license, the court concluded: "The evidence indicates that Mr. McCaffrey had operated the *Marie* frequently during the period of her ownership by Mr. Dowse, and there is no evidence that he did not properly operate the boat and, on the contrary, the testimony would indicate that he was a good operator. Although there was a violation of the (Coast Guard) statutory provision that raises the presumption that the statutory fault contributed to the disaster, this presumption may be overcome." Thus, after further review of the laws and Coast Guard Rules and Regulations, the court determined, "...a license was required by Mr. McCaffrey as the operator of the *Marie* on June 7, 1960."

Regarding the question of negligence, the court concluded, "It does not appear that the plaintiffs or claimants were negligent nor did any of them assume the risk involved, and the court finds that the *Marie*, at the time of its disappearance, was in the use and control of McCaffrey Brothers. The court further finds that Raytheon was not liable for the damages claimed by plaintiffs or claimants, nor for damage under the cross-complaint of Dowse."

Additionally, the Court offered a line of reasoning behind its judgment on Lovette, "...the fact that the said Lovette had no part in the project of Raytheon, nor in the operation of the *Marie*, and was on board solely for his own pleasure at the request of decedent Howell." The court concluded that Lovette assumed all risk.

Initially the court ruled against any financial compensation for the Lovette estate. However, that judgment would later be reconsidered with a stipulation.

At the conclusion of the trial the court offered this summary, "The court and jury having heard testimony and having examined proofs offered by the respective parties on May 28th and 29th, 1963 and June 4, 1963, and the jury having rendered a Preliminary Jury Verdict on June 4, 1963, finding that Loren Dale Howell, Deceased, was a maritime worker, not a member of the crew of the vessel *Marie* but an independent contractor on her final voyage which commenced on June 7, 1960, and that Paul Timothy Lovette, Deceased, was a guest or visitor on board the vessel *Marie* on her final voyage commencing on June 7, 1960 and the court having further considered the testimony and proofs theretofore offered by the respective parties and having heard additional testimony and additional proofs offered by the respective parties on June 4th, 5th and 6th, 1963, and the cause having been submitted for decision as to RAYTHEON on June 6th upon a motion by defendant RAYTHEON COMPANY for dismissal at the close of the plaintiffs' case on June 6, 1963, the plaintiffs having rested and the defendant RAYTHEON COMPANY having indicated that it did not intend to offer any additional proof, and the court having granted said motion, the court now makes its findings of fact and conclusions of law...."

108 Santa Barbara News-Press, $497,666 Award For Damages in '*Marie*' Tragedy, Santa Barbara News-Press, July 9 1963.

109 Santa Barbara News-Press, $497,666 Award For Damages in '*Marie*' Tragedy, Santa Barbara News-Press, July 9 1963.

110 Shipwrecks, Smugglers and Maritime Mysteries by Eugene D. Wheeler and Robert E. Kallman, Pathfinder Publishing, 1984, page 96. This book provides stories about vessels that have been battered, run aground, and sunk in the Santa Barbara Channel off the central coast of California. The "*Marie's*" disappearance is listed under the category: Strange and Unusual Accidents. The *Marie* story is afforded only two paragraphs with a word count of less than 200. Its text includes a phase that also perpetuates one of the myths concerning the *Marie*, "No trace of the seven men was found." This should read, 'no trace of *three* men was found.' I'm pleased that the book introduces the *Marie*.

111 Santa Barbara News-Press' HEADLINERS: A History of Santa Barbara From the Pages of its Newspapers 1855-1982, Edited by Dewey Schurman. This book includes

the *Marie*'s disappearance as one of the 100 most newsworthy stories of the 1900's. These stories are identified with headlines taken from the newspaper of the day and reflect only portions of the newspaper articles of the events, selected as the most newsworthy stories.

112 https://en.wikipedia.org/wiki/Bombardment_of_Ellwood

113 Bob Schwemmer, Ken and I enjoyed a lunch conversation; however, this presentation Bob gave recently at the Santa Barbara Maritime Museum about the Oil Tanker, Montebello is a reasonably fair resource for this purposes: http://www.youtube.com/watch?v=qclrEm_tL3E Another resource Bob Schwemmer for information into the Ellwood Oil Field attack is the museum Rancho La Patera at Stow House, http://www.StowHouse.com:

- 12-18-1941, Freighter, Eureka, CA, Saved

- 12-20-1941, Tanker, Blunts Reef, CA, Lost

- 12-22-1941, Tanker, Point Arguello, CA, Saved

- 12-23-1941, Tanker, North Morro Bay, CA, Saved

- 12-23-1941, Tanker, Piedras Blancas Pt., CA, Lost

- 12-24-1941, Freighter, San Pedro, CA, Saved

- 06-07-1942, Freighter, Cape Flattery, WA, Lost

- 06-20-1942, Freighter, Cape Flattery, WA, Lost

- 10-05-1942, Tanker, Cape Sebastian, OR, Lost

- 10-10-1942, Tanker, Oregon Coast, Lost

114 E-mail sent to the author by Theresa Huerta on August 19, 2009.

115 Letter sent from Raytheon to the author dated December 4, 2009.

116 www.dtic.mil/dtic/tr/fulltext/u2/666031.pdf

117 www.dtic.mil/dtic/tr/fulltext/u2/666031.pdf

118 He sent me a link to this link from which he referredto: http://www.worldcat.org/oclc/22426962

119 Maxwell Krasno, In Memoriam Dr. Niel F. Beardsley, Proc. IRIS, 6, (1961). (Declassified January 6, 2010: Code 5596.3, Research Reports Library, Naval Research Laboratory, Office of Naval Research, Boston, MA. at the request of Teresa Newton-Terres on behalf of the MARIE Commemoration Event.)

120 I e-mailed Mr. Hodges, Tuesday, December 22, 2009 asking only of the Proc. IRIS, 6, 1961. The e-mail was a head's up because I would be traveling his way as I and Ken would be sharing Christmas in DC with Dete. I went into the Navy Yard operational

archives the day after the New Year. By this time, Mr. Hodges had answered the Proc. IRIS request by e-mail; but, it was on this visit to the Navy Yard archives that I asked for insights into the Tropical Storm alerts. And Mr. Hodges returned with the STORM PROJECT booklet.

121 Craven, John Piña (2001). The Silent War. Simon and Schuster. pp. 165-166.

122 E-mail sent to the author Wed, January 6, 2010 by Judi Griffin, Code 5596.3 from the Research Reports Library, Naval Research Laboratory.

123 March 9, 2010 week in a conversation on the phone and at Light Productions studio the author and Lee Burrell met.

124 E-mails sent to the author March 3 and 26, 2010.

125 While Jeannie said as much in our phone conversation March 2010, I didn't take notes. These words were taken from Jeannie Russell Carter's Oral History recorded June, 2010. They are repeated here because they fit appropriately.

126 MARIE Story Told at CG Hearing, Santa Barbara News-Press, June 15, 1960.

127 "The Coast Guard Light Station log, noted receiving five calls from civilians reporting "flares out at sea." Investigating by landline, the CGD11 RCC informed them that a Coast Guard helicopter had been dropping flares in search of a man fallen overboard." Coast Guard Light Station Report, Thursday, June 9, 1960

128 Finding of Body at Sea Spurs Hunt for 7 Missing on Secret Mission, Los Angeles Times, Friday, 10 June 1960.

129 6 Lost in Channel Science Test; Body of 7th Man Found, Santa Barbara News-Press, Page A-1, June 10, 1960

130 Finding of Body at Sea Spurs Hunt for 7 Missing on Secret Mission, Los Angeles Times, Friday, 10 June 1960.

131 Spies, Traitors, Subtours: Fear and Freedom in America. Clinton Library. Created by the International Spy Museum in Washington, DC , "Spies, Traitors, and Saboteurs: Fear and Freedom in America" dramatically illustrates the challenge of securing our nation without compromising the civil liberties upon which it was founded. From the Revolutionary War to the today: https://www.clintonfoundation.org/get-involved/take-action/attend-an-event/exhibit-opening-spies-traitors-and-saboteurs

132 "Colossus: The Forbin Project. 1970. An artificially intelligent supercomputer is developed and activated, only to reveal that it has a sinister agenda of its own." Source: http://www.imdb.com/title/tt0064177/releaseinfo . Not to be confused with first electronic computer that was programmable Colossus computer (http://en.wikipedia.org/wiki/Colossus_computer) http://en.wikipedia.org/wiki/Colossus:_

The Forbin Project

133 Maxwell Krasno, In Memoriam Dr. Niel F. Beardsley, Proc. IRIS, 6, (1961). (De-classified January 6, 2010: Code 5596.3, Research Reports Library, Naval Research Laboratory, Office of Naval Research, Boston, MA. at the request of Teresa New-ton-Terres on behalf of the MARIE Commemoration Event.) http://www.project-tnt.com/marie/documents/Dr_Niel_F_Beardsley_in_memoriam.pdf

134 Ibid

135 Ibid

136 "He was here, but not one of ours." "It was a black project then, it's a black project still." Mr. Hancock conveyed these words to me. They were, not his words, but the words of the Wright-Patterson Air Force Base historian. I was informed that I could quote him. But, what projects(s), he was unable to offer me any insights into. This exchange of words occurred in a conversation with the author April 16, 2010.

137 The on-line news, the Noozhawk. I found it interesting that its headquarters was located in my grandparent's old Goleta buildings and Laura gave them a personal visit. In fact, the Noozhawk was located in Judge Lodges, Nell Beardsley's lawyer's office.

138 From what I know, an initial trip on this project effort was made May 31 – June 1, 1960. All of the same men went out from SB Harbor on the Marie to Santa Cruz Is-land. This included Dr. Beardsley. All the same men, except Hal Mackie whose wife's testimony said he hadn't been out with the group before.

139 The truth is that Greg Gorga at this point in our meeting, asked me to return the following day to review the display panels with a fine tooth comb, because he didn't have time that day. I combined two meetings into one single one in order to tell the story efficiently.

140 In The Mystery of the Marie: Dolphin Sculptor Bud Bottoms Among Those Spared, by Barney Brantingham, Santa Barbara Independent, June 2010, Brant-ingham clarifies for readers that three men "should have been on the Marie" includ-ing Bob Bryant, Bob Wilke, and Bud Bottoms.

141 For more information see http://www.yahoo.com/?r775=1358299806

142 Helen Wilke, Marie Commemoration Event, Saturday, June 5, 2010.

143 "All But One", 'Marie' Victim Died Of Shock, Exposure, Santa Barbara News-Press, Friday Evening, June 17, 1960.

144 The enveloped was from the National Archives, Civilian Records of Govern-ment Employees, Saint Louis, Mo. And I'm eager to get started decoding its contents!

CONTINUED (from page 362)
Dr. Niel F. Beardsley

Dr. Paul Ovrebo of ATIC, under who he was then working, reports, "It was said at Syracuse University during the early years of their detector research that a pall hung over the place for three days after his visits. And yet this vigorous insistence on rigor, turned out some of the most significant results."

Dr. Levinstein, who directed the Syracuse University research under the Air Force contract wrote, "It is my feeling that Dr. Niel Beardsley, more than any other person in the U.S., was responsible for the rapid IR detector development in the period between 1948 and 1958." When Dr. Beardsley joined Dr. Paul J. Ovrebo in infrared work at the Wright Air Development Center (WADC) in 1946, he had behind him a long career in the teaching of physics.

A native of Wadsworth, Ohio, he obtained his B.S. degree at Hiram College in 1913 and taught elementary school for four years. During WWI he taught at Ft Sill, Oklahoma. In 1920 he earned his M.S. at Northwestern University and for the next nine years was on the faculty of Georgia Tech., leaving to join the Physics Department of the University of Chicago. Here he remained for seventeen years, receiving his Ph. D. in 1932 and continued as Instructor and later as Assistant Professor.

Dr. Beardsley moved to Santa Barbara May 1959. Dr. Beardsley was lost at sea and one of the three victims never recovered.

[Source: Dr. Maxwell Krasno, IN MEMORIAM DR. NIEL F. BEARDSLEY, Proc. IRIS, 6 (1961).]

Scan for more information on
Dr. Niel Freeborn Beardley.

Bibliography

BOOKS

Craven, John P., *The Silent War: The Cold War Battle Beneath the Sea*, Simon & Schuster, New York, 2001

Earley, Pete, *Family of Spies: Inside the John Walker Spy Ring*, Bantam, 1988

Earls, Alan R. and Edwards, Robert E., *Images of America: Raytheon Company The First Sixty Years*, Arcadia Publishing, IL, 2005

Ennes, James M., Jr., *Assault on the Liberty: The True Story of the Israeli Attack on an American Intelligence Ship*, Reinteree Press, 1979

Kurson, Robert, *Shadow Divers: The True Adventure of Two Americas Who Risked Everything to Solve One of the Last Mysteries of World War II*, Ballatine Books, New York, 2005

Monroe-Jones, Edward, Edited by, *Undersea Encounters: The Stories of Over Thirty American Submarine Collisions and Groundings With Background Information on the Causes and Effects of Undersea Encounters*, Submarine Research Center, Washington, 2006

Morris, Don P. and Lima, James, *Channel Islands National Park and Channel Islands National Marine Sanctuary: Submerged Cultural Resources Assessment*, Intermountain Cultural Resource Centers Professional Papers, Number 56, U.S. Department of the Interior, New Mexico, 1996

Offley, Ed, *Scorpion Down: Sunk by the Soviets by Buried by the Pentagon: The Untold Story of the USS Scorpion*, Perseus Books Group, PA, 2007

Polmar, Norman and Noot, Jurrien, *Submarines of the Russian and Soviet Navies, 1718-1990*, Naval Institute Press, Maryland, 1991E

Powers, Francis Gary with Gentry, Curt, *Operation Overflight: The U-2 Spy Pilot Tells His Story for the First Time*, Holt, Reinehart and Winston, Canada, 1970

Sande, Ken, *The Peacemaker: A Biblical Guide to Resolving Personal Conflict*, Baker Books, Michigan, 2004

Sewell, Kenneth with Richmond, Clint, *Red Star Rogue: The Untold Story of a Soviet Submarine's Nuclear Strike Attempt on the U.S.*, Simon & Schuster, New York, 2005

Sontag, Sherry, and Drew, Chris, *Blind Man's Bluff: The Untold Story of American Submarine Espionage*, Harper Collins Publishers, New York, 1998

Tompkins, Walker A., It Happened in Old Santa Barbara, Sandollar Press, 1976

Weir, Gary E., and Boyne, Walter J., *Rising Tide: The Untold Story of the Russian Submarines That Fought the Cold War*, Penguin Books Group (USA), New York, 2003

Wheeler, Eugene E., and Kallman, Robert E., *Shipwrecks, Smugglers and Maritime Mysteries*, Pathfinder Publishing, Ventura, 1984

GOVERNMENT REPORTS AND DOCUMENTS

"2 U.S. Submarines Meet at Pole: Skate and Seadragon Surface Through Arctic Ice Pack," The New York Times, August 23, 1962

"Guided Missile Data Exchange Program; forwarding of documentation for", Memo From Commanding Officer, U.S. Naval Ordnance Laboratory, Corona, Chief, Bureau of Naval Weapons (FQ), June 21, 1960, Reproduced from the Holdings of the National Archives and Records Administration, Pacific Region (Laguna Niguel), CA

"House Realigns Defense Budget: Votes 39.3 Billion for Arms, Stressing Missile Work – Pentagon Takes Cuts," " by Hanson W. Baldwin, The New York Times, April 17, 1959

"M/B MARIE, O/N 253 652; disappearance of resulting in loss of life," United States Coast Guard, Memo from Senior Investigating Officer to Commandant (MVI), Eleventh Coast Guard District, July 27, 1960 (Originally from Howell family archives)

"Navy to Tighten Artic Air Alert: Will Shift Squadrons From Newfoundland to Iceland-Step to Cut Costs," by Hanson W. Baldwin, the New York Times, December 19, 1960

"Pacific Fleet Sees Many Red Warships," Special to the New York Times, October 21, 1954

"Polaris Shot Opens Crucial Test Series", by Richard Witkin, Special to the New York Times, March 28, 1960

"Report Symbol BUORD 8821-2 Terrier Firing Summaries; forwarding of (U)," Memo From Commanding Officer, U.S. Naval Ordnance Laboratory, Corona, California to Distribution, June 7, 1960, Reproduced from the holdings of the National Archives Pacific Southwest Region (Laguna Niguel), CA

"Soviet Submarines Held A Major Peril," Special to the New York Times, December 15, 1960

"Technical Reports; transmittal," Memo From Commanding Officer, U.S. Naval Ordnance Laboratory, Corona, California to Raytheon Company, Santa Barbara Subdivision, Santa Barbara California, June 7, 1960, Reproduced from the holdings of the National Archives Pacific Southwest Region (Laguna Niguel), CA

"Technical Reports; transmittal", Memo From Commanding Officer, U.S. Naval Ordnance Laboratory, Corona, California to Raytheon Company, Santa Barbara Subdivision, Santa Barbara California, June 21, 1960, Reproduced from the records of the National Archives Pacific Southwest Region (Laguna Niguel), CA

A Program For The Interchange of Guided Missile Parts/Components Test Data, U.S. Bureau of Naval Weapons, U.S. Naval Ordinance Laboratory, Corona, CA, June 15, 1960, Reproduced from the records of the National Archives Pacific Southwest Region (Laguna Niguel), CA

Air-Sea Search System Used To Seek Victims of 'Marie': Search Employed Coast Guard and Navy Boats and Planes Plus Air Force Helicopters and Other Volunteer Craft, , Eleventh Coast Guard District, Map, Santa Barbara News-Press, June 15, 1960

An Annotated Literature Survey of Submarines, Torpedoes, Anti-Submarine Warfare, Undersea Weapon Systems, and Oceanography: 1941-Jan 1962, by Barbara Ann Bryce, Armed Services Technical Information Agency, Reproduced from the records of the National Archives, Washington D.C.

AN/SOC (XN-1) Sonar Set: Sonar Communications System (SESCO): Production Test: Procedure & Report, Contract No. NObar 75793 (FBM) (Receiver and Transmitter Test), Technical Library, Raytheon 1958-1960, Reproduced from the holdings of the National Archives and Records Administration, College Park, MD Clark, John E. (Rear Admiral), "Problems of Anti-Submarine Warfare", 1961,

Reproduced from the Holdings of the National Archives Pacific Southwest Region, Laguna Niguel, CA

Coast Guard Auxiliary Scrapbooks 1949-1966, Box Number 4, Reproduced from the Holdings of the National Archives Pacific Region (Laguna Niguel), Record Group 26, Records of the U.S. Coast Guard, Eleventh Coast Guard District, 1960

Command History of Commander Submarine Division Eleven, 1960, Reproduced from the Holdings of the Archives Branch, Naval History and Heritage Command, Washington, D.C.

Command History of Commander Submarine Flotilla One, U.S. Pacific Fleet, 1960, Reproduced from the Holdings of the Archives Branch, Naval History and Heritage Command, Washington, D.C.

Command History of Commander Submarine Force, U.S. Pacific Fleet, 1960, Reproduced from the Holdings of the Archives Branch, Naval History and Heritage Command, Washington, D.C.

Command History of Commander Submarine Squadron One, 1960, Reproduced from the Holdings of the Archives Branch, Naval History and Heritage Command, Washington, D.C.

Command History of Commander Submarine Squadron Three, 1960, Reproduced from the Holdings of the Archives Branch, Naval History and Heritage Command, Washington, D.C.

Command History of Commander U.S. Fleet Anti-submarine Warfare School, San Diego with Statement of Mission and Tasks, Reproduced from the Holdings of the Archives Branch, Naval History and Heritage Command, Washington, D.C.

Command History of Submarine Squadron Five covering period 1 January – 31 December 1960, Reproduced from the Holdings of the Archives Branch, Naval History and Heritage Command, Washington, D.C.

Command History of the Pacific Missile Range, 1960, Reproduced from the Holdings of the National Archives and Records Administration, Pacific Region (Laguna Niguel), CA

Command History of U.S. Ship Cochino (SS 345), 1949, Reproduced from the Holdings of the Ships History Branch, Naval History and Heritage Command, Washington Navy Yard, D.C.

Command Report on U.S. Ship Cochino (SS 345), 1949, Reproduced from the Holdings of the Archives Branch, Naval History and Heritage Command, Washington, D.C.

Deck Log Book of the U.S. Ship Aspro (SS-309), June, 1960, Reproduced from the holdings of the National Archives College Park, College Park, MD

Deck Log Book of the U.S. Ship Baya (AGSS-318), June, 1960, Reproduced from the holdings of the National Archives College Park, College Park, MD

Deck Log Book of the U.S. Ship Bugara (SS-331), June, 1960, Reproduced from the holdings of the National Archives College Park, College Park, MD

Deck Log Book of the U.S. Ship Caiman (SS-323), June, 1960, Reproduced from the holdings of the National Archives College Park, College Park, MD

Deck Log Book of the U.S. Ship Capitaine (AGSS-336), June, 1960, Reproduced from the holdings of the National Archives College Park, College Park, MD

Deck Log Book of the U.S. Ship Colonial (LSD-18), June, 1960, Reproduced from the holdings of the National Archives College Park, College Park, MD

Deck Log Book of the U.S. Ship Growler (SSG-577), *(Records Restricted)* June, 1960, Reproduced from the holdings of the National Archives College Park, College Park, MD

Deck Log Book of the U.S. Ship Los Angeles (CA-135), June, 1960, Reproduced from the holdings of the National Archives College Park, College Park, MD

Deck Log Book of the U.S. Ship Nereus (AS-17), June, 1960, Reproduced from the holdings of the National Archives College Park, College Park, MD

Deck Log Book of the U.S. Ship Raton (SSR-270), June, 1960, Reproduced from the holdings of the National Archives College Park, College Park, MD

Deck Log Book of the U.S. Ship Razorback (SS-394), June, 1960, Reproduced from the holdings of the National Archives College Park, College Park, MD

Deck Log Book of the U.S. Ship Redfish (SS-395), June, 1960, Reproduced from the holdings of the National Archives College Park, College Park, MD

Deck Log Book of the U.S. Ship Remora (SS-487), June, 1960, Reproduced from the holdings of the National Archives College Park, College Park, MD

Deck Log Book of the U.S. Ship Rock (AG-274), June, 1960, Reproduced from the holdings of the National Archives College Park, College Park, MD

Deck Log Book of the U.S. Ship Ronquil (SS-396), June, 1960, Reproduced from the holdings of the National Archives College Park, College Park, MD

Deck Log Book of the U.S. Ship Salmon (SSR-573), June, 1960, Reproduced from the holdings of the National Archives College Park, College Park, MD

Deck Log Book of the U.S. Ship Sperry (AS-12), June, 1960, Reproduced from the holdings of the National Archives College Park, College Park, MD

Deck Log of the U.S. Ship Norton Sound (AVM-1), June, 1960, Reproduced from the holdings of the National Archives College Park, College Park, MD

Deck Log, U.S. Ship King County (AG-157), June, 1960, Reproduced from the holdings of the National Archives College Park, College Park, MD

Deck Log-Weather Observation Sheet, U.S. Ship Thomaston (LSD-28), June, 1960, Reproduced from the holdings of the National Archives College Park, College Park, MD

Fleet Marine Force Pacific: STORM Project, Command File Post, 1946, Records of the Naval History and Heritage Command, Washington Navy Yard, D.C.

History of Eleventh Naval District Headquarters, Command History, 1960, Reproduced from the records of the Naval History and Heritage Command, Washington Navy Yard, D.C.

History of the Pacific Missile Range: An Historical Report Covering The Period 1 July 1959 to 30 June 1960, Prepared by the Staff Historian Pacific Missile Range, Arthur Menken, The Naval Missile Center Point Mugu, CA, Records of the Naval History and Heritage Command, Washington Navy Yard, D.C.

History of the U.S. Pacific Fleet, U.S. Naval Air Station, North Island, San Diego, CA, Command History, Records of the Naval History and Heritage Command, Washington Navy Yard, D.C.

History of the U.S. Western Sea Frontier, Treasure Island, San Francisco, CA, Command History, 1960, Records of the Naval History and Heritage Command, Washington Navy Yard, D.C.

History of U.S. Naval Construction Battalion Center, Command History, Port Hueneme, California, 1960, Reproduced from the records of the Naval History and Heritage Command, Washington Navy Yard, D.C.

History of U.S. Ship Colonial (LSD-18), c/o Fleet Post Office, San Francisco, CA, Command Histories, Records of the Ships History Center, Washington Navy Yard, D.C.

History of U.S. Ship King County (AG-157) (Ex-LST 857), Command Histories, Reproduced from the records of the Ships History Center, Washington Navy Yard, D.C.

History of U.S. Ship Norton Sound (AV-11), by CW03 Robert F. Hovestadt, USN (Retired), Reproduced from the holdings of the Ships History Center, Washington Navy Yard, D.C.

History of U.S. Ship PVT Joe E. Mann (AGM-4), Records of the Ships History Center, Washington Navy Yard, D.C.

History of U.S. Ship Sperry (AS-12), Command Histories, 1960, Reproduced from the records of the Ships History Center, Washington Navy Yard, D.C.

History of U.S. Ship Yorktown (CVA-10), by Commanding Officer to Director of Naval History, 1951-1955, Reproduced from the holdings of the Ships History Center, Washington Navy Yard, D.C.

Log / Bridge Book of the U.S. Coast Guard 95334 (Cape Sable), Record Group 26, Eleventh Coast Guard District, June 1960, Reproduced from the records of the National Archives College Park, College Park, MD.

MARIE, #253652, Record Group 36, Records of the Bureau of Customs, Los Angeles Collection District Vessel Documentation Case Files, National Archives Pacific Southwest Region, Laguna Niguel, CA

Memo From Commanding Officer, U.S. Naval Ordnance Laboratory, Corona, California to Distribution, June 7, 1960, Report Symbol BUORD 8821-2 Terrier Firing Summaries; forwarding of (U), Reproduced from the records of the National Archives Pacific Southwest Region (Laguna Niguel), CA

Some Early Lead Salt Detector Development, D.J. Lovell, The University of Michigan

supported by the US Air Force of Scientific Research, Ann Arbor Michigan, Contract F44620-67-C-0051, www.dtic.mil/dtic/tr/fulltext/u2/666031.pdf
Submarine Force, Pacific Fleet, CINCPACFLNOTE 05440, 4 January 1960,

Reproduced from the Holdings of the Archives Branch, Naval History and Heritage Command, Washington, D.C.

U. S. Coast Guard Port Hueneme Light Station log, June 1960, Record Group 26, Eleventh Coast Guard District, Reproduced from the records of the National Archives, Washington D.C.

U. S. Coast Guard Rescue Coordination Center (RCC), Eleventh Coast Guard District, 9 June 1960, (Located in Record Group 36, Records of the Bureau of Customs Los Angeles Collection District Vessel Documentation Case File, Vessel 253652, MARIE), Reproduced from the records of the National Archives Pacific Southwest Region (Laguna Niguel), CA

U.S. Pacific Missile Range: 1960 Year of Achievement, News Release, 1960, Records of the Naval History and Heritage Command, Washington Navy Yard, D.C.

U.S. Pacific Missile Range: The Comptroller Annual Report, Year ending June 30, 1960, Records of the Naval History and Heritage Command, Washington Navy Yard, D.C.

United States District Court For The Southern District of California Central Division, Civil No. 235-61-EAC, Dawn Howell Hooker, etc., et al., Plaintiffs, vs. Raytheon Company, etc., et al, Defendants, In the Matter of the Petition of Richard W. Dowse, et al., Petitioners. Civil No. 235-61, 1961

United States District Court For The Southern District of California Central Division, In the Matter of the Petition of Richard W. Dowse, et al., Dawn Howell Hooker, etc., et al., Plaintiffs, vs. Raytheon Company, etc., et al, Defendants, In Admiralty No. 495-61-EC (Civil No. 235-61-EAC), 1961

USN 422812, LCVP Crew Retrieves mine sweeping equipment aboard an LCVP, Off CHINNAMPO, Korea, During Mine Sweeping Operations, Photographer E.R. Barlow, Defense Department Photo, U.S. Navy, 1950, Reproduced from the Holdings of the National Archives College Park, MD (Image 2 of 3)

USN 422812, LCVP Crew retrieves mine sweeping equipment, aboard an LCVP, Off CHINNAMPO, Korea, During mine sweeping operation, Photographer E.R. Barlow, Defense Department Photo, U.S. Navy, 1950, Reproduced from the Holdings of the National Archives College Park, MD (Image 3 of 3)

USN 422812, LCVP Making a shallow water sweep off coast of Korea during mine sweeping operations at CHINAMPO, Photographer E.R. Barlow, Defense Department Photo, U.S. Navy, 1950, Reproduced from the Holdings of the National Archives College Park, MD (Image 1 of 3)

State of California Records

"Application for Hearing Death Claim", Industrial Accident Commission, State of California Department of Industrial Relations, Case No. 61 SBA 2330, 1960
Superior Court of California, County of Santa Barbara, Case SB63293 and SB060901, 1960

Superior Court of California, County of Santa Barbara, Case SB63294 and SB060901, 1960

Superior Court of California, County of Santa Barbara, Case SB63298 and SB060901, 1960

Howell Family Archives

Howell, Dawn Darlene, "Testimony", June 13, 1960

"M/B MARIE, O/N 253 652; disappearance of resulting in loss of life," United States Coast Guard, Memo from Senior Investigating Officer to Commandant (MVI), Eleventh Coast Guard District, July 27, 1960

"Howell & Lovette vs. Raytheon: Assignment to perform the necessary investigation," Investigation by Joseph H. Mock, July 1, 1960

Other Reports, Exhibits, etc.

Foreign Relations of the United States, 1958–1960, Editors: Suzanne E. Coffman, Edward C. Keefer, Harriet Dashiell Schwar; Government Printing Office, Washington, D.C., 1992

The Museum of Science and Industry (MSI), Honor, Courage, Commitment: United States Navy, Chicago, Illinois

The Museum of Science and Industry (MSI), "U-505 *Submarine*", Chicago, Illinois

Newsletters, Pamphlets, and Documents *(1960's)*

Adams, Charles, "We Could Not Have Suffered A Greater Loss", Open Letter of Appreciation, Raytheon Communicator: Raytheon Santa Barbara Operations, page 1, July 1960

Humphrey, Gordon, Raytheon Communicator: Raytheon Santa Barbara Operations, page 1 Cover Letter, July 1960

Maxwell KRASNO, IN MEMORIAM DR. NIEL F. BEARDSLEY, Proc. IRIS, 6, (1961). (Declassified January 6, 2010: Code 5596.3, Research Reports Library, Naval Research Laboratory, Office of Naval Research, Boston, MA. at the request of Teresa Newton-Terres on behalf of the MARIE Commemoration Event.) http://www.project-tnt. com/marie/documents/Dr_Niel_F_Beardsley_in_memoriam.pdf
Raytheon Company, "Open Letter of Appreciation", Raytheon Communicator: Raytheon Santa Barbara Operations, page 1, July 1960

Newsletters, Pamphlets, and Documents *(Post 1960)*

Marie Remembered (Documentary), EdHat, May 2010, https://www.edhat. com/?nid=31954

Marie Tragedy, Cold War Museum Timeline, 1960, http://www.coldwar.org/ articles/60s/index.asp

Santa Barbara High School Alumni Association, Fall 2009, Spring 2010 Newsletter, Vol 35

The Disappearance of the Marie, by Mary Larmoyeux, Grand Connections, June 2010 https://grandconnection.blogspot.com/2010/06/disappearance-of-marie.html

NEWSPAPER ARTICLES (1960 to 2004)

$335,000 Sought In 'MARIE' Claims Filed: Boat Tragedy, Santa Barbara News-Press, Jan 11, 1961

'Marie' Fund Proposed, Santa Barbara News-Press, June 17, 1960

5 Men Mission In Channel Off Santa Barbara *, The Bee: Danville, Virginia *, June 11, 1960

6 Lost in Channel Science Test; Body of 7th Man Found, Santa Barbara News-Press, June 10, 1960

Accident at Sear Mystifies, Los Angels Mirror, June 11, 1960

BELIEVED TO BE 'MARIA' – Wreckage of Boat Found Off Island, Santa Barbara News-Press, Nov 6, 1969

Boat Project Believed Classified, Los Angeles Evening Mirror News, June 10, 1960

Body Tentatively Identified as James C. Russell, unknown**, June 22, 1960

CHANNEL Search Made for 6 Men, Santa Barbara News-Press, June 10, 1960

Coast Guard Begins 'Marie' Probe; Raytheon Official Due, Santa Barbara News-Press, June 13, 1960

Coast Guard Opens Hearing On "Marie' – Investigation To Seek Cause of Accident, Santa Barbara News-Press, June 14, 1960

Coast Guard Probes Loss of Science Craft, Los Angeles Times (Or from LA Mirror), June 14, 1960

Crash Boat Finds 2nd Ocean Victim *, The Press-Courier, Serving Ventura County, CA *, June 11, 1960

Cuts, by Hanson W. Baldwin, The New York Times, April 17, 1959
Finds Fourth body of "Marie" disaster, Goleta Valley Times, June 30, 1960

Fish Gnawed Bodies Found in Pacific, The Daily Inter Lake, Kalispell, Montana *, June 12, 1960

FIVE PRESUMED DEAD: Cutter Docks to End Vain Search for Missing Men, Santa Barbara News-Press, June 12, 1960

Four Skindivers Conquer River, Santa Barbara News-Press, Tue Evening, April 8 1958 (A story of friends two years prior to the Marie tragedy enjoying rafting down the river - Jim McCaffrey, Bud Bottoms, Dale Howell, and Jim Terres.)

Funeral Notices, Santa Barbara News-Press, June 13, 1960

Grim Lesson in Loss of Marie, Santa Barbara News-Press, Aug 26, 1960

HEARING ENDS: Inquiry Dredges Up "Marie" Facts, Santa Barbara News-Press, June 15, 1960

House Realigns Defense Budget: Votes 39.3 Billion for Arms, Stressing Missile Work – Pentagon Takes
IN SEA TRAGEDY, Santa Barbara News-Press, June 10, 1960

James Russell, Santa Barbara News-Press, June 15, 1960

LOREN HOWELL AUTOPSY: "Marie" Victim Died Of Shock, Exposure, Santa Barbara News-Press, June 17, 1960

MARIE Story Told at CG Hearing, Santa Barbara News-Press, June 15, 1960

MISSING BOAT, Los Angeles Times *, June 11, 1960

MISSING MEN Believed Dead, Ocean Hunt Off: Coast Guard Ends Search – Final Cutter Trip Due In Hunt for Five Men, By James Schermerhorn, News-Press Staff Writer, Santa Barbara News-Press, June 11, 1960

Mystery of Scientist's '53 Death Grips Son: Did father jump, or did the government push him?, by Scott Shane, Arkansas Democrat Gazette, Sunday September 12, 2004

Needed: More Answers, Santa Barbara News-Press, June 14, 1960

New Claim Is Filed in Boat Death, Santa Barbara News-Press, Jan 14, 1961

Ocean Yields Third Victim, Los Angeles Times (Or LA Mirror), June 15, 60

Officer Finds Marie Owner Violated Law, Santa Barbara News-Press, Jan 5, 1961
Pacific Fleet Sees Many Red Warships, Special to the New York Times, October 21, 1954

Possible Victim of Boat Disaster Found on Beach, Santa Barbara News-Press, June 21, 1960

Private Search On For Marie Victims, Santa Barbara News-Press, June 18, 1960

Russell Rites, Santa Barbara News-Press, June 23, 1960

Russell's Body Returned Here, Santa Barbara News-Press, June 22, 1960

Sea Gives Up 2nd of 7 Victims, INDEPENDENT, Long Beach, CA *, June 11, 1960

Search Called Off for Five Lost on Boat, Lo s Angeles Times *, June 12, 1960

Search continues for Marie victims, Goleta Valley Times, June 23, 1960

SECRET MISSION: Finding of Body at Sea Spurs Hunt for 7 Missing on Secret Mission, Los Angeles Times, June 10, 1960

SEVEN FEARED LOST AT SEA: Body, Debris Found; Los Angeles Examiner *(Part of the Hearst Syndicate)*, June 10, 1960

Six Feared Victims of Shark Pack, Los Angeles Evening Mirror News, June 10, 1960

Soviet Submarines Held A Major Peril, Special to the New York Times, December 15, 1960

Third Body Found In "Marie" Tragedy; Four Are Missing, Santa Barbara News-Press, June 16, 1960

UCSB Engineering School: Raytheon Sets Up Four Scholarships, Santa Barbara News-Press, Jan 5, 1961

NEWSPAPER ARTICLES (Post-2000)

A Missing Vessel, Seven Lives Lost and 50 Years of Mystery: Commemoration marks anniversary of Marie's disappearance on secret Raytheon mission in Santa Barbara Channel, by Michael Goldsholl, Noozhawk, June 2010

"Mystery of scientist's '53 death grips son," by Scott Shane of the Baltimore Sun, re-published in the Arkansas Democrat Gazette, Sunday, September 12, 2004

The Mystery of the *Marie*: Dolphin Sculptor Bud Bottoms Among Those Spared, by Barney Brantingham, Santa Barbara Independent, June 2010

MAGAZINE ARTICLES (Post-2000)

"Saved by Dolphins: When life pulled him under like an ocean riptide, Bud

Bottoms found meaning – and a 20-year calling – in sculpting the ever-leaping, ever-playful sea creatures", by Michael Fessier, Jr., Los Angeles Times, July 2, 2006 http://articles.latimes.com/2006/jul/02/magazine/tm-dolphins27

ONLINE SOURCES

Marie Event: https://www.MarieEvent.com

Raytheon Company: http://www.raytheon.com

Santa Barbara Maritime Museum: https://www.sbmm.org/

Stow House in Goleta, CA: http://www.StowHouse.com

The John Walker Spy Ring and The U.S. Navy's Biggest Betrayal, by John Prados, September 2, 2014, https://news.usni.org/2014/09/02/john-walker-spy-ring-u-s-navys-biggest-betrayal

Bombardment of Ellwood, https://en.wikipedia.org/wiki/Bombardment_of_Ellwood

The Shelling of Ellwood: California and the Second World War, http://www.militarymuseum.org/Ellwood.html

Laura Funkhouser: The Right 'New' Look for Old Town Goleta, https://www.noozhawk.com/article/072010_laura_funkhouser_the_right_new_look_for_old_town_goleta

Old Town Goleta, California, http://goletahistory.com/old-town/

The National Guard State Partnership Program, http://www.nationalguard.mil/Leadership/Joint-Staff/J-5/International-Affairs-Division/State-Partnership-Program/

Department of the State, Historians Office, Historical Documents https://history.state.gov/historicaldocuments

Foreign Relations of the United States, 1958–1960, United Nations and General International Matters, Volume II, Editors: Suzanne E. Coffman, Charles S. Sampson, General Editor: John P. Glennon, Government Printing Office, Washington, D.C., 1991 (Includes "Laws of the Sea") https://history.state.gov/historicaldocuments/frus1958-60v02

The Japanese attack of the Pacific Coastline, Ellwood Pier Attack:
    (*) Bob Schwemmer presentation: http://www.youtube.com/watch?v=qclrEm_tL3E (18:20 min marker)
    (*) Statement: *Bombardment of Ellwood*, https://en.wikipedia.org/wiki/Bombardment_of_Ellwood
    (*) Propaganda Art: *The Shelling of Ellwood: California and the Second World War*, http://www.militarymuseum.org/Ellwood.html
    (*) Book: *It Happened in Old Santa Barbara*, by Walker A. Tompkins, Sandollar Press, 1976.

A Missing Vessel, Seven Lives Lost and 50 Years of Mystery: Commemoration marks anniversary of Marie's disappearance on secret Raytheon mission in Santa Barbara Channel, by Michael Goldsholl, Noozhawk, June 2010 http://www.independent.com/news/2010/jun/10/mystery-emmarieem/

Krasno, Maxwell, IN MEMORIAM DR. NIEL F. BEARDSLEY, (First published in the Infrared Symposium, Sixth edition, 1961) http://www.project-tnt.com/marie/documents/Dr_Niel_F_Beardsley_in_memoriam.pdf

Figure-Image Credits

Cover design: Bernard Erlinger-Ford
Photos of author: Ryan McInerney

Inserts

FIG 1: Diego Santos Terres, Sr. and Albert Terres searching for Dad. Author's archives.
FIG 2: My drawing of the Shillelagh by Author
FIG 3: Communicator usage. Author's recreation of Dr. Bob's napkin drawing.
FIG 4: My drawing of light beam "modulation" wave or signal by Author
FIG 5: My note of Communicator transmitter and receiveeruse - side to side lined up.
FIG 6: Communicator note by Teresa Newton-Terres
FIG 7: Grandparents dancing at a Luau in honor of my Grandmother Terres' birthday. Held at Hollister apartment, Old Town Goleta. (cir 1950's)
FIG 8: Above: Dad as a sailer. Mom as a Navy Wave. Diego Terres, Jr. and Marian Terres. Terres family archives.
FIG 9: Top: My family of origin before my youngest brother's birth.
FIG 10: Above: My family at Dad's graduation with Engineering degree from Cal Poly San Luis Obispo, CA.
FIG 11: Right: My family of origin (Jim, Rick, Don, me) with my grandparents, days after the Marie's loss. I remember the photographer giving us bubbles.
FIG 12: Above: Dale Howell and family. The rest of the story to this picture is found in chapter 27 "For The Children" forward. Used with permission by the Howell family archives.
FIG 13: Above: Dale Howell and Dad show off their legendary monster lobster catch.
FIG 14: Above: Dad, friends and shark. Author's archives.
FIG 15: Below: Cal Poly San Luis Obispo scuba-diving club suit up to go on the Marie in search of monster lobster, May 1958. Author's archives.
FIG 16: Left: Dad with Jim Russell posing in front of Raytheon Santa Barbara, June 1960. Author's archives.
FIG 17: Above: I'm with Dr. Bob and Rachel Watkins at the surprise breakfast. Bob and Rachel display items they played with. Author's archives.
FIG 18: Right: I'm between Bob and Helen Wilke in Old Town Goleta. Author's archives.
FIG 19: Jeannie Russell with her father James (Jim) Russell. The story to this picture is found in chapter 42, "A Phone
Interview." Used by permission of the Russell family archives. Used with permission by the Russell family archives.
FIG 20: Above: Dale Howell, Jim McCaffrey, and Jim Terres, at the Channel Islands area. Three Santa Barbara Highschool Graduates. Three Veterans. Three friends.
FIG 21: Albert Terres sits on a whale tale bench at what I understand is the Lost At Sea Memorial. Located at the end of the Santa Barbara harbor breakwater. It was created to recognize no one and to honor all who are lost at sea, to include the men of the Marie. Author's archives.

FIG 22: Above is the "Air-Sea Search System" used to seek victims of the Marie. Created by the Coast Guard.

FIG 23: Above: Timeline, version one, that was hand carried to the National Archives on the first day of research at NARA-I, Washington D.C. Created by the Author.

FIG 24: Left: My grandparents dancing at Noches de Ronda at Santa Barbara Old Spanish Days (cir 1950's). Author's archives.

FIG 25: Below left: My parents at mom's first Old Spanish Days, (cir. 1951). Author's archives.

FIG 26: Below: I'm preparing my daughter, Dete, for the Old Spanish Days Children's Parade, (cir. 1986).
Author's archives.

FIG 27: Above: Ken, I, Aunt Lynda and Uncle Albert at Noches de Ronda for Old Spanish Days, Santa Barbara, CA. I'm wearing treasures of my great-grandmother's, grandmother's, and mom's. Author's archives.

FIG 28: Below: Ken and I are with Bob and Helen Wilke meeting at the fund-raiser for the Kiwanas Club, pancake breakfast at Old Spanish Days. Photo Todd family archives.

FIG 29: A page from the Command History of the Pacific Missile Range, 1960. Reproduced from the holdings of the National Archives, Pacific (Laguna Niguel).

FIG 30: Above: The Coast Guards Cape Sable, CG#95334. John Stites (BMCM) stands on deck, in the middle.

FIG 31: The Western Sea Frontier from the Command History of the Western Sea Frontier, 1960. Reproduced from the holdings of the Navy Yard, Washington D.D..

FIG 32: Storm Project booklet cover. Reproduced from the holdings of the Navy Yard, Washington D.C. Reproduced from the holdings of the Navy Yard, Washington D.D..

FIG 33:: Above: I'm standing with Ken on the left and F. Sutter Fox on the right as we prepare for the 50th Commemoration, the night of the "Social." Author's archives.

FIG 34: My brothers and I prepare for the 50th Commemoration, the night of the "Social." Standing in order of birth - Diego (Jim), Rick, Teresa, and Don. Author's archives.

FIG 35: Above: Dr. F. Sutter Fox at the podium to a standing room only audience at the evening commemoration, Santa Barbara Maritime Museum. Author's archives.

FIG 36: Left: The Centerpiece Quartet sings an encore to Sharon Sims, (USA Colonel ret.) in front of the Marie Remembered exhibit. Author's archives.

FIG 37: Below-Left: Santa Barbara Maritime Museum's Marie Remembered exhibit. Author's archives.

FIG 38: Below-Right: Mrs. Mackie receives a flag from the Honor Guard. Author's archives.

FIG 39: Above-Left: My daughter, Ken, and I at sunrise service standing in front of the Painted Cave located on Santa Cruz Island. Above-Right: Uncle Albert plays TAPS for servie. Author's archives.

FIG 40: Below the Jeff McCaffrey family pose for a remembrance. Author's archives.

FIG 41: Below: All the children embrace at the conclusion of the service. (My brother, Don, on right wears Dad's peacoat.)

FIG 42: Below: All the children embrace at the conclusion of the service. (My brother, Don, on right wears Dad's peacoat.) Author's archives.

FIG 43: Above: The Marie is envisioned using a white line super-imposed on top of an image of a landing craft.

FIG 44: Left: Original image of the Marie reproduced from the holdings at the College Park, MD, National Archives.

FIG 45: Left: The Marie with snoozing Cal Poly San Luis Obispo's scuba diving club after an adventure to find the legendary monster lobsters.

FIG 46: Dr. Niel F. Beardsley

FIG 47: Loren Dale Howell

FIG 48: Harold Herbert Mackie, Jr, 32,

FIG 49: Hugh James McCaffrey,

FIG 50: James Clifford Russell

FIG 51: Diego Santos Terres, Jr.,

FIG 52: Above: In the Raytheon Company, Santa Barbara Operations, Newsletter, July 1960, lease read the General Manager's words above that begin, "Man in his search for knowledge..." because I believe they hold truth.

Index

Symbols

A

L

M

O

P

V

W

X

Y

Z

Study Questions

Here are some questions for you or a group to entertain to enrich your experience with this story:

1. In your own words answer the question, "What happened?"
2. What do you KNOW? NOT-KNOW?
3. How did various people face loss? Grief? Change? What did you lean?
4. How were the children told about the loss of their fathers? What did you learn?
5. What if you were an adult facing the aftermath of a the loss of a loved one, what are good/bad ways are there to tell a child, "What happened?" How should adults, parents, loved ones handle communicating loss to a child? To an adult?
6. What are various ways to handle grief? Loss/Change?
7. What provided the "space" in life for Teresa to go on her quest?
8. How did Teresa's perspective change as a result of visiting the Maritime Museum? And wtith conversations with the Coast Guard folks?
9. Why was the change made from a beach BBQ to a commemoration with a social, ceremony, and sunrise service?
10. What were the pro's and con's of having a small gathering vs. a large gathering?
11. Teresa made a tough choice and "put-on-ice" all on-going research. What did she enjoy and experienced because she did? What may have happened if she didn't?
12. How was the choice to "put-on-ice" on going research a mature perspective?
13. So, what "shipwreck" have you or another experienced?
14. What did you observe in the journey of Teresa's maturing perspective that may serve you or another?

What questions would you add? What questions would you ask? Check out the ongoing dialogue at www.TnewtonT.com/books

Scan below, for more information on this book or the mystery:

Scan ABOVE for more on this *BOOK*:
www.TnewtonT.com/books

Scan BELOW for more on the *MARIE MYSTERY*:
www.TnewtonT.com/marie

Above: I'm sitting on the edge of the iconic Dolphin Family Sculpture by Bud Bottoms at the foot of Sterns Warf in Santa Barbara, California.

About the Authors

TERESA NEWTON-TERRES served as a solution provider for an array of initiatives across the country and internationally, and has operated from a home base in seven states. Holding a Project Management Professional (PMP®) certification since 2000 and awarded the Community Advancement Through Project Management Award for her service to National Guard Families by the Project Management Institute. Often she is found wandering in the mountains or experiencing the seas majesty where God's grace is found within each sunrise and sunset. Currently, she lives in view of the Arkansas river - a river that runs from the mountains to the sea.

www.TnewtonT.com
Facebook.com/TeresaNewton-Terres

JAMES H. PENCE is a man of many talents. He's a performance chalk artist, singer, speaker, published author, editor & collaborator, and in all his spare time he teaches karate, writing, and art to home schooled children. Jim has been called a "Renaissance man," but he prefers to be known simply as a follower of Jesus Christ and a storyteller. Jim is the author or co-author of over nine books.

www.JamesPence.com
Facebook.com/JamesPence